May 17 2022

David an

Enjoy reading about Sevier County's Revolutionary War Patriots.

      Ruth C. Davis

A Portrait of Pioneers and Patriots in Sevier County

©2020 Ruth C. Davis

Published by Silver Lining Literary Services, LLC, in conjunction with Ruth C. Davis

Silver Lining Literary Services, LLC
106 Offutt Rd.
Clinton, TN 37716
www.saralfoust.com

Printed in the United States of America

All rights reserved. No part of this publication may be reproduced, stored in a retrieval system, posted on any website, or transmitted in any form or any means—digital, electronic, photocopy, recording, or otherwise—without the prior written permission of the publisher. The only exception is brief quotation in printed reviews.

ISBN 978-1-7329047-5-0

Cover design by Sara L. Foust ©2020

Introduction

Sevier County is THE best place to find Revolutionary War patriots. Their heritage and names are all over the area, and even the county and the town of Sevierville were named in honor of Revolutionary War hero John Sevier. Spencer Clack is the namesake of the Spencer Clack Chapter, NSDAR. Several communities in the county are named for these heroes: Emert's Cove, Richardson's Cove, Wear's Valley, Henry Crossroads, and Newell Station. A book about Sevier County's Revolutionary War soldiers had never been written. The stories of a small percentage of these patriots are well known; however, the records of most soldiers have disappeared during the passage of time. I'm on a mission to search for every Revolutionary War patriot who lived in Sevier County. My desire is to learn all about them: Their fathers and mothers; wives and children, their experiences and struggles during the war for our independence and their lives after the war.

I've discovered that some of the patriots' descendants, and even the patriots themselves, were already in my Ancestry family tree. I learned my house is located on a patriot's 1808 Revolutionary War grant. I could see McGaughey Station from my bedroom; that is, if it were still standing. The famous Indian War Trail is just a few feet away, and it's still there but being rapidly reclaimed by Mother Nature and subdivisions. Newell Station, the center of the State of Franklin, is two miles down the road. It's exciting to know that these patriots, who risked their lives and fortunes for our independence, passed through these hills and valleys.

I'm on a never-ending adventure to learn all about my heritage, and I can't wait for the next discovery. It just might be about someone in your family tree, too.

~Ruth C. Davis

A Portrait Of Patriots & Pioneers In Sevier County

Ruth C. Davis

Foreword

Those of us who call Sevier County, Tennessee, our ancestral home have a wealth of stories that have been recanted through oral tradition over more than two centuries. On December 16, 1780, two months after the Battle of Kings Mountain, the Battle of Boyd's Creek took place in what is now Sevier County. According to Ramsey's Annals of Tennessee, the Battle of Boyd's Creek was considered to be one of the best fought battles in the border war of Tennessee history. The battle was fought, not against the British, but their sometime ally, the Cherokee. While it is not recorded, perhaps Sevier County was named in honor of John Sevier in appreciation of his involvement at the Battle of Boyd's Creek.

Undoubtedly, the most important historical event in the middle section of East Tennessee is the Treaty of Dumplin Creek. Signed on June 10, 1785, this important document between the State of Franklin and the Cherokee allowed "lands south of the Holston and French Broad Rivers to the Little River from the waters of the Tennessee, to be peacefully inhabited and cultivated, resided on, and inhabited by our elder brothers, the white people." This area encompassed what is now all of Jefferson, Hamblen, Sevier, Knox, and Blount counties.

Within three years, more than one thousand white families had moved in and established homesteads. Sevier County was established on September 18, 1794, almost two years before Tennessee became a state. Many of those early settlers established their homesteads on land grants they were bestowed for their service in the American Revolution.

It was these men who were the founding fathers of Sevier County.

Early military records were either lost due to inadequate colonial record keeping, were never properly recorded, or at best were somewhat sketchy. Consequently, the value recanting stories of our patriots of the Revolution is immeasurable. However, over the course of more than 200 years, certain elements of these accounts, passed down by word of mouth, were forgotten and others were simply embellished.

Therefore, I highly commend the endeavor of my friend Ruth Davis, who has painstakingly gathered the information necessary to record the stories of our Revolutionary War ancestors. This book details individual stories of the men who chose to settle in Sevier County; some living out their lives and buried in Sevier County soil, while others moved on to other enticing frontiers. These men began a progeny that, in most cases, numbers in the thousands. Importantly, the work Ruth has done will be studied by genealogists long after we are gone. I am a firm believer that it is essential to know where we came from in order to know where we are going. This book certainly chronicles where we came from.

F. Carroll McMahan

Sevier County Historian

Sevier County's Patriots and Pioneers

Alexander, Oliver
Anderson, Alexander
Atchley, Abraham
Atchley, Thomas
Baker, Henry B. Jr.
Benson, Spencer
Blair, Samuel
Boaz, Abednego
Bohannan, Henry
Brimer, William
Bryan (Bryant), Peter
Buckingham, Thomas E.
Campbell, Joseph Jr.
Carter, Samuel
Chandler, Timothy
Chapman, Robert
Childress, John
Clack, John
Clack, Spencer
Compton, Jeremiah
Creswell, Andrew
Crowson, William
Cusick, John B.
Davies (Davis), Zachariah
Davis, Joel
Derrick, Johann Jacob
Duggan, Robert
Emert (Emmert), Frederick
Evans, Andrew Sr., NC
Evans, Andrew, VA
Fain, Charles

Fancher, Richard
Fox, Adam
Gilliland, John Jr.
Gist, Joshua
Haggard, Henry Hazelrigg
Headrick, William H.
Henry, Hugh, Major
Henry, William
Houk, John Adam
Hubbard, James
Hudson, George
Isbell, Zachariah, Jr
Jenkins, James
Johnson, Solomon
Kendle, William
Kerr (Carr), Robert
Kirby, Christopher
Large, Joseph
Layman, Jacob
Lewis, Mordecai
Lindsey, David Elijah
Longley, William Campbell
Lovelady, John
Lovelady, William Marshall
McCroskey, John Blair
McGaughey, Samuel Alexander
McGaughey, William
McGee, John A.
McKissack, John II
McMahan, James
Mahan, James Irvine
Mahan, Lieut. John Michael
Maples, Josiah Sr.
Maples, William Condra
Matthews, Obediah
Millsaps, Thomas Minear

Montgomery, Alexander
Murphy, Edward
Newell, Samuel
Nichols, Flayl
Norton, David
Nucum, Solomon
Ogle, William Billy
Oldham, James
Parsons, George
Pierce, James George, Jr.
Porter, Mitchell
Rains, John Capt.
Reagan, Timothy
Richardson, William
Riggin, James
Robertson, William
Rogers, Henry
Rudd, Burlingham
Runyan, Isaac
Sharp, John, Jr.
Shields, Robert
Shields, Thomas
Smallwood, William
Stanfield, James
Stone, Ezekial
Thomas, Isaac
Thurman, John
Tipton, Joshua
Trotter, William
Underwood, John
Varnell, Richard
Walls, Randolph
Wear, John
Wear, Samuel
Webb, John
Weese, Peter

A Portrait of Patriots and Pioneers in Sevier County

Wells, Andrew
Wells, George
White, James
White, Meady
Wood, Richard
Zollinger, Alexander

Alexander, Oliver

Oliver began fighting for his country very early in the French and Indian War and continued to fight for his country's independence in the Revolutionary War. Oliver Alexander was born 26 September 1730 in Lancaster, Pennsylvania, to James (1694-1786) and Elizabeth Ross Alexander (1698-1774). Oliver served in General George Washington's Company during the French and Indian War. In 1755, General Washington joined forces alongside British General Edward Braddock in an attempt to overtake the French strong hold of Fort Duquesne at the site of present-day Pittsburg, Pennsylvania. The French and Indians overpowered the Continental Line, Oliver was wounded, and General Braddock was killed in a battle near the Monongahela River. This battle is sometimes referred to as Braddock's Defeat. (1) Later, Oliver was living in Washington County, Virginia, where he joined Captain David Beattie's Company and ultimately fought in the Battle of Kings Mountain. (2)

Oliver married Margaret Paul in 1765 in Augusta County, Virginia. She was born in 1735 in Pennsylvania and died in 1811 in Blount County, Tennessee. A survey in Washington County, Virginia, shows that Oliver owned a 190-acre tract of land at 15 Mile Creek, on which he operated a mill for several years. By 1791, he was living in Greene County, Tennessee. (1) Records show that Oliver died in Sevier County between 1812-1813. It is not clear when he moved to Sevier County or how long he lived in the county. (3), (4)

Oliver and Margaret's children:
- Ebenezer Crawford was born 21 January 1768 in Virginia, died 22 August 1835 in Maury County, Tennessee. He married

Elizabeth Rogers 22 January 1790. She was born 10 May 1772 in Virginia and died 13 Oct 1845 in Maury County, Tennessee.
- John Alexander married Polly Whitaker.
- Margaret married John Duncan at Fort Craig in July 1788 near present day Maryville, Tennessee.
- Abigail was born 16 September 1779 and married Robert Hooke in 1795 in Blount County, Tennessee.
- Benjamin was born 16 September 1779 and married Ruth Wallace in 1799 in Blount County.
- Susan married James McGinley.
- Adam Rankin was born 1 November 1782 in Washington County, Virginia, married Leah Reagan, and died in 1748 in Marshall County, Mississippi. (3)

Sources: (1) (Wiki Tree-Oliver Alexander; (2)Summers, Annals of SW VA, Part 2, pp. 1083, 1379; (3) find a grave. com; (4) Online catalog, Library of Virginia; Virginia, Land Office, Register, Land grants, 1779; Library of Virginia Archives

Anderson, Alexander

Alexander volunteered in the fall of 1777 for three months in the Frederick County, Maryland Militia under Captain Paple, Lieutenant Key, Colonel Bruce and Major John Scott. On 4 October 1777, the soldiers marched toward Germantown, but before arriving, they encountered the British and Tories in Paoli, Pennsylvania, and fought a battle at Germantown. Alexander remained at Paoli for the remainder of his three-month term, and he was discharged by Captain Paple. (1)

At some point between Fall 1777 and Fall 1779, Alexander's mother moved to Rockbridge County, Virginia. In October 1779, Alexander substituted for three months for James Anderson under Captain Samuel Wallace, Lieutenant Canton, and Colonel John Bowyer and marched to Petersburg, Virginia, then proceeded to the Dismal Swamp and all-the-while having frequent skirmishes with the British and Tories until arriving at Edmonds Hill. Alexander actually served five months instead of three and was discharged by Captain Wallace. (1)

After the war, Alexander moved to Sevier County and lived here for eleven years before moving to Dickson County, Tennessee, lived there for twenty-two years, and moved to Stewart County, Tennessee. Alexander applied for a Revolutionary War Pension, # S2340, on 25 September 1832, Stewart County. Alexander stated in the application that he was born 1761 in York County, Pennsylvania. He died March 1839 in Stewart County. No additional information is known about Alexander. (1)

Sources: (1) Southern Campaign American Revolution Pension Statements, transcribed by C. Leon Harris

Atchley, Abraham, Sr.

Abraham and his brother, Thomas, were very patriotic, as both fought in the Revolutionary War. Abraham was born 25 October 1759 in Middlesex, New Jersey, to Joshua Jesse and Elizabeth Mary Martin Atchley. Elizabeth was the daughter of Rev. David Martin, Sr. (1696-1751) of Burlington, New Jersey, and Elizabeth Doty (1695-1737). Abraham was a brother of Thomas Atchley, who later moved to Sevier County and became a community leader. Abraham married Alsey Wilhelm (1773-1843) in Greene County, Tennessee. She was the daughter of Andreas Joachim Wilhelm and Lea Kemmena. [1]

Abraham volunteered on 25 August 1778 for three months in Loudoun County, Virginia, under Captain Redican, who had been ordered by General George Washington to march to Fort Pitt, near present day Pittsburg, as reinforcement against attacks by the Shawnee Indians. After serving three months, Abraham was discharged, returned home for only a short time, and again returned to Fort Pitt on 1 December 1778. [2]

On 10 August 1781, he was drafted for six months and served as an Orderly Sergeant under Captain David May in the Regiment of Colonel Samuel Lewis, Commanded by General Peter Muhlenberg. He was at the Battle of Little York on 19 October 1781, which terminated in the capture of General Cornwallis. After the surrender of Cornwallis, he marched to Winchester Barracks to guard the British prisoners of war. He remained there until being relieved by new militiamen and then marched to Augusta, Virginia, where he was discharged after having been in service for that campaign for eight months. [3] After the war, Abraham and his family moved to Sevier County. It is not known when they moved to Sevier County or how long they remained before moving to Jackson County, Alabama, in 1828. Alsey died in Jackson County, and Abraham died after 18 January 1843, also in Jackson County. (2)

Abraham and Alsey's children:
- John was born 1798 in Sevier County, married Mary Genoa 12 December 1826 in Rhea County, Tennessee.
- Thomas was born 1807 in Sevier County, married Nancy Jane Temple, and died 1880 in Madison County, Alabama.
- Mary Esther was born 1809 in Rhea County, Tennessee, married George Washington Gipson on 14 September 1827 in Rhea County, and died 1880 in Alabama.
- James B. was born 1811 and died 30 November 1863 in a Union prison in Indiana.
- William Abraham was born 1813, married Mahala McCulley, and died 1 June 1880 in Madison County, Alabama.
- George Washington was born 1816 in Rhea County, married Letty Martin in about 1838, and died before 1870 in Madison County, Alabama. (1)

Historical Fact: Abraham was the younger brother of Patriot Thomas Atchley.

Sources: (1) Family Search, Church of Jesus Church of Latter-day Saints; (2) Alabama, Revolutionary War Residents, 1776-1783 for Abraham Atchley. (3) Pension Application of Abraham Atchley, R 68, Sevier Co. TN, 22 Sept 1820, transcribed by C. Leon Harris.

Atchley, Thomas

Thomas is one of the founding fathers of Sevierville. He settled on the French Broad River and started the Alder Branch Baptist Church in his home. Thomas Atchley was born 3 May 1756 in Middlesex County, New Jersey, to Joshua Jesse (1714-1774) and Elizabeth Mary Martin Atchley (1719-1795). He entered service in the New Jersey Line about 1775, marched from Middlesex County to Brunswick Town, and was placed under the command of Major John Dunn, marched to the town of Amboy, opposite the city of New York, then to Elizabeth Town, where he remained for some time and was discharged.

Later, he served in the Virginia Line under Captain James Reddakin and Lieutenant Thomas Cavin in Loudoun County, Virginia, marched to the confluence of the Monongahela and Allegany Rivers at Pittsburg, Pennsylvania, and went by boat to the mouth of the Wheeling River, where he was stationed for about six months, then returned home to Loudoun County.

He also served in Botetourt County, Virginia, under Captain John Lewis and marched to Guilford County, North Carolina. After staying there for about a month, he was discharged. He entered the service a fourth time to disarm suspected Tories at Walker Creek, Virginia, and after completing the assignment, returned home two weeks later. On 3 September 1832, Thomas applied for a Revolutionary War Pension, #W257 in Sevier County, Tennessee. (1), (2)

In 1780, Thomas married Lydia Richards, the daughter of William and Abigail Lay Richards in Loudon County, Virginia. They lived there until 1786 when they moved to Sevier County and settled on fertile land at Alder Branch, a tributary of the French Broad River. He organized the Alder Branch Baptist Church in his house in 1830 when he was 75 years old. Thomas died 11 October 1836 and was buried in Alder Branch Cemetery. Lydia died on 31 August 1850 and is also buried at Alder Branch Cemetery in Sevier County.
(3), (5)

Thomas and Lydia's children:
- Hannah was born 23 February 1782 in Botetourt County, Virginia.
- Mary was born 13 November 1783 in Botetourt County, married James Haggard about 1801, and died 1846 in McMinn County, Tennessee.
- Sarah was born 28 November 1785 in Botetourt County, married James Guthrie on 7 January 1808 in Cumberland, Kentucky, and died 29 November 1851 in McMinn County, Tennessee.
- Isaac was born 9 December 1787 in Loudoun County, Virginia, and married Elizabeth Emily Smith in 1812 in Sevier

- County, and died 19 August 1854 in Sevier County.
- Benjamin was born 24 January 1789 in Sevier County, married Nancy Maples about 1808 in Sevier County, and died 10 September 1875 and is buried at Alder Branch.
- Joshua was born 26 February 1796 in Sevier County, married Elizabeth Hardin in 1811 in Sevier County, and died 26 February 1872 in Sevier County.
- Lydia was born 1792, married Thomas Maples 6 December 1806 in Sevier County, and died 11 February 1865.
- Thomas was born 19 April 1796 in Sevier County, married Mary Polly Fancher in 1816 in Sevier County, and died 30 October 1875.
- Jane was born 8 January 1798 in Sevier County, married Ephriam Maples.
- Elizabeth was born 14 October 1800 in Sevier County and married John Lindsey about 1816.
- Rhoda was born 25 February 1802 in Sevier County and married Moses Long in 1819.
- Noah was born 19 January 1807 in Sevier County, married Elizabeth Pharis in 1824, and died 1850 in Sevier County.

(4)

Historical Fact: Thomas Atchley is the older brother of Patriot Abraham Atchley.

Sources: (1) Smoky Mountain Historical Society Newsletter, winter, 1984, p. 15., (2) *Revolutionary War Gravesite's of Knox and Surrounding Counties*, Stephen

A Portrait of Patriots and Pioneers in Sevier County

Holston Chapter SAR, (3) *Sevier County: Its Military Contribution to the Nation*, King Family Library, Sevierville, TN (4) Smoky Mountain Ancestral Quest, smokykin.com, maintained by David L. Beckwith, (5) *In the Shadow of the Smokies*, Smoky Mountain Historical Society, 1993, p. 86

Baker, Henry B., Sr.

Henry enlisted in the 5th Regiment of the South Carolina Line in 1779 under Captain James Conyers, Colonel Isaac Huger, and General Moultrie for a term of three years, and after three years of service, he was honorably discharged by Colonel Alexander Mcintosh. (1)

It is not known exactly when Henry first came to Sevier County, but a 1790 census lists a man by the name of Henry B. Baker living in the Gist's Creek area. The census shows that he was born in 1731 but does not list a place of birth. (2)

At the age of 90 years, Henry appeared in Sevier County, Tennessee Open Court on 27 January 1818 to apply for a Revolutionary War pension, #S39171. He stated that he was a resident of Sevier County and owned twenty-two acres in the county, which he bought for $20.00 with a down payment of $2.00. He further stated that he owned a house, one horse, four head of cattle, fourteen hogs, and a small quantity of household furniture. Henry added that due to bodily infirmity, debility of strength, and advanced age, he was not able to work. He also stated his wife, name not listed, was in her seventies and also unable to work. Henry died 16 April 1823. (1)

Henry and Unknown Wife's child:
- Henry, Jr. was born in North Carolina in 1785, married Eliza Betsy Unknown, and died before 1837 in Gist's Creek, Sevier County. (2)

Sources: (1) Revolutionary War Gravesite's of Knox and Surrounding Counties, Stephen Holston, Chapter, SAR (2) Sevier County, Tennessee and Its Heritage, 1994, Don Mills, p. 147

Benson, Spencer

Spencer is undoubtedly the ancestor of the large number of Benson families in Sevier County. Spencer was born 4 December 1755 in Sussex County, Delaware, to William Elam (1724-1772) and Tabitha Kennedy Benson (1727-1788). William and Tabitha married 9 August 1748 in Talbot, Maryland. (1), (2) Spencer enlisted in Sussex County Militia on 1 April 1776 and served three months, guarding the Chesapeake Bay beaches and inlets against acts of depredation and incursions by British seaman who frequently landed parties and carried off cattle in the bay area. In August 1776, he volunteered in the same Delaware Militia as a foot soldier to guard these same beaches and inlets against atrocities by the British seamen. During both of these times, he served under Colonel Simon Kellick, Major John Mitchell, Captain Robert Houston, Lieutenant John Craton, and Ensign James Bronton. (3)

In August 1777, he was drafted in Sussex County Militia to serve under Captain Robert Houston and marched against a company of Tories commanded by Captain Bartholomew Banner. The company surprised, routed, and dispersed the Tories at Key Ketum Branch. (4)

Spencer married Comfort Short on 18 February 1779. She was born 1758 in Sussex, Delaware, to Edward and Elizabeth Short. Spencer and his family arrived in Sevier County from Delaware by way of North Carolina in 1810. He received land grants on the East Fork of the Little Pigeon River for his service in the Revolutionary War. Spencer moved to Rhea County, Tennessee, where he applied for a Revolutionary War Pension, #S1496. Comfort died on

15 May 1819 in Rhea County, and Spencer died in 1834 in McMinn County, Tennessee. (1), (5), (6)

Spencer and Comfort's children:
- John Benson was born 1781 in Sussex, Delaware, and died 9 June 1863 in Sevier County.
- James Benson was born 1783 Sussex, Delaware, married Jane Daniels, and died 9 June 1863 in Marshall, Alabama.
- Mary May Benson was born 1790 in Raleigh, North Carolina, and married Frederick Jones in 1811.
- Benjamin Franklin Benson was born 1794 in Sevier County, married Prudence Clifton, and died 1874 in Hampton, Arkansas.
- William Frederick Benson was born 21 March 1795 in Sevier County, married Catherine Shell on 17 April 1814, and died 26 August 1881 in Madison, Alabama.
- Robert Benson was born 11 February 1796 in Sevier County, married Elizabeth Haney, and died 1875 in Walker, Alabama.
- Spencer Benson, Jr., was born about 1797 in Sevier County, married Ruth Colville on 10 November 1819 in Rhea County, and died 1850 in Hardin County, Tennessee.
- Isaac Benson was born 1798 in Sevier County, married Naomi Bryson on 20 January 1819, and died 6 May 1866 in Ouachita, Arkansas.

- Barclay Benson was born 1801 in Tennessee, married Angeline Rittle in 1830, and died in Rhea County, Tennessee. (2)

Sources: (l) Sevier County, Tennessee and Its Heritage, Don Mills, Sevier County Book Committee, 1994, p. 154, (2) Family Search, Church of Jesus Christ of Latter-day Saints, Spencer Benson. (3) Revolutionary Soldiers, Sevier Co. TN, Joseph Sharp Collection, McClung Historical Collection, (4) Revolutionary War Pension Application 51496, (5) Rhea- Sevier County, TN Archives Military Records, Compiled by Zella Armstrong, Pamphlet No. 1---Benson, Spencer, (6) Smoky Mountain Historical Society Newsletter, winter 1984, p. 16

Blair, Samuel

Samuel lived in Sevier County most of his adult life and is one of the many patriots who created the city of Sevierville. Samuel was born 14 June 1759 in Amelia County, Virginia, and according to family records, Samuel and his parents later moved to Burke County, North Carolina. While living in Burke County, Samuel enlisted in service for six months under Captain William Johnson in the latter part of 1779. In May 1780, Captain Johnson received orders from Captain McDowell for all soldiers that could be furnished horses to march to Burke County, North Carolina Court House and proceed against a party of Tories at Ramsour's Mill. Samuel marched to the court house and was placed under Captain Bowman in Colonel Bernard's Regiment. During the Battle of Ramsour's Mill, Captain Bowman was killed. Samuel received a discharge but reenlisted in July 1780 in Burke County as a substitute for William Smith, serving under Captain Clark in Colonel Williams' Regiment. He fought in the Battle of Kings Mountain, and at Cowpens and was discharged. He again reenlisted and served from July 1781 to August 1782.

After leaving the service, he returned to Virginia and lived there five years before moving to Sevier County, where he became an influential leader in the community and was a member of the team that chose the site for the town of Sevierville. Samuel was married to Elizabeth Tinder, and no further information is known about her. He lived in Sevier County for forty-three years and then moved to McMinn County, Tennessee. In December 1833, at the age of 75, Samuel applied for a Revolutionary War Pension, North Carolina Service, # 3009, in McMinn County. (1), (2)

Samuel died in August 1836 in Monroe County, Tennessee, and is buried in Madisonville Cemetery, Madisonville, Tennessee. (3)

Samuel and Elizabeth's Children:
- Hugh was born 15 October 1783 in Virginia and married Rachel Tipton, who was born on 26 November 1788 and died 1 August 1868. Hugh died in 1868 and is buried in Middle Creek Methodist Church Cemetery, Sevier County.
- Nancy Jane was born 11 February 1788 and married Samuel Henderson, who was born February 1786 and died 8 March 1867 and is buried in the Henderson Cemetery in Monroe County. Nancy Jane died 8 March 1867 and is also buried in Henderson Cemetery in Monroe County.
- Mahala was born 4 June 1802, married Adam Burn, and died 14 January 1879 and is buried in Burn Cemetery, McMinn County. (3)

Sources: (1) Samuel Blair, Revolutionary War Pension Application, NC Service, S3009, Joseph Sharp Collection, McClung Historical Collection, (2) Some Revolutionary Soldiers, Sevier Co. TN , (3) find a grave.com.

Boaz, Abednego

Abednego left Sevier County, but his daughter, Clara, remained, and she is probably the progenitor of an extremely large Loveday family in the county. Abednego Boaz was born 6 February 1760 in Buckingham County, Virginia, to Thomas, Sr. (1714-1780) of Buckingham County and Elinor Archdeacon Cody Boaz, who was born 1718 in Kilkenny, Ireland, and died 1787 in Buckingham County. Abednego was four years old when the family moved to Pittsylvania County, Virginia.

At the age of eighteen, Abednego enrolled as a private in William Cunningham's Company, 1st Virginia Brigade, 5th Division and was at Valley Forge during the bitter winter of 1777-78. In August 1778, Abednego fought in the Battle of Monmouth Courthouse in New Jersey. In the fall of 1778, he was transferred to Ball's Company with Colonel Richard Parker in command. [1]

After the War, Abednego returned to Buckingham County, and in 1782, he married Frances "Fanny" Matthews in Pittsylvania County, Virginia. She was the daughter of James Matthews, and she died 10 March 1810. [1]

Abednego received a Virginia land grant for his service in the War. [2] His farm was described in the deed dated 18 March 1786 as being 190 acres. Eleven years later, he sold the farm and evidently left Virginia for Sevier County. In 1810, Boaz received a land grant in Sevier County for 374 acres for a price of $374.00. Three years later, he bought eighty-seven acres on the north side of Little River in Blount County, Tennessee. Abednego died 25 September 1825 in Blount County.

[1]

Abednego and Frances' children:
- Agnes was born 26 October 1783 in Buckingham County, Virginia.
- Drucilla was born 12 May 1785 in Buckingham County and died at age 72, probably in Monroe County, Tennessee.
- James was born 12 January 1787 in Buckingham, County and died 17 March 1814 in Talladega County, Alabama.
- Obadiah was born 2 February 1787 in Buckingham County and died 4 April 1863 in Grainger County, Tennessee.
- Abednego, Jr. was born 27 March 1891 in Buckingham County and died in Tennessee.
- Mignon was born 2 February 1793 in Buckingham County and died 15 November 1845 in Indiana.
- Zedkijah was born 30 March 1795 in Buckingham County and died 19 December 1860 in Talladega County, Alabama.
- Claramon "Clara" was born 16 April 1797 in Buckingham County, married Amos Lovelady, and died June 1831 in Sevier County. Clara married Amos Lovelady, the son of William Marshall Lovelady.
- Meshack was born 18 February 1800 in Giles County, Tennessee, and died 5 May 1885 in Gordon County, Georgia.
- Peter was born 24 November 1805. (1)

Historical Fact: Amos Lovelady was the son of Patriot William Marshall Lovelady.

Ruth C. Davis

Sources: (1) The Next Generation Genealogy Site Building, Boaz Family Genealogy Pages. (2) *Historical Register of Virginians in the War of the Revolution.*

Bohanan, Henry

Henry's children and grandchildren married into the families of other Revolutionary War patriots in Sevier County. Henry Bohanan was born in 1753 in Halifax County, Virginia, the son of Henry Bohanan (1740-1807) of Pittsylvania County, Virginia, and Susanna Fretwell (?-1786). Recordings in the Virginia State library's "List of Revolutionary Soldiers of Virginia" shows that Henry served a three-year enlistment as a private from July 1778 to June 1781 in the 1st Virginia Regiment of the Continental Line's Light Dragoons commanded by Capt. Robert Boling. In *Virginia Soldiers of 1776* by Louis A. Burgess, it shows Henry Bohanan received Virginia land bounty warrants #1394 for 100 acres and #1390 for 200 acres, and additional records show the bounty warrants were never redeemed. (1)

Henry married Amelia Shotwell (1765-1813) of Culpeper County, Virginia, in about 1786 in Abbeville, South Carolina. Henry, his wife, and children are listed on the Abbeville census of 1790 and 1800. Around 1801, Henry and his family migrated from Abbeville to Sevier County. On 15 June 1810, Henry was granted a 150-acre tract of land in Sevier County in the District South of French Broad and Holston for $150.75. Prior to receiving this land grant the family is believed to have lived in the White Oaks Flats community (now called Gatlinburg). (2)

Amelia died March 1813 in Sevier County, and later Henry married Rachel McKissick (1795-1860) in Sevier County. Henry received another land grant on 25 January 1826 for fifty acres on the waters of Mill Creek in the area of Middle Creek and Pigeon Forge, Tennessee. It is believed Henry lived at his home on the waters of Mill Creek until he died in 1842 and is buried in the Plemons Cemetery in Sevier County (2), (3)

Henry and Amelia's children:
- Bohanan-four unnamed children born about 1786, 1788, 1790, and 1791
- Susannah was born 1793 in Abbeville, South Carolina, married Isaac "Shucky" Ogle, and died 2 September 1881 and is buried in Banner Cemetery in Sevier County.
- Nancy was born 1795 in Abbeville, married William "Black Bill" Ogle in about 1810, and died 3 June 1869 and is buried in Cole Cemetery in Sevier County.
- Elizabeth "Peggy" was born 1801 in Sevier County, married Alexander Dickson, and died 1872 and is buried in Middle Creek Methodist Church Cemetery.
- Henry, Jr. was born 1803 in Sevier County, married Catherine "Kate" Powell, and died 29 August 1877 and is buried in Shady Grove Baptist Church Cemetery in Sevier County.
- James was born 1805 in Sevier County, married Easter Ogle, and died 1824-25 and is buried in Gatlinburg in Sevier County.
- Sarah E. was born 1807 in Sevier County, married William Thomas Ogle, and died 25 September 1887 and is buried in Boogertown Cemetery in Sevier County.

Henry and Rachel's children:

- Evans was born 1829 in Sevier County and died after 1880.
- Margaret was born 1832 in Sevier County and died 1888. (1)(2)

Historic Fact: Isaac and William Ogle are sons of Patriot William and Mary Jane Huskey Ogle.

Sources: (1) Smoky Mountain Ancestral Quest, smokykin.com, maintained by David K. Beckwith, (2) find a grave.com, (3) In the Shadow of the Smokies, Smoky Mountain Historical Society, 1993, p, 710.

Brimer, William

William fought with two legends, Captain Valentine Sevier and his son Colonel John Sevier. William was born 1 February 1759 in North Carolina, the son of Benjamin Brimer and an unknown mother. He volunteered July 1777 in Wilkes County, North Carolina, under Captain Jacob Free in Colonel Armstrong's Regiment and General Rutherford's Brigade to march against the Cherokee Indians to the head of the Catawba River. The Regiment was involved in several skirmishes with the Cherokee along the Catawba River to the town of Cowee and the Hiwassee River.

In July 1778, he volunteered under Captain William Gilbreath in Colonel Hugh Brevard's Regiment and General Rutherford's Brigade, marched to Salisbury, North Carolina and then to Monk's Corner, near Charleston, South Carolina, and from there on to Savannah, Georgia. He arrived in Savannah shortly after the British captured Charleston, South Carolina. His regiment participated in a scrimmage with the British at Savannah River, and he stayed at Savannah until his term ended and he was discharged at Camp Turkey Hill by Captain Gilbreath and Colonel Brevard. [1] In 1780, William volunteered for the third time in Washington County, North Carolina (now Washington County, Tennessee), under Captain Valentine Sevier and Colonel John Sevier and marched across the mountains into North Carolina and fought in the Battle of Kings Mountain. [2]

William married Elizabeth Elgin around 1784. She was born 1764 in Washington County, North Carolina (now Tennessee). William and his family moved to Sevier County in 1810. [3] On 4 March 1839,

Elizabeth appeared in Sevier County court to apply for a Revolutionary War pension based on the service of her late husband. She stated he had died 10 July 1834 in Sevier County and is believed to be buried in the Flat Creek area of Sevier County. Elizabeth died 9 September 1844 in Sevier County. (5)

William and Elizabeth's children:
- John was born 1785 in North Carolina.
- James was born 1787 in North Carolina.
- Vineyard was born 1 May 1792 in Maywood, North Carolina.
- Tabitha was born 1793 in Jefferson County, Tennessee.
- Sabath was born 1793 in Jefferson County, Tennessee
- Sarah was born 1794 in Jefferson County, Tennessee.
- William was born 1796.
- Barbara was born 1796.
- Elizabeth was born 1798 in Jefferson County, Tennessee. (3) (4)

Sources: (1) Revolutionary War Gravesite's of Knox and Surrounding Counties, Stephen Holston Chapter, SAR, (2) Revolutionary War Pension Records, Sevier Co. TN, Joseph A. Sharp Collection, McClung Historical Collection, (3) Jefferson Co. TN Deed Book 1, p. 142, (4) Family Tree Maker, Connatser/ Staley Ancestors, (5) Smoky Mountain Historical Society Newsletter, winter, 1984, p.13.

Bryant (Bryan), Peter

Peter will always be included in Tennessee history books for his involvement in the development of the Constitution of the new State of Tennessee in 1796. Peter was born 1755 in Augusta County, Virginia (now Rockingham County), to Thomas (1721-1793) and Elizabeth Palmer Bryan (1729-1793). Peter served in the Rockingham County Militia, 1781, first as a private and then later as a lieutenant. He also served in the Third Virginia Militia. (1)(2)

In the late 1700s, Peter moved to the "Territory South of the Ohio River" and he settled on the north side of the French Broad River in Greene County (now Sevier County). He received two land grants in Dumplin Valley, and some of this land still belongs to his descendants. Peter was interested in education, religion, and politics, and he became a leader in the community, county, and state. On 11 January 1796, delegates were elected to structure a government for the new State of Tennessee. Five delegates from each of Tennessee's eleven counties were chosen, and Peter Bryan represented Sevier County. Peter was one of the signers of the first Constitution of the State of Tennessee. On 4 July 1796, new officials were appointed for Sevier County, and Peter was chosen to be Justice of the Peace. (3)

He married Betty "Molly" Hubberd in 1777 in Rockingham County, Virginia. She is thought to be the niece or cousin of Colonel James Hubberd, whose daughter Elizabeth married Allen Bryan, Peter's brother. According to legend, Peter accidently drowned in the French Broad River in 1815 and was buried in the Paw Paw Hollow Cemetery, although no marker has ever been found. (1)

Peter and Betty's children:
- Thomas was born 13 April 1785, married Nancy Cate on 15 August 1813, and died 4 March 1867 in Sevier County.
- Allen was born 1780 in Virginia, married Phoebe Boggess, and died 23 January 1848 in Madison County, Alabama.
- Phoebe was born in 1789 and died 1870 in Monroe County, Mississippi.
- William was born 25 September 1793 in Jefferson County, Tennessee (now Sevier County), married Lucy Cate, and died 5 Sept 1839 in McMinn County, Tennessee. Lucy Cate was born 24 February 1795 and died 16 September 1839. (1)

Historical Fact: Lucy and Nancy Cate (Cates) were sisters.

Sources: (1) Peter Bryan and Betty Hubbard, Jerry Bryan Web Pages, (2) Revolutionary War Pension 530290, Peter Bryan, (2) Rockingham Co. Va. Militia Book, Levinson 1778-1792, part 1, p.92, (3) Sevier County, Tennessee and Its Heritage, Don Mills, Sevier County Book Committee, 1994, pp. 8, 23, 164

Buckingham, Thomas Eldridge

Thomas's brick house is one of the oldest structures in Tennessee. Thomas was born about 1745 in Augusta County, Virginia, to Benjamin (1721-1793) and Avarilla Gosnell Buckinghan (1720-1826). He served in the Revolutionary War and was wounded at the Battle of Guilford Court House. He also served under Captain John Sevier in the Battle of Kings Mountain and in the Battle of Boyd's Creek. (1)

Thomas married Frances "Fanny" Elizabeth Terry on 22 February 1791 in Rockingham, North Carolina. Fanny was the daughter of Benjamin (1704-1760) and Elizabeth Dickerson Terry (1705-1787). Apparently, they moved to Sevier County soon after their marriage and became two of its first settlers. Thomas and his brother Alexander are credited with building the first brick house in Sevier County in 1790. The house still stands and is located on Boyd's Creek Highway in Seymour and is listed on the National Register of Historic Places. (2), (3)

On 8 November 1794, Thomas became the Sheriff of Jefferson County, Tennessee, and was appointed the first sheriff of the newly formed Sevier County by the first county court ever assembled. In 1796, he served as a delegate from Sevier County to the Tennessee Constitutional Convention and signed the original Constitution of the State of Tennessee. When Tennessee was admitted to the union on 1 June 1796, Thomas was retained as sheriff of Sevier County, which made him one of the first sheriffs in the State of Tennessee. (1)

The dates of Thomas' and Fanny's deaths are not known, but they are believed to be buried in Trundle Cemetery in Boyd's Creek.

Thomas and Fanny's children:
- Frances was born in Sevier County.
- Nathaniel Bannister was born 6 January 1771 in Virginia, married Jane Cocke in Sevier County, and died in 1848 and is buried in Odd Fellows Cemetery in Monroe, Mississippi.
- Thomas was born 1771 in Sevier County, married Elizabeth Terry on 22 February 1791 in Rockingham, North Carolina, and died 1850 in Stewart, Tennessee.
- William was born 1768 in Pittsylvania, Virginia, and married Polly Babb 23 September 1800 in Wake County, North Carolina.
- Rebecca was born about 1770 in Pittsylvania, Virginia, married Richard Caswell Cobb in 1801 in Sevier County, and died 1830 in Tennessee. (2)

Sources: (1) wwwgeocities.comjheartlandjcottagej1955textjfamiLlawmen.html, (2) ancestry.com search, Thomas Buckingham, (3) Sevier County, Tennessee and its Heritage, Don Mills, Sevier County Book Committee, 1994, pp. 4, 12, 20, 23.

Campbell, Joseph, Jr.

Joseph's loyalty to his country is evident. After his commanding officer died in battle, he continued to fight for independence. Joseph was born 1762 in Culpeper County, Virginia, to Joseph, Sr. and unknown mother. At the age of seventeen, he was drafted into the Albemarle County, Virginia Militia under Captain Bradley to guard the barracks in Albemarle that housed the Hessian and British prisoners. He was discharged after serving three months and returned home. (1)

A short time later, Joseph's father moved the family to Washington County, Virginia. He was again drafted under Captain Robert Edmondson and Colonel William Campbell and assigned to guard the Virginia frontier forts of Black, Bryant, and Edmonson. After serving for three months, he was discharged by Captain Edmondson.

In 1780, Joseph substituted for his father under Captain Edmondson and Colonel Campbell and marched to Kings Mountain. After the Battle of Kings Mountain, he remained in service as a guard until his three month substitution expired and he was discharged by Colonel Campbell because Captain Edmonson had been killed during the Battle of Kings Mountain. Upon returning home, he was elected Ensign under Captain Black to guard and assist the men cutting out the Kentucky Road, and after serving three months, he was discharged by Captain Black.

After the Revolutionary War, he remained in Virginia for ten or twelve years and then moved to Sevier County, where he remained for twenty-five to thirty years before moving to Rhea County, Tennessee, and then on to Hamilton County, Tennessee. On 27 November 1832, Joseph appeared in the Hamilton

County court to apply for a Revolutionary War Pension, Pension #2414, Service #2414. (1)

Joseph married Christiana Anderson, born 1754 in New Kent, Colony of Virginia. She died 1842 in Hamilton County. Joseph died in Bradley County, Tennessee, on 9 January 1841. (1), (2)

Joseph and Christiana's children:
- William Seymour was born 1790 in Sevier County, married Rebecca Shahan on 4 July 1816, and died September 1830 in Hamilton County.
- David was born in 1794 in Tennessee, married Jean Glasgow Cowan on 30 May 1814 in Knox County, Tennessee, and died 21 February 1873 in Philadelphia, Pennsylvania.
- John was born in 1796 in Tennessee, married Phoebe Booth, and died April 1850 in Independence County, Arkansas.

(2)

Sources: (1) Southern Campaigns American Revolution Pension Statements & Rosters, pension application of Joseph Campbell 52414, Transcribed by Will Graves, (2) Family Search, Church of Jesus Church of Latter-day Saints.

Carter, Samuel, Lieutenant

Samuel is one of many patriots who remained in Sevier County for a short period of time and then moved on to an area that could better use his wisdom and talents. Samuel was born about 1754 in North Carolina, and when the Revolutionary War began, he was living in Albemarle County, Virginia. (1), (2) He immediately enlisted in the Army after the capture of Burgoyne's Army and served in Captain John Martin's Company and Colonel William Fontaine's Regiment. About 1 November 1778, he moved to Fairfield District, South Carolina, and enlisted in Captain Robert Frost's Company, under Lieutenant John Mayfield, Colonel David Hopkins' Regiment, and Major Moses Bond and marched to the Congaree River several miles below Granby, where they remained several days waiting for General Nathaneal Greene. Once united with General Greene's troops, they marched to Eutaw, South Carolina, where they fought the Battle of Eutaw Springs on 8 September 1781. After General Greene's defeat and retreat from Eutaw Springs, Samuel was discharged.

Soon after returning home, Samuel learned that the Tories had killed Major Bond and Lieutenant Mayfield, thus the company elected him to succeed Mayfield as their Lieutenant. Shortly thereafter, Captain Richard Winn ordered his officers to reorganize their companies and keep them ready at a minute's warning to suppress the Tories and keep them under control, for which Samuel served two tours of about two months each.

In late summer of 1781, Samuel marched in command of a company to South Edisto and joined General William Henderson, where they had the task of suppressing the Tories and keeping in check the Tory leader, Colonel William "Bloody Bill" Cunningham, as the Tories were ravaging the country around South Edisto River. Two months later, Samuel was discharged, and on the way home, he heard the news of General Cornwallis' surrender at Little York on 19 October 1781.

In 1795 or 1796, he moved from Fairfield District, South Carolina, to Rutherford County, North Carolina, and lived there until 1810, when he moved to Haywood County, North Carolina. In 1813, he moved to Sevier County after which he moved to Blount and Monroe Counties, Tennessee. Samuel's wife is listed as Jane Unknown, and she was born in 1759 and died in Cherokee County, Alabama. (1)

At the age of 78, he was approved for Revolutionary War Pension #S1505 on his application of 21 September 1832 while living in Monroe County. By 1840, Samuel was living in Polk County, Tennessee, and became a leading citizen in the newly formed county, where he was called up to serve on the Grand Jury and assist in the organization of the county. (3) He also drew a pension in Polk County in 1840. Samuel died in Polk County on 28 May 1847 and was buried in the Old Ocoee Cemetery in Benton, Tennessee. (2)

Samuel and Jane's children:
- Samuel M. was born 1793 in North Carolina, married Faday Gallaher, and died 1874 in Johnson County, Illinois.
- John S. was born about 1785 in North Carolina.
- William was born about 1790 in North Carolina.

- Amos R. was born about 1802 in North Carolina, married Elizabeth Rush (1805-1850), and died in 1886 in Illinois. (1)

Sources: (1) Family Search, Church of Jesus Christ of Latter-day Saints, (2) "Some Tennessee Heroes of the Revolution," Zella Armstrong, Pamphlet No.11. (3) find a grave.com.

Chandler, Timothy

Timothy's legacy and contribution to Sevier County is the Wheatland mansion and plantation. Timothy was born 1750 in Goochland County, Virginia, to Joell and Priscilla Mimms Chandler. (1) He was a veteran of the Battle of Kings Mountain under the command of Colonel John Sevier. Timothy received a land grant in Sevier County near the site of the Battle of Boyd's Creek. He eventually acquired enough property to establish a 4,700-acre plantation and home, which eventually became known as Wheatland Plantation. Today, Wheatland still stands as a tribute to those early pioneers and is open to visitors. (2)

Timothy married Hetty Jane Temple in 1760. She was born 1740 in Mecklenburg, Virginia, and died in Sevier County on 15 July 1824. Timothy died 19 April 1819 in Boyd's Creek, Sevier County. (2)

Timothy and Hetty's children:
- Rebecca was born 1 January 1770 and married Jeffrey Johnson (1768-1830) in 1789. She died 1835 in Blount County, Tennessee.
- Nancy was born 1 January 1775 in Wilkes County, North Carolina, married John Adam Houk (1773-1839) about 1800, and died 18 June 1831 in Sevier County.
- Mary Polly was born 1 January 1781 in Sevier County, married William H. McCamy in 1801, and died 22 June 1840 in Blount County, Tennessee.
- John was born 9 May 1786 in Wilkes County, married Ann Usher Wayland

Ruth C. Davis (1808-1898) on 6 December 1859, and died 2 May 1875 in Sevier County. (1) (3)

Sources: (1) Family Search, Church of Jesus Christ of Latter-day Saints, (2) find a grave, (3) Smoky Mountain Ancestral Quest, wwwsmokykin.com, maintained by David L. Beckwith

Chapman, Robert

Fortunately, Robert's devotion to his country has been preserved by his Revolutionary War Pension. Robert was born in 1744. The names of his father and mother and location of his birth are unknown. He enlisted as a private in the South Carolina Continental Line on 24 July 1776 and served as a private under Captain Uriah Goodwyn and Colonel William Thomson's Regiment for a period of three years. During this time, he was at the capture of Savannah by the British and then later discharged. (1) He substituted for another person and fought at the Battle of Guilford Court House on March 15, 1781. (2)

After the Revolutionary War, Robert moved to Sevier County. On 7 June 1826, at the age of 69, Robert appeared before the Sevier County Court Pleas and Quarter Sessions to make an application for a Revolutionary War Pension, #49313. Robert stated in the application that he did not have a family, that he was a farmer but did not have any property or land. He had made a living by teaching school and bartering. Robert died 2 April 1829. No additional information about Robert is known. (1), (2), (3)

Sources: (1) The Roster of South Carolina Patriots of the American Revolution, Vol. 1, A-J, Bobby Gilmer Moss, (2) Southern Campaign American Revolution Pension Statements and Rosters, transcribed by Will Graves, (3) Revolutionary Gravesite's in Knox and Surrounding Counties, Stephen Holston Chapter, SAR

Childress, John

John fought alongside two legends, General George Rogers Clark and Daniel Boone. John was born 5 May 1755 in Cumberland County, Virginia, and moved to Surry County, North Carolina, in the late 1770s. He entered the service in 1780 under the command of Lieutenant Colonel William Shepherd in Surry County, North Carolina, and afterwards under the command of Captain James Shepherd and Colonel Benjamin Cleveland. He fought in the Battle of Kings Mountain and was wounded by a rifle ball in the abdomen. He became a wagon master under Colonel Martin Armstrong, Surry County, North Carolina, and was ordered to deliver sixty bushels of grain to Camden, South Carolina, every Monday morning to be used by General Nathaneal Greene's Army after the Battle of Guilford. He was dismissed as wagon master in the fall of 1781 and moved to Fayette County, Kentucky, where he sought protection at Bryan's Fort for about two years. During this time, he fought in several skirmishes with the Shawnee Indians. On 19 August 1782, under the command of Simon Girty, the Army was defeated by the Shawnee at the Battle of Blue Licks. In the fall of 1782, John was in a scouting party under the command of General George Rogers Clark and Colonel Daniel Boone when they marched to a Shawnee town, captured, and burned the town without a battle.

After the war, John left Kentucky and moved to Mansker's Station near Nashville, Tennessee, where he lived for about two years and then moved to Laurens County, South Carolina. John and his wife, Martha Calhoun, daughter of Thomas Calhoun, lived in Laurens County for about eighteen years and then

moved to Sevier County, where he resided until 1826 when he moved to Rutherford County, Tennessee. John died 1 September 1844 in Rutherford County. (1)
    John and Martha's children:
- Stephen was born on 23 June 1775.

Sources: (1) Southern Campaign American Revolution Pension Statements & Rosters, transcribed by Will Graves

Clack, Major John Sterling

The Clack family is legendary in Sevier County because of John and his brother, Spencer. John was born about 1757 in Loudon County, Virginia, to John and Mary Kennon Clack. Major Clack served under General Morgan at the Battle of Guilford Court House and at the Battle of Cowpens, where he received the surrender of the British after their defeat. He was also with General Wayne Anthony at the storming of Stoney Point in 1778. (1)

John married Sarah "Sally" Standifer, daughter of James and Martha Watkins Standifer, on 4 November 1779 in Henry County, Virginia. Sarah was born 20 July 1758 in Bristol Parish, Virginia, and died 1823 in Giles County, Tennessee. (1)

After the war, John moved with his family to Sevier County, where he became active in the community. He was the younger brother of Spencer Clack, and together, they helped settle and create both Sevier County and the State of Tennessee. He was elected Justice to the first Sevier County court that convened on 4 July 1796. He represented Sevier County in the Constitutional Convention of 1796. (1)

In 1815, John moved to Giles County, where he continued in public life, representing the county in the State Senate until his death in 1831. He died 22 January 1831 on his estate "Mount Moriah" near Pulaski in Giles County. (1)

John and Sarah's children:
- Martha was born 1782 in Henry, Virginia, married Spencer Beavers in Giles County in 1807, and died 17 April 1867 in De Soto, Mississippi.

- Hannah was born in 1787 in Sevier County and married George Rice of Giles County.
- Fanny was born 1798 in Henderson, Tennessee, married Quinton Nix Rice in 1820 in Giles County, and died 11 April 1887 in Arkansas.
- Naomi was born 1785 in Henry County, Virginia, and married Unknown Smith.
- Spencer, the namesake of his uncle, was born 1873 and married Lucy Williams Jones on 19 January 1818. She was the daughter of Wilson Jones of North Carolina. [2]

Sources: (1) The Family Chronicle and Kinship Book, Octavia Zollicoffer Bond, 1928, p. 649-53, (2) Family Search, Church of Jesus Christ of Latter-day Saints

Clack, Spencer

Spencer was one of General George Washington's officers. Spencer was born 28 March 1746 in Fairfax County, Virginia (now Loudoun County), to John and Mary Kennon Clack. He was the older brother of Major John Clack, who joined Spencer in Sevier County to create Sevier County and the State of Tennessee. He served in the Henry County, Virginia Militia during the Revolutionary War and was a First Lieutenant in Company "A" under Captain William Ryan. (1) He also served as a Lieutenant under General George Washington. (2)

Spencer married Mary Beavers 2 November 1766 and moved to Sevier County in 1788, where he received a land grant from the state of Tennessee for 442 acres. Near his home, he operated one of the first mills, as well as a cotton gin and wool carding machine. Spencer was active in the Forks of the Little Pigeon Baptist Church (now known as the First Baptist Church of Sevierville). After the original log church was destroyed by fire, Spencer gave land for a new church and a cemetery. (3)

Spencer was one of the five delegates who represented Sevier County at the Tennessee State Constitutional Convention of 1796. He was Sevier County's first State Representative in 1796 and served in both the state house and senate until his death on 9 July 1832. He was buried on the land he gave the church to use as a cemetery, The Forks of the River Cemetery. Mary died 14 August 1840 and was buried beside her husband. (3)

Spencer and Mary's children:
- Raleigh was born 4 June 1772 in Virginia and married first Mary Randles (1770-1816) on 28 October 1791, and after her death, he married Martha Kerr 12 August 1816. Raleigh died 1842 in Rhea County, Tennessee.
- Rhoda was born 1 March 1776 in Virginia and married James Randles in 1791 in Virginia.
- Catherine was born 23 June 1778 and married Reverend Elijah Rogers in 1794.
- Frances was born in 1783 and first married Mordecai Gist, and after his death, she married John Mynatt.
- Mary was born in 1785, married William Miller, and died 1860 in Meigs County, Tennessee.
- Martha married Josiah Rogers in Franklin County, Virginia, in 1786.
- Malvina married Major Beavers and moved to Talladega County, Alabama.

(3), (4)

Sources: (1) Sevier County and Its Heritage, 1994, Don Mills, p. 175, (2) Forks of the Little Pigeon Cemetery and Park History, Theresa Williams, Sevier Co. Public

Library System, (3) Smoky Mountain Ancestral Quest, www.smokykin.com maintained by David L. Beckwith, (4) Family Search, Church of Latter-day Saints

Compton, Jeremiah H.

Jeremiah witnessed an important moment in American history at Yorktown. Jeremiah was born October 1754 in Brunswick County, New Jersey, to unknown parents. Jeremiah stated in his application for a Revolutionary War Pension, #29, that he lived in Botetourt, Virginia, in the fall of 1780 and volunteered under Captain Charles Robertson, Lieutenant James Setherdale, and Major Campbell. The company marched to Salisbury, North Carolina, and on to the Catawba River to keep the British from crossing at the fords. Upon arrival, it was learned that General William L. Davidson had been killed at Cowan's Ford on 1 February 1781. The company retreated to Salisbury and then on to the Yadkin River, where the company scrimmaged with British Major Campbell. They marched to Guilford, North Carolina, and Jeremiah was discharged, having served three months. (1), (2)

Again in Botetourt County, Virginia, in the fall of 1781, Jeremiah volunteered under Captain David May and Major James Smith, marched to York, Pennsylvania, and was at the siege of Little York that resulted in the surrender of British General Cornwallis. He helped guard the Winchester Barracks for three months and was honorably discharged. (3)

Jeremiah returned to Botetourt County after the war and married Elizabeth Laymon (1763-1858) in about 1784 and continued to live there until 1793, at which time they moved to Washington County, North Carolina (now Tennessee). Eight years later, they moved to Sevier County, where Jeremiah died 19 June 1844 and is buried in Shiloh Cemetery in Pigeon Forge. Elizabeth died 18 May 1858 and is also buried in Shiloh Cemetery. (1), (2), (6)

Jeremiah and Elizabeth's children:
- Joseph born in 1788 and married Hettie Mullendore, the daughter of Abraham Mullendore and Susannah Laymon Mullendore.
- Zacharia was born 1790.
- Cyrus was born 1802 in Sevier County.
- William M. was born 1806 in Sevier County. (4)

Interesting Fact: Elizabeth Layman Compton was the sister of Revolutionary War Patriot Jacob Layman, who also moved to Sevier County after the war. (5)

Sources: (1) U.S. Headstone Applications for Military Veterans, 1925-1963 for Jeremiah Compton. (2) Southern Campaign American Revolution Pension Statements and Rosters, transcribed by Will Graves, (3) Smoky Mountain Ancestral Quest, smoky kin.com-maintained by David L. Beckwith, (4) Jacob Layman, Revolutionary Soldier, Beulah D. Linn, Sevier County Historian, (5) In the Shadow of the Smokies, Smoky Mountain Historical Society, 1993. p. 345.

Creswell, Andrew

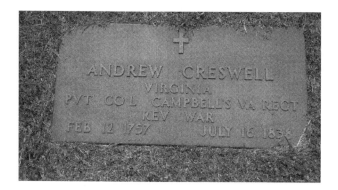

The church Andrew founded, Eusebia Presbyterian, is still going strong and is one of the oldest churches in Tennessee. Andrew was born 12 February 1757 in South Carolina to William Henry and Rebecca R. Bradley Creswell. William and Rebecca brought their family to the frontier settlements of Virginia in 1772. Andrew entered the service in the summer of 1776 in Washington County, Virginia, in the company of Captain Colville and Colonel Arthur Campbell, to perform garrison duty at Black's Station for three months, after which he was discharged. Thereafter, he was drafted each summer for the next four or five years to protect the headwaters of the Clinch River against the depredations of the northern Indians.

In September 1780, he was drafted to go to Kings Mountain, under the command of Captain Dysart, Lieutenant Newell, and Ensign Robert Campbell under the command of Colonel William Campbell. He returned home exactly one month later, after the Battle of Kings Mountain. In 1781, Colonel

William Campbell called the Washington County Regiment together and gave the soldiers a choice of either going West to defend the frontier stations against the Indians or joining General Nathanael Greene at Guilford. Andrew chose the latter and proceeded under the command of Colonel Campbell to Guilford. However, the Regiment did not arrive until after the Battle of Guilford, thus Andrew was discharged and returned home. (1)

Andrew married Dorothy "Dolly" Evans on 22 March 1780. Dorothy was born on 11 December 1756 in Abington, Virginia, to Samuel Evans and Nancy Ann Colville. In 1787, Andrew moved his wife and children; his father, William; his sister, Polly, and brother, Henry, to the Boyd's Creek area of Sevier County. He became active in the community and was one of the founders of Eusebia Presbyterian Church in Blount County, Tennessee. Andrew died 16 July 1838 in Boyd's Creek and is buried in the Eusebia Cemetery. Dorothy died 11 December 1832 and is also buried in Eusebia Cemetery. (2)

Andrew and Dorothy's children:
- Nancy was born 5 February 1781 in Virginia, married John Rundles in 1805 in Sevier County, and died 10 October 1854 in Sevier County.
- William Evans was born 10 June 1782 in Blount County, married Elizabeth McMurry, and died 7 May 1852.
- Rebecca was born 3 May 1786 in Sevier County, married Joseph Robert McMurry in 1803 in Virginia, and died in 1849 in Davis, Iowa.
- Mary Elizabeth was born 1789 in Knox County, Tennessee, married George Michael Huffaker on 18 June 1780 in

- Virginia, and died 12 June 1876 in Knox County.
- Samuel was born 14 April 1792 in Sevier County, married Margaret "Polly" Fagala, and died 13 September 1859.
- Margaret V. was born 24 March 1794 in Sevier County, married William Glasco Snoddy, and died 12 June 1876.
- Dorothy was born 22 March 1798 in Sevier County, married John A. Pitner, and died 23 August 1838 in Walker, Georgia. (3)

Historical Fact: Andrew's wife, Dorothy Evans Creswell, was the sister of Andrew Evans of Virginia, a Revolutionary War patriot who moved to Sevier County, and Andrew's sister, Sarah Jane, was the wife of Andrew Evans.

Sources: (1) Southern Campaign American Revolution Pension Statements, transcribed by Will Graves (2) find a grave memorial, Andrew J. Creswell (3) Family search, Church of the Latter-day Saints.

Crowson, William

William was a hero while serving for his country and died a hero saving the lives of two youngsters in Giles County, Tennessee. William was born in 1740 in Johnston, North Carolina, to John (1717-1780), of Accomack, Virginia, and Sarah Shook Crowson (1719-1780), of Richmond Virginia. He enlisted in the Wilmington District Militia during the Revolutionary War and served as a private. William married Mary Patience Thomas, born 1742 in Jones County, North Carolina. She was the daughter of Reverend Jonathan Thomas of Isle of Wight, Virginia, and Mary Hillard Thomas of Edgecombe, North Carolina.

In 1794, William was living in Sevier County in an area known as Crowson's Cove (now Wear's Valley). At that time, the area was plagued with attacks by Cherokee Indians, who were not happy with settlers who had moved onto their land. One such attack has become a local legend. On 14 May 1794, William's son Aaron and Aaron's friend Peter Pearcifield were out looking at land for a possible homesite when they were attacked by Indians. Pearcifield was shot and killed, but Aaron managed to escape to nearby Wear's Fort. Three men, Joseph Evans, James Hubbard, Jr., and Thomas Sellers formed a vigilante group, dressed and painted themselves as Indians, and set out to avenge the attack. The men sneaked into the Indians' camp at night and killed four Cherokees asleep around a campfire.

In 1807, William sold his land in Crowson's Cove and moved to Giles County, Tennessee. He became a well-known and beloved person in the area for helping every new settler clear their land and build a house. On 14 July 1814, William was on the Tennessee

River, a good distance from home, when he watched two boys in a boat arguing over who would tie up the boat once they reached the bank. The current pushed the boat back out into the water, and the boys yelled for William's help. While in the water, William apparently suffered cramps and drowned. (1)

William and Mary's children:
- Mary Elizabeth was born 1770 in Jones County, North Carolina, married William Hatcher (1766-1820), and died 5 March 1838 in Sevier County.
- Aaron was born 18 March 1773 in Jones County, married Jane Barnes (1774-1849), and died 18 February 1849 in Sevier County.
- Moses was born 6 October 1778 in Jones County, married Martha Wood (1775-1828), and died after 1850 in Lowndes County, Mississippi.
- Richard was born 17 April 1780 in Jones County, married Hulda Lindsay (1775-1812), and after she died, he married Sarah Moore (1775-1835). He died 12 September 1826 in Shelby County, Alabama.
- William was born 1783 in Sevier County, Tennessee, married Gilly Hightower (1783-1807), and died 1814 in Giles County.
- Jacob was born 1784 in Giles County, married Jane Greer (1792-1859), and died 1835 in Lauderdale County, Alabama.
- John was born 1786 in Giles County, married Mary Threewit (1780-1850), and died 1860 in Lamar County, Texas.

- Abraham was born 1790 in Giles County, married Jane Barnes, and died 1830 in Fayette County, Tennessee.
- Isaac was born 1792 in Giles County, married Frances Mills (1795-1830), and died 10 April in Ferndale, Pulaski County, Arkansas.
- Thomas was born 17 April 1794 in Giles County, married Jane Vinson (1794-1882), and died 2 May 1857.
- Jane was born 11 April 1798 in Giles County, married Eliah Vinson (1790-1865), and died 28 January 1857 in Giles County.

Historical Fact: Hulda Lindsay is the daughter of Patriot David Lindsey and James Hubbard, Jr. is the son of Patriot James Hubbard, Sr.

Sources: (1) Eli and Betsy McCarter Family, 2006, (2) ancestry. com, search, William Crowson, (3) rootsweb.com. Mackie-Thomas Family Tree, Larry Kinstler, owner, (4) Smoky Mountain Ancestral Quest, smokykin.com, maintained by David L. Beckwith

Cusick, John B.

A community between Sevierville and Seymour is still referred to as Cusick, in honor of John B. Cusick. He was born 1744 in Cecil, Maryland, the son of Samuel and Cynthia Vance Cusick. He moved to Washington County, Virginia, in the early 1770s and married Martha Blackburn (1743-1824) in 1771 in Washington County. She was the daughter of John and Elizabeth Colville Blackburn and the half-sister of Lieutenant Samuel Newell, Jr. After John Blackburn's death, Elizabeth married Samuel Newell, Sr. John fought in the Battle of Kings Mountain and is one of the soldiers who claimed credit for killing British commander Colonel Patrick Ferguson. John was later wounded on the way to the Battle of Guilford Courthouse. [1] [2] His grave marker at Eusebia Presbyterian Church in Blount County, Tennessee, shows that he was a member of John Sevier's "Sharp Shooters." [3]

In the late 1780s, John moved his family to Sevier County, and according to family legend, he traded directly with the Cherokee Indians for his land. He was a prominent businessman in Maryville, Tennessee, and was an associate of Sam Houston, who later became governor of Tennessee and the Republic of Texas. John was Justice of the Peace and a leading member in Eusebia Presbyterian Church in Blount County, Tennessee. [1] John died on 3 July 1816 and is buried in Eusebia Cemetery, and Martha died on 24 December 1824 and is also buried in Eusebia Cemetery.

John and Martha's children:
- John B. was born 1771 in Virginia, married Hulda Durham on 8 October

1799 in Blount County, and died in 1842 in Blount County.
- Joseph was born 1772 in Virginia, married Jane Blackburn on 31 January 1793 in Knox County, Tennessee, and died 15 October 1854 in Edgar County, Illinois.
- Rebecca was born 1779 in Virginia, married Benjamin Tipton, Sr., on 19 December 1795 in Blount County, and died about 1850 in Alabama.
- David was born on 4 June 1782 in Virginia, married Elizabeth Keeler in October 1806, and died 14 October 1864 in Edgar, Illinois.
- Samuel was born 4 November 1785 in Virginia, married Nancy Evans in 1808, and died 11 October 1862 in Blount County.
- Martha "Patsy" was born 1 June 1789 in Virginia, married John B. Tipton in 1810, and died 28 March 1866 in Blount County. (1), (4)

Historical Fact: Nancy Evans, who married Samuel, is the sister of Patriot Andrew Evans (Virginia), a Revolutionary War soldier who also moved to Sevier County.

Sources: (1) Sevier County, Tennessee and Its Heritage, 1994, Don Mills, Inc., p 181; (2) Smoky Mountain Ancestral Quest,smokykin.com-maintained by David L. Beckwith, (3) Find a Grave Memorial Family search, Church of the Latter-day Saints (4)Family search, Church of the Latter-day Saints

Davies (Davis), Zachariah

Zachariah was born 6 February 1760 in Shrewsburg, Pennsylvania. He served as a private in the Pennsylvania Continental Line under General Anthony Wayne. Zachariah's Revolutionary War Pension shows that he also served with Colonel William Butler and Captain William Stephens. He was originally placed on the Pension Rolls in Ohio but applied for a transfer to Tennessee on 16 February 1839. He received Pension #S1660 for service in the Revolutionary War. (1), (2)

Zachariah married Cathrine Elizabeth Hooft about 1784. He moved to Knox County, Kentucky, in early 1800s and lived there until about 1815. Records show that Cathrine died in Sevier County on 1 March 1815 and Zachariah died in 1842 in Sevier County. (1)

Zachariah and Cathrine Elizabeth's children:
- Jacob was born 1793 in Rockbridge County, Virginia, and married Nancy Hedrick on 12 June 1818.
- Nancy was born 26 February 1796 in Greenbrier County, Virginia, and died in 1834 in Laurence County, Ohio.
- Jesse was born 3 January 1802 in Green County, Kentucky, and married Lydia Keener on 18 October 1821 in Sevier County.
- Lydia was born 1 March 1806 in Sevier County and died 14 April 1869 in Knox County, Tennessee. (1)

Sources: (1) Joseph Sharp Collection, McClung Museum, Knoxville, TN; (2) Barbour Mountain Advocate; 8 May 2003, Nadine D. Smith, Registrar, Dr. Thomas Walker Chapter, NSDAR

Davis, Joel

After the war, Joel dedicated his life to educating children in his community. He was born 1 October 1763 in Granville County (now Wake County), North Carolina, to Joseph, Jr., (1724-1792) and Mary Barker Davis. Joseph and Mary Barker married 2 October 1744 in Trinity Parish, Charles, Maryland.

In June 1780, Joel volunteered in Johnston County, North Carolina, under Captain Edmond Griffin and Colonel Allen and marched from Johnston County to Charleston, South Carolina, served for three months under General William Caswell, and was discharged by Captain Griffin and Colonel Allen. In November 1780, he volunteered as a private under Captain Phillip Thomas, Lieutenant Hanby, and Major William Dennis and marched from Johnston County to Cheraw Hills on the Pee Dee River to fight against the British; however, a battle did not occur, and he was discharged after three months by Captain Thomas and Major Dennis.

In March 1781, Joel volunteered under Captain Asa Briant and General Butler, marched to Camden, South Carolina, and was in the Battle of Camden, commanded by General Nathanael Greene. On 12 June 1781, he volunteered under Major Reading Blount in the 3rd Regiment of North Carolina Militia, marched to Eutaw Springs, and was in the Battle of Eutaw Springs on 8 September 1781. After the Battle of Eutaw Springs, he transferred into the 1st North Carolina Regiment under Captain Thomas Armstrong, served in this company for twelve months, and was discharged by Captain Armstrong and Major James McKee. Again, in October 1782, Joel volunteered in the Johnston County Militia, under Captain Robert Gillespie, marched against the Tories in several North Carolina locations, and was discharged by Colonel Benton, having served three months.

After the war, Joel continued to live in Johnston County until 1785 and married Rebecca Coates on 4 February 1785 in Wake County, North Carolina. They moved to Halifax County, North Carolina, and lived there about three years. After 1789, he moved about every two to three years as he made a living as a school master. He taught school in Cocke County, Tennessee, for fourteen to fifteen years and then in Jefferson County for about two years and moved to Sevier County about 1825. Joel applied for a Revolutionary War Pension, #351, in Sevier County on 25 February 1832. He returned to Jefferson County on 13 February 1834 and died there 12 February 1841. (1), (2)

Joel and Rebecca's children:
- Barbara was born 22 October 1785 in Halifax County, North Carolina, married Benjamin Roberts in 1802, and died 1860 in Sevier County.
- Joel, Jr., was born 24 August 1791 in Johnston County, married Nancy Reams (1799-1845) in April 1816, and died April 1823.
- Thomas Coates was born 6 November 1804 in North Carolina and married Levina Unknown. (1), (3)

Sources: (1) Southern Campaign American Revolution Pension Statements & Rosters, transcribed by Will Graves. (2) Revolutionary War Gravesite's in Knox and Surrounding Counties, Stephen Holston Chapter, SAR, (3) Family search, The Church of Jesus Church of Latter-day Saints.

Derrick, Johann Jacob

The land Jacob donated in 1787 to create Fox Cemetery continues to be a valuable part of the community. He was born 16 May 1752 in Berks County, Pennsylvania, to Johann Simon, Sr., (1712-1787) and Catharine Margaretha Stapleton (Derk) Derrick (1721-1796). Jacob is listed on United States Revolutionary War Rolls, 1775-1783, as having served in May 1777 and June 1778 in Pennsylvania. (1), (2)

Jacob moved to Shenandoah County Virginia along with his father Simon and a brother, George, and all three became landowners. He married Eva Margaretha "Margaret" Fox, daughter of Johann Adam and Catherine Iler (Fuchs) Fox. Soon after the death of their father, Jacob and his brother, George, moved to what is now Sevier County. Jacob led a caravan consisting of their families, Jacob Bird, and Mark Fox. Both Jacob and George obtained grants for land based on their occupancy of the land prior to 1807. Jacob built Derrick's Fort, a grist mill on Flat Creek, and in 1819, St. James Lutheran Church. Mark Fox was killed by Indians on 21 June 1787, and Jacob set aside land on his property for a cemetery and named it Fox Cemetery in Mark's honor. This cemetery is still being used to this day. (3)

Jacob and Eva's children:
- Simon was born 1770 in Shenandoah County, Virginia, married Lydia Tipton 1806 in Shenandoah, Virginia, and died December 1867 in Lamar County, Texas.
- Tobias was born about 1772 in Shenandoah County, married Magdalena

Lewis on 11 December 1807 in Jefferson County, Tennessee, and died after 1830.
- George was born in 1775 in Virginia and died in 1831.
- Jonas was born 1778 in Virginia.
- Henry was born 1785 in Virginia, married Elizabeth Guyon 21 August 1815, and died 1842 in Ohio. (2)

Sources: (1) U. S. Revolutionary War Rolls 1775-1783, Publication # M236, Film Number # 83 and 129, National Archives and Records Services, (2) The Church of Jesus Church of Latter Day Saints (3) Smoky Mountain Historical Society Newsletter, summer 1983, pp. 50-51

Duggan, Robert

Sevier County was settled by the Dutch and the Irish, and Robert is an excellent example of an Irishman fighting for his new homeland. He was born 1762 in Ulster, Ireland, the son of Hugh (1740-1792) and Margaret Wilson Duggan (1749-1794). Robert came with his parents and brothers, Hugh, William and John, from Ireland to America around 1775 and first settled in Massachusetts, but by the time the Revolutionary War began, the family was living in Virginia. (1)

Revolutionary War records show Robert served three years as a sergeant in Captain Richard Edsall's Company of Colonel Oliver Spencer's Regiment of Continental troops. Muster rolls dated 18 July 1778 show Robert at Croten River tending the sick, and another muster roll dated 11 September 1778 has him at King's Ferry, again tending the sick. A company muster roll dated 21 January 1780 shows Robert was discharged 11 January 1780. In the *Historical Register of Virginians in the Revolution 1775-1783* by John H. Gwathney, it shows Robert received bounty land for his service in the war. (1)

According to family legend, the Duggan Family moved to Sevier County in 1784 and settled on the East Fork of the Little Pigeon River. Robert received 3 Tennessee land grants in Sevier County totaling over 300 acres. A school house was located on his land as early as 1826. Robert's name is listed on a petition entitled "Inhabitants of the Western Country" submitted to the North Carolina General Assembly requesting the recognition of the State of Franklin. (1)

Robert married Margaret Dunn 7 March 1792 in Greene County in the territory south of the River Ohio. (1) It is believed Robert died about 1842 and is buried in the old Duggan Cemetery now known as Mount Pleasant Cemetery in Jones Cove. (2)

Robert and Margaret's children:
- George was born 24 November 1793 and is believed to have gone to Missouri.
- Mary Jane was born 24 August 1796 in Sevier County, married Hugh Duggan on 5 March 1811 in Sevier County, and died 14 February 1878 in Bradley County, Tennessee.
- Margaret was born 21 October 1798.
- Wilson was born 23 September 1803 in Sevier County and married Elizabeth Keeler, daughter of Joseph and Catherine Keeler. He died 14 February 1875 in Sevier County.
- Robert, Jr., was born 5 March 1805 in Sevier County, married Cassandra Dunn in 1825, and died in 1853 in Sevier County.
- Elizabeth was born 11 December 1811 in Sevier County, married John Lee McNabb in 1830, and died 22 January 1881 in Cocke County, Tennessee.
- James was born 15 August 1812 in Sevier County and married Mary Evans in 1843-1845.
- Campbell was born 24 June 1815.

Sources: (1) Smoky Mountain Historical Society Newsletter, summer, 1999, p. 14. (2) Robert Duggan, Revolutionary Soldier, Beulah D. Linn, Sevier County Historian, Sevier County News-Record & Gatlinburg Press-Section D-Page1, 10 June 1976. (3) Family Search, The Church of Jesus Christ of the Latter-day Saints.

Emert (Emmert), Frederick

The beautiful and serene area known as Emert's Cove is Frederick's legacy. He was born 11 October 1754 in Berks County, Pennsylvania, to John George (1716-1796) and Eva Marie Graff Emmert (1716-1717). Frederick fought in the early years of the Revolutionary War, returned home, and married Barbara Neidig (Knight) in 1778. He was drafted again, and because he did not want to leave his new wife, he hired a substitute to serve in his place. Later, Frederick enlisted and served until the end of the war and was under the command of General George Washington and Colonel Anthony Wayne in Berks County, Pennsylvania. He was present for the surrender of General Cornwallis at Yorktown on October 9, 1781. (1)

After the war, Frederick migrated to Tennessee and settled in the area of the East Fork of the Little Pigeon River in Greene County, Tennessee (now Sevier County). This area became known as Emert's Cove. (2) Frederick died 7 January 1829 in Emert's Cove, and Barbara died 7 July 1842 also in Emert's Cove, and both are buried in Emert's Cove Cemetery. (1), (2), (3), (4)

Frederick and Barbara's children:
- Barbara Ann was born 27 December 1778 in Berks County, Pennsylvania, married Johan Martin Shults, Jr., and died 23 September 1875 and is buried in Emert's Cove Cemetery in Sevier County.
- Mary "Polly" was born about 1780 in Hampshire, Virginia, married Arnett Shields, and died after 1843.
- K. Catherine was born 27 December 1780 in Tennessee, married Reverend

Richard Evans, and died 1888 and is buried in Emert's Cove Cemetery.
- Mary was born 5 November 1782 and died in 1842.
- Elizabeth was born 27 November 1783, married Reverend John Roberts, and died 1888 and is buried in Middle Creek Methodist Church Cemetery in Sevier County.
- Philip was born 17 October 1786, married Elizabeth Reagan, and died 23 July 1821 and is buried in Middle Creek Methodist Church Cemetery.
- Margaret was born 9 March 1788, married Robert Shields, and died 1862 and is possibly buried in Primitive Baptist Church Cemetery, Cades Cove, Blount County, Tennessee.
- Louisa was born 11 February 1789-1790, reportedly married Robert Nelson Reagan, and died before 1843.
- Frederick E., Jr., was born 12 January 1790, married Celia Drusilla Reagan, and died 10 April 1871 and is buried in Tuckaleechee Campground Cemetery in Blount County.
- Daniel was born 13 June 1793, married Sarah Reagan, and died 28 August 1851 and is buried in Emert's Cove Cemetery.

(2), (3)

Historical Fact: Elizabeth, Celia Drusilla, Sarah, and Robert Nelson Reagan are the children of Patriot Timothy Reagan.

Sources: (1) Ancestry. Com- Johan Frederick Emert, (2) findagrave.com, (3) Smoky Mountain Ancestral Quest, smokykin.com, maintained by David L. Beckwith , (4) In the Shadow of the Smokies, Smoky Mountain Historical Society, 1993, p. 404

Evans, Andrew Sr., North Carolina

As soon as Andrew came to Sevier County, he received permission to start a ferry service on the French Broad River, which was a valuable commodity to farmers and travelers at that time. He was born 28 September 1759 in Mecklenberg County, North Carolina, to David William and Dorothy Moore Evans. (1) Andrew first served as a volunteer in the Virginia Militia under Captain William Neil and Colonel Campbell. During this time, the troops were in pursuit of Tories in the New River area of Montgomery County, Virginia.

A short time later, Andrew was ordered by Colonel Campbell to aid in the guarding of Tory Captain James Carr for two weeks while he was being transferred to Richmond, Virginia. This tour took about one week. Again, he was called on by Colonel William Campbell to march with a body of troops to the mountains bordering North Carolina to guard against the Tories who were living in the area, and this tour lasted seven to eight weeks.

Soon after Andrew returned home, a call went out to all the troops to be ready at a moment's notice. Again, he entered service as a volunteer under Captain William Edmondson, marched to Abingdon, Virginia, and joined the troops in the company of Colonel William Campbell. These combined forces marched into North Carolina, met Evan Shelby's troops, and marched on to Kings Mountain. The Battle of Kings Mountain followed, but, sadly, Major Edmondson was killed. Andrew is later quoted as saying that he saw British Major Patrick Ferguson fall from his horse, mortally wounded. He continued in service for two months and returned home in late-November 1781.

Shortly after returning home, he joined John Sevier's troops, marched into Cherokee country and had one small engagement, in which several Indians were wounded and seventeen killed. A few days later, the troops continued to march south and had Christmas dinner in the Indian town of Chota. (This was possibly the Battle of Boyd's Creek.)

Andrew married Elizabeth Fain on 5 December 1781 in Jonesborough, Washington County, Tennessee. Elizabeth was born 29 July 1764 in Chester County, Pennsylvania, to Nicholas Thomas and Elizabeth Taylor Fain. (2)

It is not clear when Andrew and his family moved to Sevier County, but he was living here in 1787, as proven by North Carolina Land Grant No.1268 dated 20 September 1787. The land located in Greene County (now Sevier County) consisted of 250 acres on the north side of the French Broad River. The Great Indian War Trail transverses this land, and located nearby is the site of the Battle of Boyd's Creek. In 1790, Andrew was given permission by Greene County Court to operate a ferry at his plantation on the French Broad River. A document dated 16 April 1798 called "intent to sell property" shows that Andrew's son, John, owned the ferry and it was later sold to John Brabson, whose heirs operated the ferry until 1918. Today, this property is still owned by the Brabson heirs. (3) Andrew lived in Sevier County for thirteen years and then moved to Pulaski, Kentucky, lived there for twenty-seven years and later moved to Owen, Illinois, where he died 5 December 1840. Elizabeth Fain Evans died 8 August 1850, also in Owen, and both are buried in Asher Graveyard in Owen County, Indiana.

Andrew and Elizabeth's children:
- David was born 11 January 1783 in Washington County, Tennessee, married

Elizabeth McCullough on 26 January 1802, and died 1837 in Owen, Indiana.
- Nathaniel was born 21 January 1785 and died in 1834-1837 in Owen, Indiana.
- Jesse was born 13 March 1787 in Washington County, married Hester M. Newell in 1810, and died 13 December 1875 in Owen County, Indiana.
- John Fain was born 27 June 1789 in Kentucky, married Mary "Polly" Hodges on 8 January 1822 in Sevier County, and died 1891.
- Elizabeth was born 1792, married Matthew Wilson on 19 January 1809 in Pulaski, Kentucky, and died before 1850 in Lauderdale, Alabama.
- Andrew, Jr., was born about 1794 in Jefferson, Kentucky, married Susannah Newell in 1814, and died 3 April 1863 in Tipton, Indiana.
- Nancy was born 2 February 1793 in Knox County, Tennessee, married Lewis Morgan in 1812 in Pulaski, Kentucky, and died 1837 in Owen County, Indiana.
- Samuel was born 2 April 1795 in Kentucky, married Marjorie Modrell on 1 January 1818 in Pulaski, Kentucky, and died 2 February 1875 in Owen, Indiana.
- Mary "Polly" was born 1799 in Pulaski County, Kentucky, married Joel Richardson on 9 February 1818 in Pulaski, Kentucky, and died 22 May 1871 in Boone, Indiana.

- William was born in 1792 in Kentucky and married Maximilia Cunningham in Chester, Pennsylvania in 1816.
- James was born 28 August 1803, married Jane Newell on 20 April 1837 in Owen, Indiana, and died 24 July 1866 in Tipton, Indiana.
- Rachel was born 28 December 1805 in Pulaski, Kentucky, married John Couchman in 1825 and then James Burcham in 1831, and died 5 February 1885 in Washington, Indiana. (1)

Historical Fact: Hester, Susannah, and Jane Newell are daughters of Patriot Samuel Newell. Also counted among Andrew and Elizabeth's descendants are Birch Evan Bayh, Jr., a former US Senator from Indiana and his son, Birch Evan Bayh, III, also a former US Senator and Governor of Indiana.

Sources: (1) Family Search, Church of Jesus Christ of Latter-day Saints, (2) Revolutionary Soldiers, Sevier Co. Joseph Sharp Collection, McClung Museum, (3) Ferries on the French Broad River in Sevier County, Smoky Mountain Historical Society Newsletter by Stella Underwood, Elaine R. Wells, Bobby G. Wilhoite, Cherel B. Henderson and Beulah D. Linn.

Evans, Andrew, Virginia

    Andrew is connected to the prominent Creswell family of Boyd's Creek. He was born 1 April 1763 in Frederick County, Virginia, the son of Samuel II and Nancy Ann Colville Evans. The Evans family moved to Washington County, Virginia, before the war. In April 1779, Andrew substituted for his father, Samuel, who had been drafted into the Washington County Militia. He served six weeks under Lieutenant Benjamin Cooper and Captain Duncan, guarding the frontiers against the Shawnees, and was honorably discharged by Captain Duncan. (1), (2)

    In his next tour, he was drafted in a horse company in Washington County under Lieutenant Robert Campbell to suppress the Tories. After rendezvousing at Abingdon, Virginia, they marched to Wilkes County, North Carolina, crossed Stone Mountain at Deep Gap and New River, then continued on to the Wilkes County Court House. Andrew remained there for four weeks and was discharged.

    In late summer of 1780, he volunteered under Ensign James Vance, Lieutenant John Bradley, and Captain Andrew Colville to go against the Tories at Mulberry Hollows. After serving there for three weeks, he was discharged by Captain Colville and returned home.

    In September 1780, Andrew substituted for his brother, Joseph, who had been drafted in Washington County under Lieutenant Robert Campbell, Captain Andrew Colville, and Lieutenant Colonel William Campbell. After rendezvousing in Abingdon, the troops crossed the Doe River and marched across Yellow Mountain into North Carolina and on to Kings Mountain. The troops consisted of a thousand horsemen commanded by Colonels William Campbell, Isaac Shelby, John Sevier, James Williams, and Benjamin Cleveland. The five colonels elected William Campbell to be the principal commander. The Battle of Kings Mountain lasted just over an hour before the British surrendered. The next day, the British prisoners were divided among the regiments. Andrew's regiment, along with their prisoners, marched to the Burke County Court House, where they were relieved by the North Carolina Militia. He was discharged after having served six weeks.

About the first of March 1782, Andrew volunteered again in Washington County under General Nathaneal Greene, Ensign James Vance, Captain Joseph Black, and Colonel William Campbell, marched across New River at Fort Chiswell and on to Wetzel's Mills, where they unexpectedly met the British General Cornwallis, and were defeated. Andrew remained there for six weeks, taking care of the wounded and then returned home. (2)

After the war, Andrew moved to Knox County, Tennessee, and from there to Grainger County, Tennessee, then to Sevier County. He married Sarah Jane Creswell on 22 March 1780 in Virginia. She was born about 1767 in Virginia and died about 1802 in Rhea County, Tennessee. Andrew moved to Rhea County, Tennessee, where he applied for a Revolutionary War Pension, #S3341, on 24 September 1832. He died in Rhea County on 9 April 1839. (1), (2)

Andrew and Sarah's Children:
- Henry Andrew was born 7 November 1783 in Washington County, Virginia, married Mary "Polly" Yadon in April 1782 in Grainger County, Tennessee, and died between 1850 and 1860.

- Mary was born 27 September 1785 in Knox County, Tennessee, married Peter Millard Huffaker (1796-1827) in about 1810 in Knox County, and died 1 November 1865 and is buried in Seven Islands Cemetery in Knox County.
- Samuel was born 13 October 1787 in Washington County, Tennessee, married Elizabeth Kennedy McCullah on 7 August 1810 in Jefferson County, Tennessee, and died 20 August 1863 in Davis, Iowa.
- Ann Colville was born 27 September 1789 in Washington County, Tennessee.
- Andrew C., Jr., was born 25 December 1791 in Washington County, Tennessee, married Sally Sarah Yadon on 9 April 1812 in Grainger County, Tennessee, and died 25 March 1868 in Davis, Iowa.
- Henry Vance was born about 1793 in Tennessee, married Virginia Ellen Jane Capps about 1818 in Tennessee, and died about 1827 in Union County, Tennessee.
- William was born 13 November 1793 in Tennessee, married Mary Elizabeth Evans on 1 April 1819 in Knox County, Tennessee, and died 22 April 1827 in Monroe County, Tennessee. (3)

Historical Fact: Andrew's wife, Sarah, is the sister of Patriot Andrew Creswell and Andrew Creswell's wife, Dorothy, is Andrew's sister.

Ruth C. Davis

Sources: (1) Some Heroes of the Revolution, Zella Armstrong, Pamphlet No. II, (2) Southern Campaigns American Revolution Pension & Rosters, transcribed by Will Graves, (3) Family Search, Church of Jesus Christ of Latter-day Saints.

Fox. Adam

Adam is listed as being in the Virginia 15th Regiment in May 1775. Adam was born in Shenandoah County, Virginia, in 1759, the son of Johann Adam and Anna Catheine Fuch (Fox). Adam's father died when he was about seven or eight years old. Even though his mother did not remarry, she managed to provide for seven children, the family's farm, and even add more land to the family's holdings. (1), (2)

Adam married Elizabeth Derrick in 1783. She was born 1762 in Berks County, Pennsylvania, to Johannes H. and Anna Marie Dunkelberger Derrick. In 1786, Adam, along with his wife and their children, his brother, Mark, plus his brother-in-law, Jacob Derrick, and several other relatives and friends, formed a large caravan of wagons, horses, and mules and moved to Sevier County. Shortly after their arrival, Mark was killed by Indians on 21 June 1787. Jacob Derrick donated land for Mark's burial, and that became Fox Cemetery. Fox Cemetery is still used today. Mark's grave marker is one of the oldest in the county. Adam died after 1819 and is buried in Fox Cemetery, and Elizabeth died in 1830 and is also buried in Fox Cemetery in Sevier County. (1), (2)

Adam and Elizabeth's children:
- John was born 19 February 1784 in Shenandoah County, Virginia, married Nancy Patterson in 1802, and died 25 October 1852 in Sevier County.
- Catherine was born 1785 in Shenandoah County, Pennsylvania,

married Joseph Reinhardt Keeler in 1803, and died 1843 in Sevier County.
- Martha was born 1788 in Sevier County.
- George was born 24 July 1789 in Sevier County, married Christine Eversall about 1811, and died 1859 in Sevier County.
- Adam was born 1794 in Sevier County, married Mary Polly Strader about 1815, and died 8 November 1867 in Jefferson County, Tennessee.
- Mark was born 13 July 1798 in Sevier County, married Anna Dickey in 1818, and died 1862 in Sevier County.
- William was born 12 December 1803 in Sevier County, married Rebecca Dickey in 1823, and died 13 December 1874 in Sevier County.
- Elizabeth was born 1804 in Sevier County, married Alfred Allen in 1828, and died 1850 in Sevier County. (3)

Sources: (1) Smoky Mountain Ancestral Quest, smokykin.com, maintained by David L. Beckwith, (2) Ancestry, U.S. Revolutionary War Rolls, 1775-1783, (3) Family Search, The Church of Jesus Christ of Latter-day Saints

Fain, Charles

Charles experienced the tragic loss of his parents at a young age; however, he persevered and built a successful life for himself and his family. He was born in August 1742 to Richard (1708-1752) and Sarah Burford Fain (1706-1746). Charles was orphaned at a young age and raised by an uncle in Chesterfield County, Virginia. When the Revolutionary War was declared, he was living in Halifax County, Virginia, and from there he moved to Surry County, North Carolina. Charles was drafted in Surry County for a tour of six months under Captain Reed and Colonel Joseph Williams. They marched south to assist the town of Charleston, but upon reaching Moncks Corner, they were informed by Colonel William Washington that the route to Charleston was heavily guarded by the British, so they changed their route and went to Haddrell's Point and from there by boat into Charleston. So many soldiers deserted along the way that only six arrived in Charleston. Charles was then placed under the command of Captain Joseph Collins. Charles remained in Charleston but was taken prisoner by the British and released nine days later and returned home. (1), (2)

Charles married Judath Catharine Spurlock, the daughter of John "Iron Pott" (1722-1794) and Sarah A. Caldwell Spurlock (1730-1764) in1776 in Elbert County, Georgia. On 14 August 1832, Charles appeared in Bedford County, Tennessee Court of Pleas and Quarter Sessions to apply for a Revolutionary War Pension, #S3353. In the application, Charles stated that after the war he moved to Georgia. Afterwards, he moved to Blount County, Tennessee, then to Sevier County, and in 1806(7), moved to Bedford County, Tennessee, where he died in 1834 at the age of 90. (1)

Charles and Judath's children:

- John was born about 1770 in North Carolina and died 1840 in Elbert, Georgia.
- Jesse was born 1780 in Georgia, married Jenny Canway, and died 13 October 1801 in Blount County.
- David Fain was born 26 July 1781 in North Carolina, married Katherine Wood in 1805 in Elbert, Georgia, and died 8 February 1831 in Marshall, Tennessee.
- Katherine was born 20 February 1776 in Granville County, North Carolina, and died 2 May 1859 in Bedford County. (3)

Historical Fact: Katherine Wood Fain was the daughter of Revolutionary Patriot Reverend Richard Wood.

Sources: (1) Southern Campaign American Revolution Pension Statements & Rosters, transcribed by Will Graves, (2) Revolutionary War Gravesite's in Knox and Surrounding Counties, Stephen Holston Chapter, SAR, (3) Family Search, Church of Latter-day Saints

Gilliland, John III

John will forever be remembered for his actions during the Battle of Kings Mountain. He was born about 1725 in Pennsylvania to John II (1706-1780) and Hester Roome (1721- 800) Gilliland. John and Hester were married 3 August 1742 in Philadelphia, Pennsylvania. (1) John fought under Colonel John Sevier at the Battle of Kings Mountain, and even though he had been shot three times by a .69 caliber musket ball, he ascended the mountain on the final push to the top alongside his father-in-law Robert Young. John spotted the British commander Colonel Patrick Ferguson atop his white horse, wearing a red checkered shirt with a sword in one hand and a whistle in his mouth. Gilliland fired, but his flint snapped. He then said to his father-in-law, "There's Ferguson, shoot him." Robert Young is credited with firing the fatal shot that knocked Ferguson out of his saddle, with his spur catching in the stirrup. Earlier that day, Ferguson declared that "God himself and all his angels couldn't get him off that mountain," and he was right. He is still there today, buried under a pile of rocks. (2)

John married Elizabeth Young (1752-1795), the daughter of Robert Young and Mary Douglass, in about 1773. Before the war, Gilliland was instrumental in the establishment of the Watauga Association, a governing body created in 1772 by settlers living along the Watauga River in what is now Elizabethton, Tennessee. After the war, John was an early settler in neighboring Cocke County. He was active in the organization of the State of Franklin and was a member of the 1785 Convention that wrote the Constitution of the new state.

John and Elizabeth's daughter, Mary, was the second wife of Colonel Samuel Wear who was a comrade of Gilliland's at the Battle of Kings Mountain and served with Gilliland as a delegate to the State of Franklin's constitutional convention. Colonel Wear lived in Wear's Fort in present day Pigeon Forge, Tennessee. On 11 August 1795, John was returning home to Cocke County from a visit with his daughter at Fort Wear when he was killed by Indians. John was buried in the Wear Cemetery at Fort Wear. On April 23, 2016, a ceremony honoring John was held at his gravesite, and a new plaque in his memory was unveiled. (2)

John and Elizabeth's children:
- Robert Young was born 1773 in Virginia, married Margaret Claunch on 12 April 1792 in Guilford, North Carolina, and died before 23 December 1803 in Pulaski, Kentucky.
- John was born 1774 in Greene County, Tennessee (now Cocke County), married Axley Unknown in 1795, and died 23 June 1829 in Cape Girardeau, Missouri.
- James was born in 1776 in Greene County, married Elizabeth Raney on 15 October 1801 in Knox County,

Tennessee, and died 25 October 1842 in Henry, Missouri.
- Priscilla was born 1778 and married Anthony Walsh on 20 January 1791 in Greene County.
- Mary "Polly" was born about 1779 in Greene County, married Colonel Samuel Wear (1750-1817) on 30 September 1799, and died on 30 September 1840 in Blount County, Tennessee, and was buried at Wear's Cemetery in Sevier County.
- James Abel was born 1782 in Washington County, Tennessee, married Mary Haynie, and died 6 June 1827 in St. Clair, Alabama.
- Elijah "Eli" was born 1784 in Greene County, married Keziah Haynie (1788-1850), and died 25 August 1867 in Angelina County, Texas.
- Harvey was born in 1786 in Tennessee and died 2 February 1823 in St. Clair, Alabama.
- Isaac was born in 1788 and died in Kansas.
- Josiah was born 1790 in Tennessee and died 6 June 1837 in Aransas, Texas. (1)

Sources: (1) Family Search, Church of the Latter-day Saints, (2) Revolutionary War hero John Gilliland is buried in Pigeon Forge, Carroll McMahan, "Upland Chronicles," ,Mountain Press, Sevierville, TN, (3) In the Shadow of the Smokies, Smoky Mountain Historical Society, 1993, p. 680.

Ruth C. Davis

Gist, Joshua

Joshua provided excellent leadership in the formation of Sevier County before leaving for further ventures. He was born 11 July 1739 in Baltimore County, Maryland, to Nathaniel and Mary Howard Gist. The Gist family moved to Cumberland County, North Carolina, when Joshua was a young boy. He served as captain in the North Carolina Militia under Colonel Thomas Brown's Battalion of Ashe's Brigade. He was also at Camp Wilmington, North Carolina, in July 1776. (1)

After the war, Joshua received and sold several land grants in Cumberland County, North Carolina. He was active in a number of public offices, including the office of Justice of the Peace in Cumberland County. After living in Cumberland County for several years, Joshua moved to Greene County, North Carolina (now Sevier County), in 1783. He was one of the first justices for the Sevier County Court and a delegate to the 1783 convention in Jonesborough to consider the formation of the State of Franklin. When the State of Franklin was formed, he was named Assistant Judge to the Franklin Supreme Court. Joshua was also present at the signing of the Treaty of Dumplin on 19 June 1785 at the home of Major Hugh Henry on Dumplin Creek. This treaty was the most important accomplishment of the State of Franklin. Joshua's home was near the mouth of Dumplin Creek and Gist's Creek. Gist's Creek runs through a large part of western Sevier County and was named for him. (2)

Joshua married Elizabeth Kellam (1749-1818) on 25 November 1766 in Cumberland County. In 1806, Joshua sold his Sevier County land and moved to Henderson County, Kentucky, and he died soon afterwards in 1810. (2)

Joshua and Elizabeth's children:
- Sarah was born 19 September 1772 in Cumberland County, married John Brown on 30 January 1793, and died 30 November 1801 in Jefferson County, Tennessee.
- Mordecai was born in 1775 in North Carolina, married Frances Clack (1783-?) about 1799 in Sevier County, and died in Sevier County in 1812.
- Rachel was born 5 April 1777 in North Carolina, married James Porter in December1794 in South Carolina, married Alexander Smith 1801 in North Carolina, and died in Pickens County, Alabama, on 11 August 1828.
- Nathaniel was born in 1778 in Cumberland County, married Patsy Brooks on 30 April 1807 in Knox County, and died in Union County, Kentucky, about 1842.
- Jane was born 27 January 1780, married Pearcy Yell about 1801 in Coffee County, Tennessee, and died in Bedford County, Tennessee. (3)

Sources: (1) Sevier County, Tennessee, Genealogy & History, Muir and Dorsey, Christopher Gist and Some of his Descendants, (2) Sevier County, Tennessee and Its Heritage, 1994 Don Mills, pp. 4, 5, 10, submitted by D. Morton Rose, Jr., Knoxville, (3) Family Search, Church of Jesus Christ of the Latter-day Saints.

Haggard, Rev. Henry Hazelrigg

Henry took his talent for spreading the Gospel to the new frontier of Alabama. He was born 27 March 1744 in Albemarle County, Virginia, the son of Henry Randolph IV, and Tabitha Poythress Haggard. Henry is listed on Revolutionary War Pay Voucher #2120, Roll #S.115.93. In 1887, he also received a Revolutionary War Land Grant, #1623, in Greene County, Tennessee, for 300 acres. (1)

Henry married Doratha "Dolly" Randolph, daughter of Henry Randolph and unknown mother in about 1766 in Albemarle County, Virginia. Dolly was born 1745 in Chesterfield, Virginia. In 1789, Henry moved his family to the rapidly growing area at the Forks of the Little Pigeon River, where Sevierville was later established. He was instrumental in establishing the Forks of the Little Pigeon Baptist Church. Henry represented Forks of Little Pigeon Church numerous times at Holston Association meetings between 1789 and 1805, as documented in Forks of Little Pigeon Church by Harold Ownby. (2)

After Doratha's death in Sevier County in about 1813, Henry moved to Bibb County, Alabama, with his children James, Martin, Nancy, Noah, Lucy, and Susan and organized the Cahaba Valley Baptist Church in Bibb, Alabama. On the 1840 Bibb County Revolutionary War Census of Pensioners, Henry is listed as living with his daughter Nancy and James Fancher. Henry died in 1842 and is buried in Cahaba Valley Baptist Church Cemetery in Bibb, Alabama.

Henry and Doratha's children:
- Henry, Jr., was born 1769 in Albemarle County, married Lucy Randolph on 6 October 1797 in Dandridge, Tennessee,

and died 1 July 1829 in Jefferson County, Tennessee.
- David was born 9 January 1770 in Albemarle County, married Amelia Elkin on June 27 1793 in Clark County, Kentucky, and died 1850 in Clark County.
- Joel was born 1770 in Albemarle County, married Letta Unknown in 1798 in Jefferson County, and died 1 July 1860 in Huntsville, Texas.
- Mary was born 1778 in North Carolina, married John Sevier Trotter in 1799 at White Oaks Flats (now Gatlinburg, Tennessee), and died 24 January 1803 in Jefferson County.
- James was born about 1779 in Albemarle County, married Mary Atchley 1801 in Sevier County, and died 1851 in McMinn County, Tennessee. Mary died in 1856 in Sevier County.
- William Martin was born 1780 in Jefferson County, married Prudence Morris about 1809 in Sevier County, and died 24 April 1820 in Bibb County, Alabama.
- Susan was born 1782 in Sevier County, married John West Fancher (1782-1864) about 1802 in Jefferson County, and died 1868 in Noxubee, Mississippi.
- Elizabeth was born 1783 in Jefferson County, married John Claubough III about 1801 in Jefferson County, and died 1860 in Madison County, Texas.
- Noah was born 1788 in Green County, North Carolina, married Sarah Randolph

on 28 January 1807 in Jefferson County, and died 2 January 1866 in Shelby County, Alabama.
- Lucy was born 1793 in North Carolina, married Robert Longbotham on 21 March 1821 in Catawba, Alabama, and died 21 August 1873 in Freestone County, Texas.
- Nancy was born 1794 in Jefferson County, married James S. Fancher about 1814 in Sevier County, and died 12 July 1869 in Bibb County, Alabama. (3), (4)

Historical Fact: John Clabough III is the son of John, Jr., and Margaret Ferguson Clabough, and Mary Atchley is the daughter of Thomas and Lydia Richards Atchley.

Sources: (1) Alabama Revolutionary War Residents 1776-1783 for Henry Haggard, (2) Forks of Little Pigeon Church, Harold Ownby, The Buckhorn Press, Gatlinburg, TN, 1989, (3) Descendants of Rev. Henry Hazelrigg Haggard, Web Page, (4) Family Search, Church of Jesus Christ, Latter-day Saints.

Headrick, William J.

The large number of Headrick families living in Sevier County today are undoubtedly William's descendants. He was born 25 December 1744 in Lancaster, Pennsylvania, the son of Georg (1729-1785) and Catherine Elizabeth Haideberg Hedrick (1729-1786). Georg and Catherine Hedrick were born in Germany. (1) On 6 March 1833, at the age of 88, William applied for a Revolutionary War Pension, #S4355, in the Sevier County Court of Pleas and Quarter Sessions. In the application, William stated that in the fall of 1775, he volunteered in Lancaster County for a six-month tour under Captain Thomas Cassenhefner in Major Abraham Ledrour's Regiment as a fifer.

William stated the regiment marched to Philadelphia, Pennsylvania, and remained there for a time and were later joined by another large regiment. These regiments marched to Elizabethtown, then on to New York, where a large battle with the British ensued, and the British were defeated. He does not remember the name of the battle or names of any other officers. After this battle, he marched to Trenton, crossed the Delaware River, returned to Lancaster County, and was discharged in the spring of 1776, having served six months.

In the summer of 1776, he enlisted as a rifle man for a term of eighteen months under Captain Grubb in the 5th or 6th Regiment of the Pennsylvania Infantry. The regiment marched to Philadelphia and then on to Trenton, where he participated in the Battles of Trenton, Princeton, and Brandywine. After fighting in the Battle of Germantown, he marched back to

Philadelphia and was honorably discharged by Captain Grubb, having served eighteen months. (2), (3)

William married Marie Margaretha Myers, the daughter of Ludwig and Anna Margaretha Geigele Meyer, before 1775 in Pennsylvania. After the war, William continued to live in Lancaster County for a few years and then moved to Sullivan County, Tennessee, where he lived for nineteen years. He later moved to Greene County, Tennessee, and lived in the Horse Creek community. In 1821, he moved to Sevier County, where he lived until his death on 21 October 1839. He is one of the first to be buried in Headrick Chapel Cemetery in Wear's Valley in Sevier County. (3), (5)

William and Marie's children:
- John was born 20 July 1775 in Lebanon County, Pennsylvania, married Elizabeth "Lizzie" Myers in 1796, died 16 November 1867, and is buried in Headrick Chapel Cemetery in Sevier County.
- Katherine "Katy" was born in 1776 in Lancaster, Pennsylvania, married George Caylor, Sr., before 1800, and died 1835 in Townsend, Tennessee.
- Henry was born 1778 in Lancaster County, Pennsylvania.
- Daniel was born about 1788 in Sevier County, married Lucinda Bennett on 20 February 1812 and died about 1800.
- Jacob was born about 1791 in Sullivan County, married Mary "Polly" Rice on 4 February 1823 in Blount County, Tennessee, and died 1863 in Murray County, Georgia.
- Rebecca was born 2 April 1796 in Greene County, married' William B.

Dunn 31 January 1816 in Greene County, and died 25 April 1870 in Murray County, Georgia. (4)

Sources: (l) Geni Profile-Wiltiarn Hedrick, (2) Revolutionary War Pension Application-William Hedreik, Maples History Center, King Family Library, Sevierville, TN. (3) Smoky Mountain Historical Society Newsletter, winter 2002, p. 12-13, by Jim Shular, (4) Family Search, Church Of Jesus Christ Latter-day Saints, (5) In the Shadow of the Smokies, Smoky Mountain Historical Society, 1993, p, 644.

Henry, Major Hugh

One of the most important events in the history of Tennessee happened at Henry Station, the signing of the Treaty of Dumplin Creek. Hugh was born in 1756 in Pittsylvania County, Virginia, to Samuel and Rachel Elizabeth Hickman Henry. In the spring of 1777, Hugh volunteered as lieutenant under Captain John Donalson's Company in Colonel Evan Shelby's Regiment to go on a six-month expedition against the Cherokee Indians into Georgia and Tennessee. He volunteered again as a sergeant in 1778 under Captain Thomas Dillard and John Montgomery's Company in Colonel George Roger Clark's Illinois Regiment of Virginia and marched to the junction of the Kaskaskia and Mississippi River, where they captured a town, and Hugh was discharged 29 August 1779. (1)

In 1780, he moved to Tennessee and immediately joined the "Over the Mountain Men" under Captains John Shelby and John Sevier, marched to Kings Mountain, and fought in the Battle of Kings Mountain. Soon after the Battle of Kings Mountain, Hugh fought against the Cherokee Indians at the Battle of Boyd's Creek under Captain John Sevier.

Hugh settled on 450 acres of land beside the Indian Warpath at the mouth of Dumplin Creek in the early 1780s and built a home and fort. The fort was known as Henry's Station and became one of the most important places in Sevier County. It was the location of the signing of the Treaty of Dumplin Creek on 6 May 1785 by Chiefs of the Cherokee Nation and the Governor of the State of Franklin, John Sevier. This treaty opened up the land south of the French Broad and Holston River, which resulted in an immediate influx of homesteaders. (2)

Henry married Mary "Polly" Long in 1775 in Jamestown, Virginia. She was born about 1760, died 29 July 1813 in Sevier County, and is buried in Hugh Henry Cemetery. Henry married Mary Upton on 29 July 1814 at Eusebia Presbyterian Church in Blount County, Tennessee. Nancy was born 1781 to James and Nancy Bogle Upton. She died in 1865 and is buried at Henry Crossroads Cemetery in Sevier County, and Henry died in 1838 and is also buried in Henry Crossroads Cemetery. (4)

Henry and Mary L.'s children:
- Samuel was born 13 July 1787 in Sevier County, married Margaret Bryan in 1821, and died 16 March 1835 and is buried in Bryan (Saffell) Cemetery in Sevier County.
- Hugh was born 19 April 1796 at Henry's Crossroads, married Ann Claunch (1820-1881), and died 29 April 1856 in Marshall County, Alabama.
- William was born 5 October 1798 at Henry's Crossroads, married Catherine Underwood on 18 March 1821, and died 7 October 1830 in Alabama.
- Ezekial was born 6 April 1804 at Henry's Crossroads, married Elizabeth Vaughn on 21 April 1842, and died April 1862 in Blount County, Alabama.

Henry and Mary Upton Henry's children:
- Isaac was born 3 July 1815 and died 11 February 1881 in Marshall County, Alabama, and is buried in Henry Cemetery.
- Albert was born 7 January 1817, married Nancy Routh, and died in 1861 in Sevier

County and is buried in Hugh Henry Cemetery.
- Patrick was born 21 January 1821, married Martha Carmichael Brimer on 29 October 1870, and died 2 June 1895 and is buried in Henry Crossroads Cemetery in Kodak, Tennessee.
- Rachel was born 7 March 1823 in Sevier County, married Ephriam Johnson on 10 September 1841, and died 3 July 1885 and is buried in Hugh Henry Cemetery.
- Luke Lee was born 18 December 1824, married Sarah C. Henry, and died 1902 in Ray County, Missouri, and is buried in the Knoxville Cemetery in Ray County.
- J. Pleasant was born 11 December 1825 at Henry Crossroads, married Mary Bryan, and died 26 July 1865 in Mercer County, Missouri, and is buried in South Linville Cemetery, Mercer County.
- Thomas was born 17 September 1828 at Henry Crossroads, died 10 February 1896, and is buried in Henry's Crossroads Cemetery. (3)

Historical Fact: Henry's brothers William, James, and Samuel fought in the Battle of Kings Mountain during the Revolutionary War.

Sources: (1) Fold 3 by Ancestry-Hugh Henry, (2) Sevier County Tennessee and Its Heritage, 1994, Don Mills, p. 217, (3) findagrave.com, (4) In the Shadow of the Smokies, Smoky Mountain Historical Society 1993, p. 34.

Henry, William, Sr.

The Henry brothers, James, Samuel and William, were very patriotic. All three served in the Revolutionary War. William was born 1749 in Hanover County, Virginia, to Samuel and Rachel Elizabeth Hickman Henry. Sometime before the beginning of the Revolutionary War, William moved to Botetourt County, Virginia. In 1776, at the age of twenty-seven, he enlisted for two years in Botetourt County, Virginia, under the command of General Edward Hand, Colonel Andrew Donnally, Captain William McKee, Ensign James Gilmore, and Lieutenant James Thompson, and marched to Greenbrier County to rendezvous with other units and then marched to Fort Randolph at the mouth of New River (now Point Pleasant, West Virginia). He remained there for two years, was honorably discharged on 10 August 1788, and returned home to Botetourt County. (1) He entered service again for three months under the command of General Peter Muhlenberg and Colonel Samuel Lewis and was at the Siege of Little York (Yorktown). William applied for a Revolutionary War Pension in Sevier County on 1 September 1832. (1) Elizabeth applied for Revolutionary War Widow's Benefits (#364) in Sevier County on 5 August 1839 in Sevier County. (1)

William married Elizabeth Jones, the daughter of John and Elizabeth Linglan Jones, on 15 February 1780. She was born 11 November 1765 in Botetourt County and died 11 May 1847 in Jones Cove (Sevier County) and is buried in the Henry Cemetery in Kodak, Tennessee. William died 1 February 1835 and is also buried in the Henry Cemetery. (2), (5)

William and Elizabeth's children:
- Mary "Polly" was born 12 September 1781 in Botetourt, Virginia, married

John Williams, and died after 1860 and is buried in the Huff Cemetery in Sevier County.
- John was born 24 December 1783 in Botetourt, Virginia, married Sarah Unknown, and died 1852 in Jones Cove.
- Hugh was born 5 May 1786 in Botetourt, married Lydia Jenkins Whaley on 11 September 1827 in Sevier County, and died 22 November 1872 and is buried in Henry Cemetery, Sevier County.
- William, Jr., was born 28 February 1789.
- Robert was born 28 August 1791 and died before 6 June 1855. (3), (4)

Sources: (1) Southern Campaigns American Revolution Pension Statements and Rosters, transcribed by C. Leon Harris, (2) Smoky Mountain Historical Society Newsletter, submitted by Olene Large Cagle, transcribed by Betty R. Davis, summer, 1990, (3) Family Search, Church of Jesus Christ of Latter-day Saints, (4) Smoky Mountain Ancestral Quest, smokykin.com, maintained by Robert l. Beckwith, (5) In the Shadow of the Smokies, Smoky Mountain Historical Society, 1993, p. 470.

Houk, Captain John Adam

John fought in the Revolutionary War, and after moving to Tennessee, he continued to serve his country in the Knox County Militia. John was born in 1750 in York, Pennsylvania, to John Adam Haugch (Houk) and an unknown mother. The elder John Adam emigrated from Germany to Pennsylvania. Captain Houk is listed in the Pennsylvania Revolutionary War Battalions and Militia Index as a Private in the Pennsylvania Militia. John married Mary Malone about 1771. She was born in 1753 in Somerset, Maryland, to John Joseph, Sr., and Sarah Mary Harrison Malone. The Houk family moved from Pennsylvania to Botetourt County, Virginia, and later to a portion of Greene County, Tennessee, that is now Sevier County. After the war, John continued to serve as a private in the McGaughey Militia in Knox County, Tennessee, from 1892-1894. Mary died in 1830 and is buried in the Old Boyd's Creek Cemetery in Sevier County, and John died about 1838, and he is also buried in the Old Boyd's Creek Cemetery. (3)

John and Mary's children:
- Martin was born about 1772 in Botetourt County, Virginia, married Margaret Houk about 1830 in Sevier County, and died after 1850 in Sevier County.
- John was born 23 September 1773 in Virginia, married Nancy Chandler about 1800 in Sevier County, and died 28 October 1839 in Sevier County.
- Margaret Elizabeth was born about 1780 in Tennessee and married unknown Hicks.
- Sarah "Sally" was born 10 October 1782 in Tennessee, married Charles B. Hicks

on 22 November 1805, and died 21 February 1869 in Tennessee.
- Elizabeth was born about 1783 in Tennessee, and no additional information is known.
- Archimedes was born about 1785 in Tennessee, and no additional information is known.
- Mary was born about 1789 in Tennessee, and no additional information is known.
- Catharine was born about 1793 in Tennessee, and no additional information is known.
- Flora was born about 1795 in Tennessee, and no additional information is known.
- Mary Polly was born 1795 in Madison County, Tennessee, and married George Hicks.
- Rebecca was born 1800 in Tennessee, married Royal J. Adkinson on 24 December 1821 in Wilson County, Tennessee, and died June 1855 in Hamilton County, Tennessee. (2)

Historical Fact: Nancy Chandler is the daughter of Patriot Timothy Chandler, and George and Charles Hicks are brothers.

Sources: (1) Pennsylvania, Revolutionary War Battalions and Militia Index, H-Ho, 1775-1783, Vol. 1, p 620, (2) Family Search, Church of Jesus Christ of Latter day Saints, (3) In the Shadow of the Smokies, Smoky Mountain Historical Society, 1993, p. 228.

Hubbert/Hubbard, James

James experienced a life changing tragedy as a youngster, and that event forged his life-long desires and goals. James was born 18 July 1747, possibly in England or Virginia, to Colonel James Hubbert and an unknown mother. He fought in the Revolutionary War as Private in the Battle of Guilford Court House and alongside Colonel John Sevier in the Battle of Kings Mountain and as a captain in the Battle of Boyd's Creek. James married Elizabeth Anderson on 20 December 1770 in Virginia. She was born 13 July 1750 and died 8 October 1821 in Warren County, Tennessee.
(1)

James received a Revolutionary Land Warrant for several hundred acres of land along the French Broad River and become one of the first settlers in what is now Sevier County. He built a cabin for his family on the north bank of the French Broad River in 1782-83. James' land was beautiful and serene, but he was well aware of the dangers that could be imposed by those who viewed him and other early settlers as intruders, James knew all about Indian atrocities.

In Virginia, a young James Hubbert witnessed the brutal massacre of his parents, brothers, and sisters by the Shawnee Indians. So great was his grief that it affected the rest of his life, his reputation, and his place in history. His agony turned into revenge, and he became known as the "Indian Hater." James was a respected leader among his fellow settlers. His courage, fortitude, and willingness to face danger and uncertainty were traits admired and needed on the frontier. The settlers were glad to have a man of Hubbert's caliber on their side.

It is not known when James left Sevier County and moved to Rhea County, Tennessee, but he was evidently living with his son Matthew in Rhea County after the death of Elizabeth. In early February 1824, James left Matthew's home to visit another son, Benjamin, in Warren County, Tennessee. While in Warren County, James became ill and went to the home of a man known to have "drugs," but the man was not at home and his wife accidentally gave James arsenic instead of calomel. James died 8 February 1824 in Warren County. (1)

James and Elizabeth's children:
- Robert, Sr., was born 15 September 1771 in Virginia, married Patty Unknown, and died in 1830 in Marion County, Alabama.
- James, Jr., was born 12 September 1774 in North Carolina, married Elizabeth McDonald before 1800, and died in Benton County, Arkansas, sometime after the 1850 census.
- Elizabeth was born 19 January 1777, married Allen S. Bryan, Sr., died before 1810, and is believed to be buried in Bryan Cemetery, Sevier County.
- Matthew was born 5 June 1779, married first Rachel Henry, and after her death, married Mary Woodward on 20 February 1817 in Rhea County, and died 10 August 1852 in Barry County, Missouri.
- Margaret "Peggy" was born 10 March 1782, and no further information is available.
- Phoebe was born 7 January 1784, married Hugh McClung in Sevier County, and died 1 November 1844 in Limestone County, Alabama.

- Polly was born 8 April 1787, and no further information is available.
- Benjamin was born 3 July 1790, married Rebecca Calvert on 19 January 1809 in Sevier County, and died 16 March 1872, probably in Saline County, Arkansas. (1)

Historical Fact: Allen S. Bryan, Sr., was the son of Patriot Peter and Mary Bryan.

Sources: James Hubbert (1742-1824) Sevier County's Paradoxical Pioneer, Cherel Bolin Henderson, Smoky Mountain Historical Society Newsletter, fall 1987 and winter 1987.

Hudson, George

George is believed to have moved to Sevier County after the death of his first wife, Mary. He was born on 12 October 1764 in Chesterfield, Virginia, to George, Sr., and Nancy Holland Hudson (1740-1776). Although George was born in Virginia, Revolutionary War records list him as serving as a private in the North Carolina Line. He is on the muster roll from September to December 1778 in Captain Jeremiah Burroughs' Battalion, commanded by Colonel Seth Warner. These records also show he lived in both Washington County and Sullivan County, North Carolina (now Tennessee). (1)

George married Mary "Molly" Berry on 11 December 1786 in Mecklenburg County, Virginia. Mary was born in 1765 to Thomas and Catherine Babcock Berry in King and Queen County, Virginia, and died 1813 in Campbell County, Virginia. (2) George married Rebecca Lindsay Conway Scruggs about 1813 in Greene County, Tennessee. She was born in 1775 in Virginia and died about 1862 in Kodak, Sevier County. George died 8 January 1850 and is buried in the Hudson Cemetery near Kodak. (4)

George and Mary's children:
- Martha was born 20 November 1787 in Pittsylvania County, married Jacob Walter Grimmett in December 1807 in Sevier County, and died 13 December 1872 in Wilson County, Tennessee.
- George was born 1789, married Mary Polly Knight on 6 March 1816 in Greene County, Tennessee, and died 1822 in Anderson County, Tennessee.

- Sarah was born 1790 in Virginia, married George Taylor on 22 March 1809 in Campbell, Virginia, and died 1809 in Campbell, Virginia.
- Thomas was born 1792 in Pittsylvania County, Virginia, married Frances Jackson Manley in 1814 in Anderson County, Tennessee, and died 1860 in Roane County, Tennessee.
- Elijah was born 1793 in Pittsylvania County, Virginia, married Rebecca Tatum Barker in 1824 in Marion County, Tennessee, and died October 1842 in Marion County, Tennessee.
- John William was born 1796 in Campbell, Virginia, married Nancy Ann Davis in 1820 in Roane County, Tennessee, and died 1849 in Wilson County, Tennessee.
- Armistead D. was born 1797 in Pittsylvania County, Virginia, married Nancy Webb in 1817 in Roane County, Tennessee, and died 18 December 1867 in Marion, Arkansas.
- Benjamin Berry was born 1800 in Pittsylvania County, Virginia, married Catherine Wright on 19 April 1842 in Roane County, and died 1842 in Monroe County, Tennessee.
- Amanda was born 4 June 1810 in Culpeper, Virginia, married Wingfield Meredith Cosby on 7 February 1829 in Culpeper, and died 19 December 1893 in Fayette, Kentucky. (2)

George and Rebecca's children:

- Mary was born 24 April 1814 in Kodak, Tennessee, married Samuel Huffaker on 26 May 1836 in Sevier County, and died August 1842 at Seven Islands, Knox County, Tennessee.
- Joel was born 1816 in Sevier County, married Agatha Huffaker on 17 March 1840 in Knox County, and died 21 January 1867.
- Anna Porter was born about 1818 in Kodak, Tennessee, married Jesse Huffaker around 1850 in Knox County, Tennessee, and died about 1881 in Kodak. (3)

Sources: (1) U. S. Revolutionary War Rolls, 1775-1782 for George Hudson, (2) ancestry.com, search, George Hudson, (3) Family Search, Church of Jesus Christ of Latter day Saints, (4) In the Shadow of the Smokies, Smoky Mountain Historical Society, 1993, p. 36

Isbell, Lieutenant Zachariah, Jr.

Zachariah and his father served in the war together. Zachariah was born in 1745 in Virginia to Zachariah William, Sr., and Elizabeth Day Calloway Isbell. (1) Based on family legend, Zachariah, Jr., was at the Battle of Kings Mountain with his father Captain Zachariah Isbell. While there were no muster rolls or rosters showing every soldier that fought at Kings Mountain, researchers and armchair historians are satisfied with family lore recited in numerous sources that both men were Revolutionary War soldiers and both were at Kings Mountain. (2)

Zachariah married Elizabeth Miller, the daughter of John and Hannah Crawford Miller. She was born 1750 in Augusta, Virginia. (1) Records do not show when Zachariah and Elizabeth moved to Sevier County, but on 6 November 1795, Zachary bought 190 acres of land in a portion of Jefferson County, Tennessee, that is now Sevier County. Elizabeth died in 1796 and was buried in Forks of Little Pigeon Cemetery in Sevier County. Zachariah died in 1799 in Sevier County and was also buried in Forks of Little Pigeon Cemetery. (1)

Zachariah and Elizabeth's children:
- William was born 1769 in North Carolina, married Sarah Richardson, and died 1826 in Jackson County, Alabama.
- Levi was born in 1770 in North Carolina, married Sara Jane Todd in 1797, and died before 1860 in Jackson County, Alabama.
- John Miller was born in 1777 in Washington County, Tennessee, married Mary Adaline Hawkins on 2 July 1845

in Monroe County, Tennessee, and died 25 August 1853 in Monroe County.
- Jason was born 1779 in Sevier County, Tennessee. (1)

Sources: (1) Family Search, Church of the Latter-day Saints (2) www.geni.com/people/zachariah-isbell-jr.

Jenkins, James

James was a true patriot. He served during the entire duration of the war in numerous battles and skirmishes. He was born about 13 May 1760 in Cheraw Hill District (now Chesterfield County), South Carolina, to unknown parents. He was living on the Pee Dee River in the Cheraw District when called into service in February 1776. He entered service as a sergeant under Captain Thomas Ellerbee and Colonel George Hicks and marched from Cheraw to Charleston, South Carolina. At the end of the month, he was honorably discharged and ordered to return to Cheraw but rendezvous again in ten days. As ordered, he marched to Orangeburg, South Carolina, then to the Black Swamp on the Savannah River, and then on to Charleston. Four months later, he was discharged and sent home. (1), (2)

In September 1776, he was called into service as 1st Sergeant under Captain Ellerbee and served every third month until being honorably discharged in September 1779. In late September 1779, he received a commission as Lieutenant that was signed by South Carolina's Governor Rutledge and Peter Freeman, Secretary of State.

In March 1781, James volunteered in the South Carolina Line under Colonel Wade Hampton and General Sumter, marched to Charlotte, North Carolina, where they met the main North Carolina Militia, and then marched to the Congaree River in South Carolina, surrounded a fort, and had a scrimmage in which some British and Tories were killed. (1), (2)

Again in July 1781, James volunteered as a lieutenant under Captain Claudius Pegues and Major Tristam Thomas, marched to the Santee River, where they were joined by General Marion, and, from there, they marched toward Beaufort. After marching a short distance, they found a party of British troops, and about twenty-five were killed and some were taken prisoner. Later, they marched to the Santee River, met General Nathaneal Greene near Eutaw Springs, and marched with him on to Eutaw and engaged in the Battle of Eutaw Springs. James served until the first of September 1781, which amounted to about forty days.

    After the war, James returned to Cheraw District and resided there until 1805 when he moved to Sevier County. James appeared in Open Court in Sevier County on 5 December 1832 before Justices of the Peace Josiah Rogers, John Mullendore, and John Brabson to apply for a Revolutionary War Pension #R5569. In the application, he stated he was born in Cheraw District, South Carolina, and lived there until 1805, when he moved to Sevier County.

    On 10 January 1844, Hannah Jenkins filed for a widow's pension in Sevier County, stating that James died in Sevier County on 26 August 1839. Hannah made another application 30 June 1849 and stated she and James were married 15 August 1799 in South Carolina. In an affidavit dated 10 May 1852 given in Sevier County Court, William Jenkins stated he was the son of James and Hannah Jenkins, who were now both deceased and that he believed his parents were married in Chesterfield District, South Carolina, in the year 1799. (1) Hannah is listed as living in the household of William Jenkins in the 1850 Sevier County Census. (3)

    James and Hannah's child:
- William was born in 1808 in Sevier County and married Nancy Jenkins.

Sources: (1) Revolutionary War Gravesites of Knox and Surrounding Counties-Sevier Co., Stephen Holston Chapter, Sons of the American Revolution, (2) Southern Campaigns American Revolution Pensions Statements and Rosters,

Ruth C. Davis

transcribed by Will Graves, (3) Family Search, Church of Jesus Christ of Latter-day Saints.

Johnson, Solomon

Solomon is an example of another patriot about whom much information has been lost in the passage of time. He was born in Accomack County, Virginia, in 1759 to unknown parents. He volunteered in July 1782 as a Private in the Virginia Militia under Colonel John Cropper, Captain Birton, and Lieutenant James Cropper, rendezvoused at the Accomack Court House, and marched to the Block House on the eastern shore of Virginia. The company marched up and down the shoreline day and night for eighteen months to prevent the invasion of the British. (1), (2)

Solomon married Sarah Morris on 4 June 1787 in Halifax County, Virginia. (3) On 15 March 1834, Solomon appeared in Sevier County Court before acting Justice of the Peace, Isaac Love, to apply for a Revolutionary War Pension (R5664). In the application, Solomon stated that he moved to Sevier County about 1804. Ashley Wynn and George McCown gave the court supporting affidavits. Solomon's date of death is unknown. (1), (2), (3)

No children have been identified.

Sources: (1) Revolutionary War Gravesite's of Knox and Surrounding Counties, Stephen Holston Chapter, SAR, (2) Southern Campaign American Revolution Pension Statements & Rosters, transcribed by Will Graves, (3) ancestry.com-Public member trees, Solomon Johnson

Kendle, William

William was born in England and later kidnapped to fight for the King and eventually escaped from his captors and fought for American independence. William was born 21 August 1752 in Suffolk County, England, to unknown parents. William was a blacksmith's apprentice in Fakenham, England, and in May 1777, he met a British Army sergeant. The sergeant gave him a shilling and informed him that he was enlisted to serve King George for three years. William refused to comply but was compelled and put on board a ship and brought to the American Colonies.

(1), (2)

After landing in New York, William went to Philadelphia and was placed on a ship headed to Charleston, South Carolina. He participated in the capture of Charleston in May 1780. After the capture of Charleston, he was stationed at Haddrell's Point, and about the first of October 1780, he and another soldier deserted during the night, went to Georgetown, and swapped their regimental clothing for civilian clothes. He was befriended by a man by the name of Stewart, who hid him out for two weeks.

The British and Tories were committing atrocities every day and the only safe place was in a military camp; therefore, William volunteered under Captain William Dick, who immediately took him to General Marion in Santee. He was furnished a horse and entered the cavalry. His regiment reconnoitered the country in search of Tories and the British and had a skirmish at Singleton's Mill and totally defeated the British. From there, he marched to the Tyger River, then to the Sampit Bridge and destroyed that bridge. He then marched toward the Congaree River and had a siege at Georgetown on 28 May 1781 and at Fort Motte on 8-12 May 1781. He remained at Fort Motte to guard the roads and intercept Tories on their way to Charleston. From Fort Motte, he went to James Island and remained there until the British surrendered Charleston, and he was honorably discharged about the middle of December 1782. (1), (2)

After the Revolution, William went to live in Moore County, North Carolina and lived there until moving to Sevier County in 1820s. At the age of eighty, William appeared in Sevier County Court of Pleas and Quarter Sessions on 8 May 1833 to make application for a Revolutionary War Pension. On 19 April 1855, Elizabeth Kendle appeared in Knox County, Tennessee, court to file for a widow's pension (W7978). She stated she and William were married by Mr. Hill, Justice of the Peace, in Sevier County in the fall of 1827, and she continued to live with him until his death on 18 November 1836 at their home and she was still a resident of Sevier County. (1), (2) Elizabeth Kendle was listed in the 1840 Sevier County Census as head of household. (3)

No children have been identified.

Sources: (1) Revolutionary War Gravesite's of Knox and Surrounding Counties, Stephen Holston Chapter SAR, (2) Southern Campaign American Revolution Pension Statements and Rosters, transcribed by Will Graves, (3) wwwfamilysearch.org, Sevier Co., TN 1840 census

Kerr, (Carr) Robert

Robert fought in the first battle of the Revolutionary War, the battle of Point Pleasant. Robert was born 15 May 1758 in Virginia to Robert, Sr., (1732-1806) and Martha Hayes Kerr (1733-1786). Robert fought in the Revolutionary War at Point Pleasant under Evan Shelby and at Kings Mountain under Colonel Isaac Shelby.

On 23 November 1809, the State of Tennessee granted Robert 342 acres lying in the County of Sevier in the District South of the French Broad and Holston on the French Broad River and signed by Governor William Blount, The land was bordered by the property of Joseph Beavers and Peter Brian (Bryan). On 24 May 1810, the State of Tennessee and Governor Blount granted Robert an additional 21 acres for the sum of $21.82 that adjoined the 342, warrant #1301. (1)

Robert married Amy George on 12 December 1786 in Sevier County. Amy was born in Berks County, Pennsylvania, to Edward (1733-1789) and Martha Woolaston George (1735-1798) on 19 May 1767. Both Edward and Martha George died in Jefferson County, Tennessee. Robert died 8 May 1819 and is buried in Saffell Cemetery in Sevier County. Amy died after 1830 in Sevier County and is probably buried in Saffell Cemetery. (2)

Robert and Amy's children:
- Martha was born 16 October 1787 in Sevier County, married Raleigh Robert Clack on 12 August 1816, and died 20 April 1858.
- Jesse was born 25 December 1789 in Sevier County, married Sarah Miller in 1808 in Blount County, Tennessee, and

- died 29 October 1872 in Greenback, Loudon County, Tennessee.
- William was born 11 March 1791 in Sevier County, married Anne Nancy Hubbert on 2 January 1812 in Sevier County, and died 27 March 1875 in Green County, Missouri.
- Margaret was born 5 June 1796 in Tennessee, married Micajah Clack on 28 September 1820 in Sevier County, and died 10 September 1877 in Rhea County, Tennessee. (2)

Historical Fact: Raleigh and Micajah Clack are sons of Patriot Spencer Clack,

Sources: (1) North Carolina and Tennessee, Early Land Records, 1753-1931. Ancestry.com, search Robert Kerr, (2) Family Search, Church of Jesus Christ of Latter-day Saints

Kirby, (Kerby) Christopher

Christopher volunteered and fought in the Battle of Kings Mountain. Christopher was born 10 September 1760 in Halifax County, Virginia, to unknown parents but lived in Surry County, North Carolina, at the time of the Revolutionary War. Christopher enlisted in the Surry County Army in July 1779 in the company of the light horse dragoons commanded by Captain William Underwood, Colonel Martin Armstrong, and Colonel Joseph Williams and was selected as the company's ensign. The company marched into the Virginia counties of Henry, Patrick, Wyeth, and Washington to take, dispose, or kill any and all Tories who tried to pass into Virginia from North Carolina. Christopher was honorably discharged near Flower Gap, Virginia, in December 1779 after having served five months. [1], [2]

Christopher volunteered in July 1780 as a private in a dragoon company commanded by Captain James Shepherd and marched from Surry County to Wilkes County, where the company was joined by troops under the command of Colonels Isaac Shelby, John Sevier, and William Campbell, and they proceeded to Kings Mountain, South Carolina, and engaged in the Battle of Kings Mountain on 7 October 1781. [1]

Christopher appeared in Washington County, Arkansas' Third Circuit Court to apply for a Revolutionary War Pension on 19 December 1835. According to Christopher's sworn statement in court, after the Revolutionary War, he moved to a portion of Greene County, Tennessee, that is now Sevier County and lived in the county for twenty years. The dates of his arrival and departure are not known. Also on that same date, Thomas Pogue appeared in court and stated under oath that he had lived in Sevier County within one-half- mile of Christopher for twenty years. He also stated that during those years he saw commission documents in Christopher's possession constituting him an ensign during some of the Revolutionary War. Thomas Pogue added that he recollected the burning of Christopher's house and believes all those papers were burned in that fire. Christopher was approved for Revolutionary War Pension #S32356. The name of his wife and/or mother of his child is not known. Christopher died after 8 February 1836 in Washington County, Arkansas. (1)

Christopher's child:
- Henry was born about 1812 in Greene County, married Rebecca in 1850, and died about 1860 in Washington County, Arkansas. (2)

Sources: (1) Southern Campaigns American Revolution Pension Statements & Rosters, transcribed by Will Graves, (2) DAR Patriot Index, Vol. II

Large, Joseph

Joseph served his country by guarding British and Tory prisoners. He was born in 1761 in Halifax County, Virginia, to Robert (1716-1774) and Rhonda Wildman Large (1719-1798). He was living in Lincoln County, North Carolina, when called into service. Joseph volunteered in February 1781 for a term of ten months in the North Carolina cavalry under Captain Kinzey, Major Boykin, and General Thomas Sumter. He rendezvoused at the Lincoln County Court House, marched to the Mecklenburg County Court House, and then on to Camden, South Carolina, where he was assigned the duty of guarding the Tory prisoners. (1)

During the summer of 1781, he marched to a place called Ninety Six and scouted for the British and Tories. From there, he marched to Eutaw Springs, joined the main Army commanded by Colonel Middleton and General Wade Hampton and continued guarding soldiers who were taken prisoner at Camden. He was honorably discharged by General Wade Hampton in December 1781 after having served a term of ten months. (1)

Joseph appeared in Jefferson County, Tennessee Court of Pleas and Quarter Sessions on 12 March 1833 to apply for a Revolutionary War Pension #6163 and was granted a pension based on ten months' service only after appearing in the court again on 21 September 1833 with additional pertinent information. On 4 May 1844, Joseph's son John Large filed an affidavit in Jefferson County Court stating that his father died on 9 October 1842, leaving his mother, Mary, a widow and he was seeking to obtain the pension due his mother being the widow of a Revolutionary War pensioner. (1)

Joseph married Mary Jane "Mollie" Emmitt in 1791 in Pittsylvania County, Virginia. Mary was born in 1760, died 7 November 1843 in Jones Cove, and was buried in Huff Cemetery in Sevier County. Joseph died in Jones Cove and was also buried in the Huff Cemetery in Sevier County. (2), (3)

Joseph and Mary's children:
- William was born about 1785, married Phoebe Hankins 23 April 1804 in Knox County, Tennessee, and died about 1830 in Jefferson County.
- Thomas was born in 1792, married Hannah Minter (1796-1860), and died in 1865.
- John was born 10 August 1794 in Peria, South Carolina, married Elizabeth Webb (1792-1872) in 1829, and died 11 July 1865 in Sevier County and was buried in Huff Cemetery in Sevier County.
- Lucinda "Lucy" was born about 1800, married William H. Carmon on 13 September 1824 in Jefferson County, and died about 1850 in Grainger County, Tennessee.
- Phoebe was born 1801 in Jefferson County, Tennessee, married John Cook (1800-1850) in 1822, and died 1855 in Bledsoe, County, Tennessee.
- Adam was born about 1805, married Jane Roulman (1833-1880) on 31 January 1868 in Jefferson County, and died about 1880 in Sevier County.
- James E. was born 15 September 1809, married Mary Williams (1810-1870), and died 14 August 1869 and is buried in Huff Cemetery in Sevier County. (2)

- Sarah was born 1812, married James Harper, and died 1850 in Jefferson County. (2), (3)

Historical Fact: Elizabeth Webb is the daughter of Patriot Jesse Webb.

Sources: (1) Southern Campaign American Revolution Pension Statements and Rosters, transcribed by Will Graves, (2) Smoky Mountain Ancestral Quest, smokykin.com, maintained by David L. Beckwith, (3) findagrave.com, (4) In the Shadow of the Smokies, Smoky Mountain Historical Society, 1993, p.474.

Layman, Jacob

Jacob's ability to speak fluent German was an invaluable asset in the fight for American independence. He was born 20 November 1758 in Reading County, Pennsylvania, to George (1733-1788) and Elizabeth Bleister Layman. The Layman family moved to Virginia before the start of the Revolutionary War. Jacob entered the war as a substitute for Reuben Beaver in Shenandoah County, Virginia. He marched to Richmond under Captain Bonywitt, joined the infantry under General Peter Muhlenberg and Major William Boyce for ten weeks, was honorably discharged, and returned home to Culpeper County, Virginia.

Later, Jacob entered the 8th Division of the Virginia Line under Colonel James Barbour as one of the many German speaking soldiers who guarded 900 Hessians prisoners (Burgoyne's men) captured by General George Washington, while they were being moved to Albemarle barracks near Charlottesville, Virginia. Jacob was honorably discharged after five months and returned home. (1), (2)

Jacob married Nancy Unknown in about 1800. The exact date of Jacob's arrival in Sevier County is not known; however, he was appointed Captain of the Tennessee Militia in Sevier County on 30 July 1800. According to his land grant surveys, he may have settled on the West Fork of the Little Pigeon River, and this assumption is strengthened by the fact that Joseph and Mary's names are listed as members of the Forks of Little Pigeon Baptist Church in Sevierville. Jacob appeared in Sevier County Court of Pleas and Quarter Sessions on 3 September 1832 to make application for a Revolutionary War Pension (S4504). He stated that he moved to Sevier County after the Declaration of Independence and had lived in the county ever since. (1)

Mary died in 1838 and was buried in Mount Pleasant Cemetery in Sevier County. Jacob died between 1840 and 1850 and is also buried in Mount Pleasant Cemetery. (4)

Jacob and Nancy's children:
- John was born 20 December 1803 in Sevier County, married Martha Unknown, and died 4 December 1893 in Laclede County, Missouri.
- George was born 13 November 1805 in Sevier County, married Nancy Selvidge (1809-1887), and died 11 January 1878 in Laclede County, Missouri.
- Michael was born 1806 in Sevier County, married Nancy Unknown, and died after 1850.
- Jacob, Jr., was born 1809 in Sevier County, married Susannah Baker in Tennessee and died 5 December 1858 in Cocke County, Tennessee.
- Ambrose was born 9 June 1810 in Sevier County, married Charlotte Temple Selvidge, and died 1888 in Benton, Arkansas.
- Absalom was born 30 August 1811 in Sevier County and died 25 January 1890 in Rush County, Indiana.
- Nancy was born between 1810 and 181515 in Sevier County, married George W. Selvidge, and died in Laclede County, Missouri.
- Preston was born 14 July 1816 in Sevier County, married Malvina L. Baker, and died 13 December 1892 and is buried in

Cummings Chapel Cemetery, Sevier County.
- Mary was born about 1817 in Sevier County and died about 1832 in Sevier County. (1), (2), (3)

Historical Fact: Nancy and Charlotte Temple Selvidge are sisters.

Sources: (1) Jacob Layman-Revolutionary Soldier, by Beulah D. Linn, News-Record, Section B, p. 1, 20 November 1975, (2) Southern Campaign American Revolution Pension Statements & Rosters, transcribed by Will Graves, (3) Smoky Ancestral Quest, smokykin.com, maintained by David L. Beckwith, (4) In the Shadow of the Smokies, Smoky Mountain Historical Society, 1993, p. 495.

Lewis, Mordecai

Mordecai became an active member of the government, after moving to Sevier County, by serving as a Justice of the Peace and county coroner. Mordecai was born 26 October 1741 in Shenandoah Valley, Virginia, the son of John and Margaret Reese Lewis. John was born October 1713 in Wales and died 1788 in Long Meadows, West Virginia. Margaret was born 1713, also in Wales, and died in Virginia. Mordecai served as a private in Captain Jacob Holleman's Company of the Dunmore County, Virginia Militia, and he also served in the Shenandoah County, Virginia Militia during the Revolutionary War. He was recommended to become Captain of the Militia on 31 May 1782. [1]

Mordecai married Mary Ziegler on 21 January 1777 in Frederick County, Virginia. Mary was born 1757 in Shenandoah County, Virginia, to George Jacob and Barbara Mary Schmidt Zeigler. After the War, they moved to Sevier County, and on 29 September 1794, Mordecai was appointed Justice of the Peace, and on 9 October 1794, he was appointed county coroner. He was present at the first Sevier County Court that met on 4 July 1796.

On 12 January 1807, Mordecai was issued Land Grant # 905 containing 151 acres by Governor William Blount, located in present day Pigeon Forge. The land adjoined that of patriots Isaac Runyan and Richard Fancher on the eastside of the West Fork of the Little Pigeon River. The Historic Old Mill is located on this land. Mordecai died August 1817 in Sevier County, and Mary died 10 December 1832 in Marion County, Tennessee. [1]

Mordecai and Mary's children:

- Amos was born 20 October 1777 in Shenandoah County, Virginia, married Agnes Wilson in 1805, and died in 1856 in Marion County.
- John was born in 25 September 1779 in Shenandoah County, married Mary Lewis in 1812, and died 6 August 1850 in Humphreys, Tennessee.
- George Henry was born in 14 October 1781 in Frederick Virginia, married Rebecca Ann Walker 1808 in Sevier County and died 1860 in Marion County.
- Levi was born in 5 January 1784 in Shenandoah, Virginia, married Elizabeth Ballard (1791-1872) on 25 November 1808 in Sevier County, and died 25 April 1865 in Sevier County.
- Archibald was born 14 October 1786 in Virginia, married Nancy Mitchell in 1808 in Marion County, and died 16 November 1856 in Marion County.
- Mary "Polly" was born 9 June 1788 in Shenandoah County, married Isaac Love on 28 September 1805 in Sevier County, and died 9 January 1853 in McDonald County, Missouri.
- Margaret was born 17 October 1790 in Shenandoah County, married James Mitchell on 7 May 1807 in Sevier County, and died 1837 in Jackson, Mississippi.
- Elizabeth "Betsy" was born in 20 January 1793 in Shenandoah County, married (first) Charles Walker in 1812 in Sevier County, and (secondly), she

Ruth C. Davis

married Robert Shields. Betsy died 6 August 1845 in Sevier County. (2)

Sources: (1) Mordecai Lewis-militiaman in the Continental Army, Sevier County News-Record & Gatlinburg Press, Beulah D. Linn, 26 February 1976, Section B, p.1. (2) Church of Jesus Christ of Latter-day Saints, Mordecai Lewis

Lindsey, David Elijah

In 1927, a group of ladies in Montevallo, Alabama, formed the David Elijah Lindsay Chapter of the Daughters of the American Revolution. David was born 1750 in Washington County, Pennsylvania, to David, Sr., (1695-?) and Katharine Ruth Lindsay (1697-?). David served as Private under Captain Robert Millar's Company in the 4th Pennsylvania Battalion. Research also shows David served in the 2nd, 3rd, 4th, and 6th Virginia Regiments. The area where David lived was claimed by both Pennsylvania and Virginia at the time of the Revolutionary War, and people often appeared in both Pennsylvania and Virginia records. Fort Pitt was located here and was used by both Virginia and Pennsylvania military units during the War. (1)

David married Mary "Molly" Casey in 1769 in Washington County, Pennsylvania. She was the daughter of Henry (1726-1785) and Elizabeth McCarthy Whealand Casey (1720-1820). David moved to Greene County, Tennessee, in 1783 and received two land grants for 640 acres and 400 acres of land on Lick Creek, Churn Camp Creek, and Plum Creek in Greene County.

David sold his land in Greene County in 1789 and moved to Sevier County. In 1789, people living in Sevier County were considered to be trespassers after the disbanding of the State of Franklin. David and many other settlers signed a petition to the North Carolina Assembly in 1789, appealing for protection and legal ownership of their land. Militia records show that David and his oldest son, Thomas, were in the Tennessee Company of the Rangers commanded by Abraham Slover in 1794. Later in the same year, David was listed in a company that included Richard Crowson and William Lovelady. David, Mary, and their adult children also appear on church records in Sevier County.

In 1818, David, his wife Mary, and children plus their spouses moved to Madison County, Alabama, and then to Shelby County, Alabama, around 1820. David died 1835 in Shelby County and is buried in the David Lindsay Cemetery, and Mary died in 1747, also in Shelby County.

The David Lindsay Chapter, Daughters of the American Revolution, was chartered in 1927 in Montevallo, Alabama. In the early 1950s an elderly resident in the area mentioned that a Revolutionary War soldier was buried in his family's cemetery plot. A search began when members of the David Lindsay Chapter heard this might be the grave of their chapter's namesake. After a ten month search, conclusive evidence was found that it was the grave of David Lindsay, and a gleaming bronze marker was erected over his grave in December 1953. [1], [2], [3]

David and Mary's children:
- Thomas was born 1771 in Washington County, Pennsylvania, married Elizabeth Frazer on 14 August 1786 in Frederick County Virginia, and died 14 September 1830 in Fairfax County, Virginia.
- Rachel was born around 1773 in Pennsylvania, married William Morgan Lovelady in 1794 in Greene County, Tennessee, and died around 1850 in Shelby County, Alabama.
- Huldah was born 8 January 1775 in Pennsylvania, married Richard Thomas Crowson on 14 June 1792 in Madison

County, Alabama, and died around 1814 in Madison County.
- John was born 1775 in Pennsylvania, married Elizabeth West on 1 September 1797 in Greene County, and died 6 May 1844 in Talladega, Alabama.
- Lydia was born 1779, probably in Greene County, married Isaac Skillman in 1799 in Sevier County, and died 6 July 1864 in Tishomongo, Mississippi.
- Elizabeth was born 1781, married Joseph Hale, died 1842 in Shelby County, Alabama and is buried in the David Lindsay Cemetery.
- Elijah was born 1783, probably in Greene County, married Mary "Polly" Harrison on 29 November 1811 in Madison County, Mississippi, and died 21 April 1836 in Shelby County, Alabama.
- David, Jr., was born 1785 in Greene County, Tennessee, married Martha Susan Crouch on 1 January 1820, and died 9 March 1855 in Talladega, Alabama.
- Mary Ann was born 1788 in Greene County, Tennessee, married Patrick Smith in 1806, and died 1860 in Alabama.
- Joseph was born 1789 in Tennessee, married Vina Landman on 28 March 1815 in Madison County, Alabama, and died 1861.
- James was born 12 April 1791 in Sevier County, married Martha Torrance Moore

on 11 March 1820, and died 14 February 1846 in Coosa County, Alabama.
- Rebecca was born on 17 November 1794 in Sevier County, married David Fulton on 3 July 1816 in Madison County, Mississippi, and died 12 July 1871 in Shelby County, Alabama. (2)

Historical Fact: William Thomas Crowson is the son of Patriot William Crowson, and William Morgan Lovelady is the son of Patriot John Lovelady.

Sources: (1) mimipickles.com/lindsey/group2/david/david ala/david.htm#tennessee, (2) Family Search, Church of Jesus Christ of Latter- day Saints, (3) Alabaster Reporter, Phoebe Robinson, September 17, 2018.

Longley, William Campbell

William was present at the Battle of Yorktown and was assigned to guard the British prisoners. William was born 1 September 1761 in Hunterdon, Monmouth, New Jersey, to Joseph (1735-1810) and Augustine Steel Longley (1745-1790). The Longley family moved to Loudoun, Virginia, shortly before the start of the Revolutionary War. William was drafted into the Virginia Militia in October 1780 under Captain Thomas Humphries, Lieutenant John Bartlett, and Major Armistead. William marched from Loudoun County to Williamsburg, Virginia, and was stationed there for several months to keep in check the British forces under Benedict Arnold. When the British landed at Burrell's Ferry at the mouth of the James River, the Virginia Militia stood their ground, fired upon the enemy until all their ammunition was exhausted, and then retreated to Williamsburg. With all the troops in Williamsburg, the British marched to the barracks and overtook and occupied the barracks that night. After dark, the militia returned to their barracks and fired on the British until outnumbered. The next morning, William's company marched to Richmond and was stationed there for six weeks and marched from there to join the Army of General Lafayette at Yorktown. Shortly afterwards, General George Washington and his army arrived, and the Battle of Yorktown began. Upon the surrender of British General Cornwallis, many prisoners were captured, and William was one of the guards who marched the British prisoners to Winchester, Virginia, where he remained for three months guarding the prisoners. William was honorably discharged at Shephardtown, Virginia, by Colonel Niswonger in February 1782. (1)

After the war, William returned to Loudoun County and married Mary Ann Bodine, the daughter of James (1747-1810) and Mary Rose Bodine (1746-1802), on 1 September 1784. Then, William moved to the Shenandoah Valley, to Rockbridge County, and then to Washington County, Virginia, before arriving in Sevier County about 1803. The Longleys lived in Sevier County a very short time before moving to Polk County, Tennessee. William appeared in McMinn County, Tennessee Court on 3 June 1833, at the age of 72, to make application for a Revolutionary War Pension #R6435. William died 7 November 1841 in Polk County, and Mary died 9 June 1844, also in Polk County. (2)

William and Mary's children:
- Andrew Jonathan was born 1 July 1788 in Burlington County, New Jersey, married Sarah Oldham on 28 August 1810 in Sevier County, and died 1851 in Polk County.
- Joel was born 1 September 1791 in Rockingham County, Virginia, married Mary Unknown about 1808, and died 29 November 1830 in McMinn County.
- James was born 1 October 1792 in Rockbridge, Virginia, married Nancy Ann Long in 1815 in Catoosa, Georgia, and died 14 July 1870 in Ringgold, Georgia.
- Mercy was born about 1793.
- Joseph was born about 1794 in Rockbridge, Virginia, married Priscilla Patterson in Sevier County, and died 1829 in McMinn County.
- Abigail was born about 1799 in Loudoun County, Virginia, married William

Tryon Patterson in Sevier County in 1815, and died 23 May 1854 in Catoosa, Georgia.
- Sarah was born 1803 in Sevier County.
- John C. was born 4 November 1806 in Polk County, married Hannah Ray about 1828, and died 7 November 1878 in Dalton, Georgia. (3)

Historical Fact: William Preston Longley (1851-1878) AKA "Wild Bill Longley" regarded as one of the deadliest gunfighters in the Old West, is the great grandson of William and Mary Longley, the grandson of Joseph and Priscilla Patterson Longley, and "Wild Bill's" parents are Campbell Longley, born 1816 in Sevier County, and Sarah Ann Henry. (2)

Sources: (1) Some Tennessee Heroes of the Revolution, Pamphlet #2, Zella Armstrong, (2) Longley Family, Jefferson County. Missouri, Kay Clerc- Fakhar, (3) Family Search, Church of Jesus Christ Latter-day Saints.

Lovelady, John, Sr.

A plaque on the Macon County Courthouse lawn honors John for his service in the Revolutionary War. John was born 1736 in Orange County, North Carolina, to Thomas, Sr., and Hannah Hix Lovelady. Based on family legend, John and his wife, Sarah, both served in the Revolutionary War. Sarah is credited with molding bullets for the men while they fought. The John Lovelady listed as being at the Battle of Kings Mountain is thought to be this John. A plaque at the Parker Cemetery in Macon County, Tennessee, honors several patriots, including John Lovelady, Sr., for serving in the Revolutionary War. (1)

John married Sarah Morgan in 1759. Sarah was born 1736 in North Carolina to Ebenezar Morgan and Unknown mother. The date of their arrival in Sevier County is not known. Ancestry.com and Find a Grave show that John died and was buried in Sevier County in 1795, but the location of his burial is not noted, and the date and place of Sarah's death is not known. (1), (2)

John and Sarah's children:
- John, Jr., was born 1760 in Orangeburg, South Carolina, married Clarissa Hughes in 1785, and died 1815 in Bledsoe County, Tennessee.
- James was born 1760 in Tennessee, married Dorcas De Whitt in 1803, and died 23 January 1837 in Smith County, Tennessee.
- Thomas was born 1767 in Orange County, North Carolina, married Jane Elizabeth Wear on 8 October 1792 in Greene County, Tennessee, and died 1830 in White, Tennessee.

- Ann was born in North Carolina in 1769, married Curtis Mills on 28 January 1784 in Greene County, and died 1820 in Tennessee.
- William Morgan was born 1770 in Tennessee, married Rachel Lindsey in 1794 in Greene County, and died 22 December 1857 in Shelby County, Alabama.
- Sarah was born about 1773, married Amos Isaac Ellard, and died 1794 in Virginia. (3)

Historical Fact: John, Sr., is the brother of Patriot William Marshall Lovelady and Rachel Lindsey is the daughter of Patriot David Elijah Lindsey.

Sources: (1) Our Family History, John Loveday, Sr. Rev War, GEDCOM, transcribed by Catherine Trumm, (2) Ancestry.com www.findagrave.com. (3) Family Search, Church of Jesus Christ of Latter-day Saints.

Lovelady, William Marshall

The Lovelady brothers John and William fulfilled their patriotic duty by fighting at the Battle of Kings Mountain. Marshall was born 1735 in Orange County, North Carolina, to Thomas, Sr., and Hannah Hix Lovelady. Marshall is listed as being at the Battle of Kings Mountain during the Revolutionary War. [1], [2] Records show he served as a chain bearer in 1757 for his father's land survey company. [3] Washington County, Tennessee, records of 1781/82 also show Marshall is on the Lantry Armstrong List, an inventory of taxable property. [3] He is listed in Greene County, Tennessee, in 24 June 1779 for receiving a Land Grant #1480 for 100 acres. [4]

Marshall married Hannah M. Wear (Weir) about 1765 in Greene County. Marshall died January 1793 in a portion of Jefferson County that is now Sevier County and is thought to be buried in an unmarked grave at Shiloh Cemetery in Pigeon Forge, Tennessee. [1]

Marshall and Hannah's children:
- Elizabeth was born about 1767 in North Carolina, married Unknown Brumley, and died in 1792.
- Sarah "Sally" was born about 1769 in North Carolina and married David Duncan on 2 February 1789 in Greene County.
- Jesse was born about 1774 in North Carolina and is thought to have married a woman named Polly. Jesse died after 1802 in Overton County. Tennessee.
- Obediah "Obed" was born 1772 in Mecklenburg, North Carolina, married

- Christian Mahan, and died 18 August 1842 in Noxubee County, Mississippi.
- Amos was born about 1781 in Washington County, North Carolina (now Tennessee), married Claramon "Clara" Boaz, and died before 1860 in Sevier County. Both Amos and Clara are buried in Shiloh Methodist Cemetery in Sevier County.
- Rhoda "Rhody" was born 1 February 1786 in Washington County, North Carolina (now Tennessee), married John Prentice 7 April 1804 in Sevier County, and died 23 September 1855 in Shelby County, Alabama.
- Eleanor was born about 1788 in Tennessee and died after 1792 at the age of 5 years. (1)

Historical Fact: Christian is the daughter of Patriot Major John Mahan, Claramon "Clara" is the daughter of Patriot Abednego Boaz, and William Marshall is the brother of Patriot John Lovelady, Sr.

Sources: (1) Smoky Mountain Historical Society Newsletter, winter, 1996, p. 7-8, Wilma Baldwin Moore, (2) *Tennessee Soldiers in the Revolution*, Penelope Allen, (3) Washington County, Tennessee Deeds, 1775-1800, (4) Greene County, Tennessee Deed Book 2, p. 165.

McCroskey, John Blair

John fought with the Indians, Tories, and finally with the British at the Battle of Kings Mountain. He was born 26 September 1757 in Rockbridge County, Virginia, to Samuel and Charlotte Taylor McCroskey. (1) In 1776, John was drafted as a private into the Virginia Militia under Captain Andrew Moore for a three-month term to protect the frontier from the Shawnee Indians.

In May 1776, John marched from Rockbridge to Jackson River, through the mountain country to Donala's Station, which had been attacked by Indians, served three months, and was honorably discharged in August by Lieutenant John Caruthers.

John moved to Washington County, Virginia, in 1779 and volunteered in the company of Captain Aaron Lewis and Lieutenant Robert Edmonson and marched from Abington, Virginia, along with Captain Montgomery's Company to the "Big Island of Holston River." These companies rendezvoused with Colonel Evan Shelby and Colonel Robertson, got into canoes, and descended the river to the mouth of Chickamauga Creek into the Cherokee Nation, where they had a skirmish with the Indians on the Tennessee River.

John volunteered again in June 1779 under Lieutenant Samuel Edmonson to protect the settlements along the Clinch River, served two months, and was discharged. In June 1780, he was drafted again, served under Captain William Edmonston and Colonel Arthur Campbell, and marched to Baker's Settlement, a Tory stronghold, hung one Tory, and dispersed many into the mountains.

On 23 September 1780, John volunteered to protect the Carolinas from the British and Tories. He joined Captain William Edmonston's Company, marched to Sycamore Shoals, and rendezvoused with Colonel John Sevier and Colonel Evan Shelby's troops. They crossed Yellow Mountain into North Carolina, where they were joined by Colonel William Cleaveland and Colonel Blandon, and marched into South Carolina and fought the Battle of Kings Mountain. (2)

John married Elizabeth Ann Houston Montgomery about 1779 in Rockbridge, Virginia. She was born 15 August 1756 in Virginia to John and Esther Houston Montgomery in Virginia. John applied for a Revolutionary War Pension (S2781) in the Sevier County Court of Pleas and Quarter Sessions on 1 August 1832 under Justice of the Peace John Pitner. Elijah Rogers and William Porter provided affidavits to the court that supported John's residency and status in the community. John and Elizabeth's home was located near current day King's Academy (formerly known as Harrison Chilhowee) in Seymour. (3)

Elizabeth died 13 March 1829 in Sevier County and is buried in Eusebia Cemetery in Blount County, Tennessee. John died 17 August 1843 in Blount County and is also buried in Eusebia Cemetery. (1)

John and Elizabeth Ann's children:
- Samuel was born 24 July 1782 in Jefferson County, Tennessee, and first married Mary "Polly" McCollum on 9 November 1816 in Blount County and then married Sarah Tucker on 1 July 1828. Samuel died 28 September 1848 in Monroe County, Tennessee.
- Esther Blair was born 10 April 1784 in Tennessee, married Alexander McCallie on 10 November 1803, and died 31 August 1868 in Sevier County.

- Mary was born 8 May 1786 in Greene County, Tennessee, married William Wilson in 1805, and died 20 October 1866 in Blount County, Tennessee.
- John was born 17 March 1788 in Greene County, Tennessee, married first Lucinda Ann Grant on 2 April 1820 in Blount County and secondly Priscilla McCray on 12 January 1836 in Washington County, Tennessee. John died 10 November 1866 in Monroe County, Tennessee.
- Robert Scott was born 5 November 1790 in Sevier County, married Mary McChesney Sharp in 1811, and died 12 February 1846 in Blount County.
- Dorcas was born 1793 in Tennessee, married John Sharp Wear in 1812, and died 19 August 1853 in Blount County.
- Lavinia was born 11 January 1799 in Sevier County, married John Eagleton on 8 December 1814 in Sevier County, and died 5 December 1880 in Blount County.
- Elizabeth was born 23 December 1803 in Sevier County, married Andrew Bogle on 28 January 1830 in Sevier County, and died 9 October 1885 in Blount County. (1)

Historical Fact: Elizabeth Ann Houston Montgomery is the sister of Patriot Alexander Montgomery, and Mary McChesney Sharp is the daughter of Patriot John Sharp, Jr.

A Portrait of Patriots and Pioneers in Sevier County

Sources: (1) Family Search, Chuch of Jesus Christ of Latter-day Saints, (2) Revolutionary War Pension Applications, Joseph Sharp Collection, McClung Historical Library, (3) McCroskey Family Records, Charles Wright Johnson, Jr., King Family Library, Sevierville, Tennessee.

McGaughey, Lieutenant Samuel Alexander

In the spring of 1778, Samuel substituted for his brother, William, and he continued to serve his country's fight for independence until spring 1781. He was born 15 July 1763 in York, Pennsylvania, to William and Elizabeth Lackey McGaughey. Samuel stated in his application for a Revolutionary War Pension that around 1771 or 1772, his father moved the family to the Holston River area of Washington County, Virginia, and was living in a fort when the war began. In the spring of 1778, the Indians were making war, and William was called to serve, but Samuel substituted in his father's place for one month as a guard under Captain John Shelby on the Clinch River. In August 1788, Samuel served in the same capacity and same place for one month under Captain James Montgomery.

Samuel volunteered again in March 1779 under Captain James Montgomery to fight against the Chickamauga Indians. Six hundred troops were raised by Colonel Evan Shelby, 300 troops were raised by Colonel Montgomery of Virginia and these combined forces proceeded down the Tennessee River in boats to engage with the Chickamaugas. After landing, three towns were destroyed, several Indians killed, and a number of women and children were taken prisoner. Samuel returned home in mid-May. In the fall of 1779, he again agreed to serve for seven months under Captain John McKee of Rockbridge, Virginia, as a mounted rifleman. Samuel volunteered again in the summer of 1780 under Captain Andrew Cowan to go against the British and Tories in South Carolina.

In the fall of 1780, every able man was called on to fight the British and Tories and their leader

Colonel Patrick Ferguson. Colonel Shelby from Sullivan County, Tennessee, Colonel John Sevier from Washington County, North Carolina (now Tennessee), and Colonel William Campbell from Washington County, Virginia, gathered their troops and met at Sycamore Shoals. They marched over the mountains into North Carolina and were in pursuit of the enemy, who had retreated to Kings Mountain in South Carolina. On 7 October 1780, at the Battle of Kings Mountain, the British were attacked and defeated and Colonel Ferguson was killed.

In early winter of 1780, Samuel volunteered as a mounted rifleman under Captain Andrew Cowan and Colonel Russell to go against the Cherokee Indians. The troops proceeded to towns on the Tennessee and French Broad Rivers, destroying towns and killing many warriors. In April 1781, Samuel was appointed First Lieutenant, and his last tour of duty was at Eutaw Springs under General Nathaneal Greene. This tour of duty lasted eight months. (1)

Samuel and his father, William, received a North Carolina Land grant for 3,000 acres on Boyd's Creek in Sevier County. They established McGaughey Station in 1785 shortly after the signing of the Treaty of Dumplin Creek. This treaty signaled a great migration of many settlers into the valleys of the French Broad and Holston Rivers. McGaughey Station was located on Porterfield Gap Road one-half mile north of Boyd's Creek Highway and near the Great Indian Warpath. This Fort provided shelter for many early settlers in the French Broad and Holston River valley. Samuel's mother was buried on this land. (2)

On 24 February 1784, Samuel married Mary Jane Laughlin, the daughter of John Luke, Sr., and Mary "Polly" Price Laughlin, in Sullivan County, North Carolina (now Tennessee).

Samuel and Mary Jane moved to Lawrence County, Alabama, around the late 1820s. On June 15, 1833, Samuel appeared in Lawrence County Open Court to apply for a Revolutionary War Pension #9981. He died 5 January 1841 in Lawrence County. Mary applied for Widow's Benefits on 22 March 1842 and stated in her application that they were married on 4 February 1784 and he died on 5 January 1841 in Lawrence County. Mary died 1 April 1847 also in Lawrence County. (2)

Samuel and Mary's children:
- Mary Polly was born about 1784 in Tennessee, married James Denton Henry 1806 in Blount County, Tennessee, and died after 1870 in Leake, Mississippi.
- William was born December 1785 in Greene County Tennessee, married Elizabeth Wingfield in 1804 in Blount County, and died 1838 in Lawrence County, Alabama.
- Elizabeth F. was born 12 January 1790 in Greene County, Tennessee, married William Maxwell Randles, Sr., on 5 September 1808 in Blount County, and died 4 August 1869 in Lawrence County.
- John was born 12 July 1792 in Greene County, married Hannah Jane Robison on 12 February 1812 in Blount County, and died 20 May 1784 in Greene County.
- James Harvey was born about 1795 in Knox County, Tennessee, married Martha Patsy Norton on 21 February 1820 in Lawrence County, Alabama, and

died about 1860 in Franklin County, Alabama.
- Sarah was born 1800 in Blount County, married John Mose Ewing on 26 September 1816 in Blount County, Tennessee, and died 1 April 1857 in Itawamba County, Mississippi.
- Margaret Isabel "Peggy" was born about 1802 in Tennessee, married Pleasant Wright Stephenson 22 October 1823 in Lawrence County, and died 4 August in Shelby County, Tennessee.
- Merry Anne was born 1802 in Tennessee, married Asbury Simpson on 22 October 1823 in Lawrence County, Alabama, and died about 1860 in Itawamba County, Mississippi.
- Jane was born 1805 in Sevier County, married John Ladell Stinson on 25 June 1823, and died after 1860 in Lawrence County, Alabama.
- Samuel Ellison was born in 10 August 1810 in Blount County, married Sarah Stephenson on 2 December 1829 in Lawrence County, and died 11 January 1887 in Benton, Mississippi. (3)

Historical Fact: Samuel is the son of Patriot William McGaughey.

Sources: (1) Southern Campaigns American Revolution Pension Statements & Rosters, transcribed by Will Graves, (2) Sevier County, Tennessee, and Its Heritage, 1994, Don Mills, pp. 11, (3) Family Search, Church of Jesus Christ of Latter-day Saints.

McGaughey, William

William began serving his country before the Revolutionary War began, and later during the war, he served with General George Washington. William was born 1738 in Scotland to William, Sr., and Margaret Boyd McGaughey, and after the family arrived in America, they settled in York, Pennsylvania. William served as a private in Colonel Neville's Company, and on 11 August 1775, the Provincial Convention of Virginia ordered Colonel Neville to march his company and take possession of Fort Pitt (present day Pittsburg).

William moved to the Holston River Settlement in Washington County, Virginia, in the late 1770s and served in the Virginia Militia. At one point in a campaign, General Washington camped in Abingdon, Virginia, near the McGaughey home, which enabled William to be with his wife during childbirth. According to family legend, William sent word to General Washington of the birth of his namesake, George Washington McGaughey, and not having a more fitting gift, General Washington sent a little iron camp kettle as a gift for the newborn. [1]

On 26 December 1791, the State of North Carolina issued land grant # 952 to William and Samuel McGaughey and John McCroskey for 3,000 acres on Boyd's Creek (now Sevier County). William and his son, Samuel, established McGaughey Station at Boyd's Creek in 1785 shortly after the Treaty of Dumpin Creek between the Cherokees and the State of Franklin. The station was located in a valley next to a large spring near the Great Indian Warpath. McGaughey Station was located thirteen miles southeast of present day Knoxville, Tennessee, and one-half mile north of

Boyd's Creek Highway on present day Porterfield Gap Road in Seymour, Tennessee. (2)

William married Elizabeth Lackey about 1760 in York County, Pennsylvania. Elizabeth was born in Scotland in 1742, died in 1804, and was buried at McGaughey Station. After Elizabeth's death, William left immediately for Maury County, Tennessee, with his two sons, George W. and James. He died sometime after 1812 in Maury County and is buried near the Duck River. (1), (2)

William and Elizabeth's children:
- Samuel Alexander was born 15 July 1763 in York County, Pennsylvania, married Jane Laughlin on 24 February 1784 in Sullivan County, North Carolina (now Tennessee), and died 5 January 1841 in Lawrence County, Alabama, and Mary died 1 April 1847, also in Lawrence County.
- Elizabeth was born about 1764 and first married James Edmondson, and later she married William Johnson.
- Agnes was born about 1765 and married Jeremiah Alexander.
- Margaret was born 1766, married David Robinson on 2 October 1786 in Greene County, Tennessee, and died 1813 in Greene County.
- William was born 1773 in the Watauga Settlement, married Margaret Boyd in 1794, and died 24 August 1820 in Boyd's Creek, Sevier County.
- Ann was born 24 September 1774, married William Gamble on 12 October 1797, and died 12 November 1847.

- James Harvey was born 9 April 1777 in Washington County, Virginia, married Margaret McCain 12 May 1798, and died 8 June 1837 in Lawrence County, Alabama.
- George W. was born 12 January 1781 at the Holston River Settlement, married Mary Unknown, and died 12 March 1861 in Tawamba County, Mississippi.
- Mary was born 1786, married Eli McCain, and died about 1833. (3)

Historical Fact: William McGaughey is the father of Patriot Samuel McGaughey.

Sources: (1) "Family Tree" database, Familysearch.org, (2) suesimplestories.blogspot.com/../ the-mcgaughey-family, (3) Family Search, Church of Jesus Christ of Latter-day Saints

McGee, John Alexander, Sr.

John could have been a fatality of the war, but fortunately he survived two serious injuries and returned home to build a good life for himself and his large family. John was born 30 January 1757 in Rockbridge County, Virginia. While residing in Rockbridge County, John served as a private in Captain William McKee's company of the 12th Virginia Regiment for two years. He fought in Captain Lewis' campaign against the Shawnee Indians in 1774 and at the Battle of Guilford Court House under the command of General Nathaneal Greene. During this battle, John was wounded by two bullets, one entered between his elbow and the wrist and the other went through his shoulder. He was honorably discharged by Captain William McKee of the 12th Regiment on 10 October 1778 at Fort Randolph, Virginia (now West Virginia).
(1)

John married Esther Clendenon in 1792 in Sevier County. Esther was born 30 January 1769 in Virginia, the daughter of John (1744-1790) and Mary Margaret Clendenon (1745-1790). Both John and Mary Margaret were born in Virginia and died in Jefferson County, Tennessee. Esther died 24 March 1846 in Warren County, Tennessee, and John died 24 January 1820, also in Warren County. They were both laid to rest in the family cemetery near their home.

John and Esther's children:
- Jane was born 28 May 1797, married James Hennessee in 1828 in Warren County, and died 1857 in Warren County.
- Mary "Polly" was born 11 January 1799 and married Ezekial M. McGregor in Warren, County.

- Clendenon was born 9 September 1800, married Martha England in 1823 in Warren County, and died 2 May 1846 in Warren County.
- Sarah was born 4 April 1802 and married Gabriel Bryant in Warren County.
- Richard was born 5 March 1804.
- John Alexander, Jr., was born 5 March 1804 in Sevier County, married Martha Walker in Nelson County, Kentucky, and died 12 March 1878 in Warren County.
- Samuel was born 13 December 1805, married Minerva Ann Hammonds in about 1840 in Warren County, and died 31 December 1884 in Warren County.
- Elizabeth was born 21 December 1808 in Warren County.
- James L. was born 2 June 1813 in Warren County and married Martha Ross. (2)

Sources: (1) Revolutionary War Pension Application Extract-John McGee, files, usgwararchives.net, (2) The Hennessee Family Genealogy Pages, maintained by David A. Hennessee

McKissack, John II

John is listed on the muster rolls of Pennsylvania's 5th Regiment for having served eighteen months from 6 July 1778 to 27 January 1780. John was born about 1740 in Pennsylvania to John (about 1720-?) and Rebecca Simmons McKissack (about 1720-?). (1), (2)

John married Lucinda Jane Hudson, the daughter of William and Susannah P. Allen Hudson, about 1759, in Haralson, Georgia. She was born about 1745 in Caswell Beach, Brunswick County, North Carolina. It is not known when John and Lucinda arrived or left Sevier County; however, it is well documented that their three youngest children, Lucinda, John, and Nancy, were born in Sevier County. John died 1815 in Putnam County, Georgia, and Lucinda died about 1818 also in Putnam County. (1)

John and Lucinda's children:
- James was born 1761 in Caswell County, North Carolina, married Rachael Morrison in 1798 in Tennessee, and died 1830 in Henry, Alabama.
- Mary "Polly" was born 1760/61 in Caswell County, Georgia, married Samuel Penington, and died 1840 in Jasper County, Georgia.
- William was born 1770 in Caswell County, married Mary McConnell, and died April 1848 in Polk County, Tennessee.
- Duncan was born 1771 in Caswell County, married Jane Allen in 1793 in Putnam, Georgia, and died 1850 in Jasper, Georgia.

- Jonathan was born 1772 in Caswell County, married Nancy Gray in 1797 in North Carolina, and died 9 January 1813 in Person, North Carolina.
- Thomas was born 1773 in North Carolina, married Mary Browning about 1798 in Putnam, Georgia, and both died 9 May 1836 in Russell, Alabama.
- Archibald was born 1775 in Caswell County, married Lucy Ann Ellis on 1 March 1802 in Clarke, Georgia, and died 1857 in Henry, Alabama.
- Elizabeth was born 1766 in Caswell County, married George Breeding, and died March 1870 in Oglethorpe, Georgia.
- Lucinda "Lucy" was born in 1784 in Sevier County, married John Lumpkin Stewart in 1799 in South Carolina, and died March 1870 in Clarke, Georgia.
- John was born 1785 in Sevier County, married Rachel Simmons in 1815, and died 1840 in Meriwether, Georgia.
- Nancy was born 1788 in Sevier County, married Clement Jeremiah Allen on 6 April 1802, and died 27 June 1855 in Coweta, Georgia. (1)

Historical Fact: Thomas and his wife, Mary, were massacred on 9 May 1836 during the Creek Indian war. Thomas, his wife, and several neighbors were fleeing their Russell County homes and heading for safety in nearby Columbus, Georgia.

Sources: (1) Family Search, Church of Jesus Christ of Latter-day Saints, {2} Ancestry.com, U. S. Revolutionary War Rolls, 1775-1783 for John McKissack

McMahon, James

James served in the Revolutionary War with his older brother, John, and while in battle, James was seriously wounded by a Tory during a skirmish. Yet, after a lengthy recovery, he volunteered to fight the Cherokee Indians under Colonel John Sevier. James was born circa 1750 in Ireland, and according to family legend, James, along with his father and brothers, sailed across the Atlantic Ocean on a ship with the Calvert's of Maryland. During the six-month voyage, James' father died and was buried at sea. (1) James settled in Botetourt, Virginia, and served in the Montgomery County, Virginia Militia. He also signed the Oath of Allegiance.

James moved to what is now Sevier County soon after the war. The Forks of the Little Pigeon River was chosen as the county seat in 1795, and the name of the settlement was changed to Sevierville, in honor of Colonel John Sevier. James donated twenty-five acres along the south bank of the river for the purpose of establishing the county seat. He was the first Register of Deeds in Sevier County. (2)

James married Rachel Calvert, the daughter of Robert and Jane Calvert, on 1 December 1788 in Botetourt, Virginia. Rachel was born about 1760 in England. She was a descendant of George Calvert, Lord of Baltimore. She died 1840 in Sevier County. James died 16 September 1831 in Sevier County and was buried in Forks of Little Pigeon River Cemetery.

James and Rachel's children:
- Robert was born 12 February 1794 in Tennessee, married Hulda Hatcher about 1818, and died 8 December 1867 and was buried in Blount County, Tennessee.

- William was born 6 November 1796 in Sevier County, married Charlotte "Lottie" Porter about 1821, and died 4 August 1860 in Sevier County.
- Abraham was born 22 April 1800 in Sevier County, married Susannah Hardy Bush in 1831, and died 23 January 1883 and is buried in Shiloh Cemetery in Pigeon Forge, Tennessee.
- John Calvin was born 10 May 1807 in Sevier County, married Dicey Elizabeth Waters in 1847, and died 1 May 1886 and was buried in Shiloh Cemetery in Pigeon Forge.
- James Isaac was born 26 May 1811 in Sevier County, married Nancy Henderson, and died 14 April 1880 and was buried in Shiloh Cemetery in Pigeon Forge.
- Samuel was born 8 February 1812 in Sevier County, married Mary J. Henderson, and died 13 October 1868 and is buried in McMahan Cemetery in Sevier County.
- Wellington was born 16 September 1817 in Sevier County, married Catherine Hammer on 16 February 1843, and died 18 March 1887 and was buried in Middle Creek Methodist Church Cemetery in Sevier County.
- Mary—no additional information is available. (1) (3)

Sources: (1) Smoky Mountain Ancestral Quest, Smoky Kin.com, maintained by David L. Beckwith, (2) Sevier County, Tennessee and Its Heritage, 1994, Don Mills, pp.8, 9, (3) Family Search, Church of Jesus Christ of Latter day Saints

Mahan, Captain James Irvin

James was born 2 December 1755 in Winchester, Virginia, to Thomas, Jr., and Margaret James Mahan. James was living near the Monongahela River in Virginia when he volunteered on 4 May 1774 to serve under Captain Jacob Drenin as an Indian spy and guard for less than six months. During this time, James marched to Fort Pitt, crossed the Ohio River, and fought against the Shawnees on the Chillicothe River. (1)

In the fall of 1775, he enlisted at Fort Pitt under Captain Astor, Captain Gibson, and Captain David Scott to guard the Indian prisoners until they returned home. James served less than a year and was honorably discharged to return home. He remained inactive until hearing Fort Laurens was under siege, and then he immediately raised a company to go to the relief of the fort. James received a severe abdominal wound in an altercation with a Tory and was incapacitated for twelve months.

James moved to Greene County, Tennessee (now Sevier County) in about 1780 with his brother, John Mahan, who was also a Revolutionary War soldier. (2), (3) James volunteered as a captain in the Greene County Militia under Colonel John Sevier, marched against the Cherokee Nation, and rendezvoused with the Indians at Hiwassee and Chilhowee.

James married Nancy Ann Goodwin, the daughter of Benjamin and Hannah Urquhart Goodwin of Monongahela Valley in 1773 at Winchester, Virginia. (3)

James and his family moved to Knox County, Kentucky (now Whitley County), between 1796 and

1800 and then in 1830, they moved to Missouri to live with their daughter, Elizabeth Miller. James died 17 December 1839 in Livingston County, Missouri, and The Daughters of the American Revolution erected a monument in James' memory in the Liggitt Cemetery in Livingston County, Missouri. Nancy Ann died 7 October 1840 and is also buried in the Liggitt Cemetery. (4)

James and Nancy Ann's children:
- Thomas was born about 1778 in Augusta, Virginia, married Amy Cox on 8 September 1800, and died 1826 in Whitley County, Kentucky.
- Hezekiah was born about 1781 in Greene County (Sevier County), married Sarah Hickey on 13 February 1803 in Knox County, Kentucky, and died in Ozark, Missouri. (4)
- Elizabeth was born 26 May 1784 in Greene County (Sevier County), married David Miller on 15 May 1806 in Knox County, Kentucky, and died 23 September 1870 in Cole, Missouri.
- James was born 1791 in Greene County (Sevier County), married Rebecca Trosper on 2 February 1810 in Whitley County, Kentucky, and died 5 September 1863 in Whitley County.
- Catherine was born 1802 in Knox County, Kentucky, married James Miller on 3 September 1820, and died 31 August 1860 in Knox County, Kentucky.
- Permelia was born 22 October 1804 in Pulaski County, Kentucky, married Francis Berry on 2 November 1823 in

Whitley County, Kentucky, and died 28 January 1882 in Linn, Oregon. (5)

Historical Fact: James is the brother of Patriot John Mahan.

Sources: (l) Historic Register of Virginians in the Revolutionary War, p. 494, (2) Sons of the American Revolution membership application, for James Mahan, (3) ancestry.com, James Mahan - Revolutionary Spy, Ed Beard, 2004, (4) findagrave.com, (5) Family Search, Church of Jesus Christ of the Latter-day Saints.

Mahan, Major John Michael

John served as a Major in the Virginia 13th Continental Line during the Revolutionary War. After the war, he was appointed Major of the Sevier County Regiment by Governor John Sevier. John was born 27 April 1750 in Winchester, Virginia to Thomas, Jr., (1731-1779) and Margaret James Mahan (1735-1801). James served thirteen months as a major in the 13th Virginia Continental line from 1 January 1777 to 23 September 1778. Sometime before 1783, John and his brother, James, and their families moved to Greene County, North Carolina (now Tennessee). John served as captain in the Greene County Militia's campaign against the Chickamauga Indians in 1788. (1)

John married Mary Scott about 1771. Mary was born in 1754 to Henry and Isabel Scott in Frederick County, Virginia, and reportedly, she is the niece of General Winfield Scott. In 1792, John moved his family to Sevier County and settled in the West Fork of the Little Pigeon River area, just three or four miles south of Sevierville. His land joined that of Alexander Montgomery, Flayl Nichols, and Samuel Wear.

Governor John Sevier appointed John the captain of the Sevier County Regiment on 4 April 1799, and a year later Governor Sevier appointed him to 2nd Major of the Regiment. Land records in Sevier County show that he received a land grant for 344 acres. After U. S. Congress established the Alabama Territory from Creek Indian land in 1816, John and Mary moved for the last time to be near their children in Cahaba (now Bibb) County, Alabama. John died on 7 April 1820 and is buried in the Community Baptist Church Cemetery in Bibb County, and Mary died in June 1823. She is also buried in Bibb County. (2)

John and Mary's children:
- Edward "Ned" was born 1772 in Frederick County, Virginia, married Rachel Reagan in 1798 in Sevier County, and died 1 October 1855 in Bibb County.
- Christian Mahan was born about 1780 in Frederick, Virginia, married Obediah Lovelady in 1799 in Pittsylvania County, Virginia, and died 10 September 1842 in Noxubee, Mississippi.
- John, Jr., was born 8 August 1781 in Sevier County, married Rebecca Crowson in 1806 in Shelby County, Alabama, and died 4 August 1843 in Talladega, Alabama.
- James was born 30 June 1782 in Sevier County, married Mary Polly Nowlin, and died 29 May 1849 in Bibb County.
- Mary "Polly" was born about 1790 in Sevier County, married Elijah Thomas in 1817 in Bibb County, and died 9 March 1866 in Philadelphia, Mississippi.
- Archimedes was born 1797 in Sevier County, married Mary Edwards Bennett on 21 June 1832 in Perry, Alabama, and died 11 February 1863 in Perry, Alabama. (2), (3)

Historical Fact: John is the brother of Patriot James Mahan, Rebecca is the daughter of Richard Crowson and granddaughter of Patriot William Crowson, Obediah Lovelady is the son of Patriot William Marshall Lovelady, and Rachel is the daughter of Patriot Timothy Reagan.

Sources: (1) Virginians in the Revolution, John H. Gwathney, p. 183, (2) Smoky Ancestral Quest, smokykin.com, maintained by David L. Beckwith (3) The Book of Ragan/Reagan 193, p 242, 408-409

Maples, Josiah, Sr.

All too often family legend is the only "record" of a patriot's participation in the war, and fortunately, records of Josiah's fight for American independence were handed down for generations by his family. Josiah was born about 25 January 1746 in Pittsylvania County, Virginia, to William and Prudence Comstock Maples. Josiah's tombstone at Murphy Chapel Cemetery in Sevier County shows he served in the Virginia Militia. (1), (2)

Josiah married Ruthea Sweeney about 1765 in Pittsylvania, Virginia. She was born in 1749 to Moses, Sr., and Ann Query Sweeney in Halifax, Virginia. Josiah and Ruthea moved to the Red Bank community of Sevier County around 1802. Josiah died 12 November 1820 in Sevier County and is buried at Murphy's Chapel Cemetery. Ruth died after 1830 and is also buried at Murphy's Chapel Cemetery.

Josiah and Ruthea's children:
- William Cordra was born 1 July 1766 in Halifax County, married Nancy Long on

6 October 1790, and died 26 October 1847 in Madison County, Alabama.
- Ruthea was born January 1770 in Pittsylvania County and died in 1784.
- Nancy Elizabeth was born about 1772 in Pittsylvania County, Virginia, married George Washington Long on June 9, 1791, and died 3 February 1850 in McMinn County, Tennessee.
- Ephriam was born March 1774 in Pittsylvania County, Virginia, married Martha Jane Atchley about 1817 in Sevier County, and died 1840 in Sevier County.
- Josiah, Jr., was born 1776 in Pittsylvania County, Virginia, married Mary Ann Dyer on 16 September 1807 and died 1855 in Christian County, Missouri.
- Elijah was born in 1783 in Pittsylvania County, Virginia, married Elizabeth Maples about 1830 in Sevier County, and died between 1860 and 1870.
- John W. was born June 1784 in Pittsylvania County, Virginia, married Susan Elizabeth Adams in 1824 in Alabama, and died 24 September 1851 in Limestone, Alabama
- Jesse was born March 1786 in Pittsylvania County, Virginia, married Jeminah Atchley in 1805 in Pittsylvania County, and died on 28 April 1866 in Bradley County, Tennessee.
- James was born 1788 in Pittsylvania County, Virginia, and died 1840 in Sevier County.

- Thomas was born 20 March 1790 in Pittsylvania County, Virginia, married Lydia Pauline Atchley on 6 December 1809 in Sevier County, and died 15 March 1871 and is buried in Bethel Cemetery in Sevier County. (1), (2), (3)

Historical Fact: Lydia Pauline and Martha Jane are sisters and the daughters of Patriot Thomas and Lydia Richards Atchley. Jeminah is a cousin and the daughter of Daniel Atchley.

Sources: (1) Smoky Mountain Ancestral Quest, smokykin.com., maintained by David L. Beckwith, (2) Ancestry, Family Tree for Josiah Maples, Sr. (3) Family Search, Church of Jesus Christ of Latter-day Saints.

Maples, Sergeant William Condra

According to family legend, William served alongside his father, Josiah, at the Battle of Guilford Court House. William was born 1 July 1766 in Halifax, Virginia, to Josiah (1746-1820) and Ruthea Sweeney (1749- after 1830) Maples. At the age of fifteen, William was with his father at the Battle of Guilford Court House. The British Army, commanded by General Cornwallis, was heavily outnumbered by General Nathaneal Greene's troops. However, Cornwallis' redcoats advanced and overcame American resistance. General Greene ordered a retreat rather than risk more lives. General Cornwallis is credited with winning the battle, but the victory was costly, more than one-fourth of his men were either killed or wounded. [1], [2], [3]

He married Nancy Long, the daughter of Edward and Jane S. Jones Long on 6 October 1790 in Pittsylvania County, Virginia. She was born in 1768 in Loudoun County, Virginia. William and Nancy moved to Jefferson County, Tennessee, in 1796 and were living in Sevier County in 1802. After the war, William served as a sergeant in Captain William Mitchell's Company of Mounted Infantry, East Tennessee Volunteer Militia, commanded by Colonel Samuel Wear.

William, Nancy, and several of their children moved to Alabama in 1833. William died on 26 October 1847 in Madison County, Alabama, and is buried in Bethel Cemetery in Madison County. Nancy died 11 January 1839 in Madison County and is also buried in the Bethel Cemetery. [4] A bronze and granite marker on the Madison County Court House lawn lists all the Revolutionary War soldiers buried in Madison County, and William is included. (1)

William and Nancy's children:
- Josiah was born 25 January 1794 in Pittsylvania County, Virginia, married Mary Butler on 29 June 1815 in Sevier County, and died 11 September 1840 in Jackson County, Alabama.
- William, Jr., was born 6 December 1795 in Pittsylvania County, Virginia, married Jane L. Reynolds in 1814 in Sevier County, and died 1883 in Bell County, Texas.
- Edward was born 1798 in Jefferson County, married Jane Moon in 1818 in Jefferson County, and died 17 October 1838 in Madison County.
- John Henry was born 1797 in Jefferson County, married Elizabeth Sharp on 7 February 1818 in Grainger County, Tennessee, and died in 1875 in Morgan County, Alabama.
- Moses was born 17 September 1802 in Sevier County, married Catherine Manning on 8 May 1820 in Sevier County, and died 24 June 1880 in Woodville, Alabama.
- Peter was born 30 October 1804 in Sevier County, married Mary Moon in 1823 in Sevier County, and died 8 January 1885 in Madison County.
- James was born 1806 in Sevier County, married Edith Caroline Patterson in 1830, and died in 1854 in Madison County.

- George was born 1 December 1808 in Sevier County, married Winey Bodine in Sevier County in 1826, and died 26 November 1887 in Madison County.
- McCampbell was born 8 June 1818 in Sevier County, married Elizabeth Wilder on 9 February 1837 in Jackson County, Alabama, and died 11 January 1905 in Bell County, Texas. (4)

Sources: (1) Revolutionary War Soldiers in Alabama, Thomas Owen, p. 82, (2) History of Alabama and Dictionary of Alabama Biography, Thomas Owen, Vol. IV, p. 1157, (3) findagrave.com, (4) Family Search, Church of Jesus Christ of Latter-day Saints.

Matthews, Obediah

Although Obediah served in the war, he is most remembered for the tragedy that happened on 29 December 1792. Obediah was born 1756 in Buckingham County (now Appomattox County), Virginia, to James and Agnes Allen Matthews. (1) Obediah is credited with receiving nine pounds of specie as payment for his service in the Revolutionary War. A "specie" is a colonial form of money used as currency, such as the precious metals gold or silver. (2), (3)

Obediah married Lydda Richardson on 1 April 1786 in Greene County, Tennessee. Lydda was born 1764 in Virginia to William and Mary Schull Richardson. Obediah and Lydda, along with her parents, the Richardson's, moved to what would later become Sevier County. The family built a cabin beside a spring in the area that became known as Richardson's Cove, named for his father-in-law, William Richardson. Later, the Matthews family settled on Dunn's Creek in the Rocky Flats Community, and Obie's Branch is named for Obediah.

On 29 December 1792, Indians attacked the home of Obediah's in-laws and massacred Mrs. Richardson, her two younger children, and her sister, Miss Schull. This massacre is still the topic of interest 200 years later. The dates of Obediah and Lydda's deaths are unknown. (4)

Obediah and Lydda's child:
- Robert was born 19 February 1786 in Greene County, State of Franklin (now Tennessee), married Leah Dobbins (Dobkins) in 1809 in Sevier County, and died 19 March 1870 in Sevier County. (1)

Historical Fact: William Richardson is also a patriot of the Revolutionary War.

Sources: (1) Family Search, Church of Jesus Christ of Latter-day Saints, (2) North Carolina Army accounts: Secretary of State, Treasurer's and Comptroller's papers, Weynette Parks Haun, 1988-1995. (3) roots web, Dennis Nicklaus genealogy, (4) Sevier County, Tennessee, and Its Heritage, 1994, p. 9, Don Mills.

Millsaps, Thomas Minear

Thomas volunteered to assist in his country's fight for independence. He is one of the thousands of Revolutionary War heroes who honorably fulfilled their orders and then returned home to build a future for themselves and their family.

Thomas was born 23 December 1752 in Rowan (now Randolph) County, North Carolina, the son of Robert and Ellender King Millsaps. Thomas volunteered in March or April 1780 as a private in the North Carolina Militia under the command of Captain Aaron Hilt, Lieutenant Elijah Williams, and Colonel Andrew Belfour as a minute-man and continued in service for twelve months until peace was made with the British. Thomas commenced his service as a light horseman but was frequently on foot and assigned to follow the Tories. In one tour, Thomas marched from Rowan County to Chatham County, North Carolina, below Deep River, caught a Tory hiding in a fodder stack, captured the Tory, and took him to headquarters above Deep River. Once peace was made with the British, Thomas was permitted to return home, but he did not receive a written discharge. [1]

Thomas married Bathsheba Williams in May 1777 in Guilford County, North Carolina. After the war, Thomas moved from Rowan County to Carter County, Tennessee, and then to Greene County, Tennessee (now Sevier County); however, the date of Thomas' and Bathsheba's arrival in Sevier County is not known. Bathsheba appeared in Sevier County Court on 15 July 1844 before Justice of the Peace, J. N. Siles, to file for a Revolutionary War Widow's Pension #7173. Bathsheba stated in the application that she and Thomas were married in May 1777 by a minister of the gospel by the name of Shackelford. She further stated that Thomas died 1 April 1837 and she remained his widow. Bathsheba was born in 1759 in North Carolina and died before 25 March 1857 in Sevier County, and Thomas died 4 January 1837, also in Sevier County. (1)

Thomas and Bathsheba's children:
- Thomas James was born 23 December 1782 in North Carolina, married Mary Sutton on 10 March 1811 in Cocke County, Tennessee, and died 23 August 1870 in Fannin County, Georgia.
- Edward was born 1784 in North Carolina, married Lydia Brickey on 10 December 1820 and died 1840 in Haywood County, North Carolina.
- Isaac was born in 1795, married Mary Blackburn on 23 September 1819 in Pike County, Mississippi, and died at the Alamo on 6 March 1838 in Bexar County, Texas.
- David was born in 1802 in Tennessee, married Lavennia Unknown in 1827, and died in 1880 in Van Buren County, Arkansas. (2)

Sources: (1) Southern Campaigns American Revolution Pension Statements & Rosters, transcribed by Will Graves, (2) Ancestry.com., public member trees- Thomas Millsaps.

Montgomery, Alexander

Alexander came to Sevier County and actively participated in the county's government. He was appointed the first surveyor during the State of Franklin, and when Tennessee became a state, he was elected to the county court. Alexander was born about 1760 in Augusta County, Virginia, to John (1730-1795) and Esther Houston Montgomery (1724-1798). Alexander's maternal grandparents, John and Margaret Cunningham Houston, are the paternal grandparents of Sam Houston. Family legend passed down from generation to generation is that Alexander fought in the Battle of Kings Mountain under Colonel John Sevier. Alexander is listed in the Daughters of American Revolution Index as having served in the Revolutionary War.

Alexander married Margaret Eaune Napier on 13 May 1798 in Montgomery, Virginia. She was born in 1766 in Montgomery, Virginia. Alexander and Margaret settled in Sevier County about 1790 and lived in a cabin on the West Fork of the Little Pigeon River, near the mouth of Walden's Creek. In 1808, he obtained a land grant for 263 acres on the bank of the river that was bounded on the north by Patriot Flayl Nichols, on the south by Abraham Mullendore, and on the west and southwest by John McMahan. He was appointed the first surveyor for Sevier County, State of Franklin, and when the area became part of the State of Tennessee, Alexander was elected to the first Sevier County Court that met for the first time on November 8, 1796, at Newell Station (now Seymour).

Alexander died 19 December 1817 and is buried in Shiloh Cemetery in Pigeon Forge, and Margaret died 12 December 1830 and is also buried in Shiloh Cemetery. (1)(4)

Alexander and Margaret's children:
- John Alexander was born 17 November 1784, married Mary Cunningham Winton, and died 9 August 1860 in Roane County, Tennessee, and is buried in the Winton Family Cemetery.
- William H. was born 12 January 1788 in Washington County, North Carolina (now Tennessee), married Elizabeth "Betsy" Winton on 1 April 1824 in Sevier County, and died 28 May 1840 in Sevier County and is buried in Shiloh Cemetery.
- Margaret was born 17 June 1793 in Sevier County, married Captain Andrew Lawson on 19 January 1825, and died 4 August 1848 in Sevier County and is buried in Shiloh Cemetery. (2), (3)

Historical Fact: Alexander's sister Elizabeth married Patriot John McCroskey; his sister Esther married Patriot Samuel Doak, the founder of Tusculum College in Greeneville, Tennessee; his sister Jane married Samuel Newell, Jr.; and his sister Mollie married Patriot Captain Robert Edmonson, who was killed during the Revolutionary War.

Sources: (1) Sevier County, Tennessee, and Its Heritage, 1994 Don Mills, pp. 223, 232, 275, 277, (2) Family Search, Church of Jesus Christ of Latter-day Saints- Alexander Montgomery, (3) Smoky Mountain Ancestral Quest, smokykin.com, maintained by David L. Beckwith, (4) In the Shadow of the Smokies, Smoky Mountain Historical Society, 1993, p. 360 .

Murphy, Edward

Edward stated in his application for a Revolutionary War Pension that he was told by his parents he was born 25 December 1742 in York, Pennsylvania. He further stated there is no record of his birth and he couldn't read or write. Edward stated he was living in Rockbridge County, Virginia, when drafted for a term of three months into the militia commanded by Captain Morrow. The Company rendezvoused in Greenbrier County and marched to the junction of the Ohio and Elk Rivers and engaged in a battle with the Shawnee Indians. After the battle, the company was ordered to build a barracks at the junction, and after completing the barracks, the company was discharged. (1)

Edward was living in Botetourt County, Virginia, when again called into service in a company led by Captain Marlow to go against the Cherokee Indians. The company marched from Rockbridge County to Long Island of the Holston River (near present day Kingsport, Tennessee). At Long Island, the company was joined by the main Army commanded by Captain William Christian. Edward remained there until he was discharged.

In the fall of 1780, Edward was drafted for three months in a company commanded by Captain William Christian, they rendezvoused at Reedy Creek, Virginia, and marched to Kings Mountain, South Carolina. At Kings Mountain, they were joined by the additional companies of Colonels Isaac Shelby, John Sevier, and William Campbell. After the battle on October 7, 1780, Edward's company marched to General Campbell's home and was discharged.

After returning home to Botetourt County, Edward was forced by the Tories to move to Washington County, Virginia. In late-summer of 1781, Edward was drafted for a three-month term as an orderly sergeant in a company led by Captain James Gilmore, Lieutenant McCampbell, and Ensign Cunningham. The company rendezvoused at the Nolichucky River, marched to Lexington, Virginia, and then on to Yorktown, and remained there until the battle on 19 October 1781. (1)

After the war, Edward moved to the Tennessee counties of Greene, Sevier, Rhea, and McMinn. He appeared in McMinn County Court on 6 September 1832 to apply for Revolutionary War Pension # S1569. Edward's wife is listed as Elizabeth Unknown. He died after 1 June 1835 in McMinn County. (1), (2)

Edward and Elizabeth's child:
- Mary was born 1 July 1766 in Augusta County, Virginia, married James Bates (1760-1814) on 25 November 1786, and died 30 January 1848 in Bradley County, Tennessee. (2)

Sources: (1) Southern Campaign American Revolution Pension Statements & Rosters, transcribed by Will Graves, (2) Family Search, The Church of Jesus Christ of Latter-day Saints.

Newell, Samuel

After the Revolutionary War, Samuel migrated to Sevier County and became active in establishing the State of Franklin, and later, he was a delegate to the convention that drafted the Constitution of the State of Tennessee. Samuel was born 4 November 1754 in Frederick Virginia, the son of Samuel, Sr., and Elizabeth Colville Newell. He entered service April 1776 in Washington County, Virginia, in the company of Captain John Shelby and marched to Washington County, North Carolina (now Tennessee), to go against the Tories, who were about to unite with the Indians. About forty Tories were taken prisoner, three or four joined the United States Army, and the rest of the Tories took the Oath of Allegiance to the United States and were permitted to remain with their families.

In July 1776, Samuel volunteered in the company of Captain Cook, marched to Eaton's Fort about five miles east of Long Island Fort on the Holston River (near present day Kingsport, Tennessee), and defeated the Indians in the Battle of Long Island. After the defeat of the Indians, Samuel marched to Fort Black (now Abington, Virginia), was appointed Sergeant by Captain Andrew Colville, and served in that capacity for twelve months. In July 1777, he was appointed Lieutenant in Captain Colville's company and directed to march to Glade Hollow Fort on the Clinch River to guard the frontiers, and after completing this tour, the company returned home.

In the fall of 1779, Samuel again volunteered as Lieutenant in the company of Captain Colville, Ensign John Beattie, and Colonel William Campbell and marched toward Kings Mountain, in South Carolina, to join the company of General McDowell. He fought in the Battle of Kings Mountain and was severely wounded in the left thigh and groin. In late January 1781, Andrew was appointed Captain and proceeded to Rock Spring Station at the head of Powell Valley and was involved in several skirmishes with the Indians. At the end of four months, Samuel was discharged by Colonel Campbell and ordered to return home to raise a company to fight against General Cornwallis, but before the company was ready to march, Cornwallis surrendered and the order was countermanded. (1)

Samuel married Jane Montgomery, the daughter of Reverend John and Esther Houston Montgomery in Raphine, Virginia, in 1782. Jane was born in September 1764 in Raphine and is a first cousin to Samuel Houston, later Governor of Tennessee and President of the Republic of Texas. By 1783, Samuel had moved to Greene County, North Carolina (now Sevier County), and built Newell's Station at the headwaters of Boyd's Creek in present day Seymour. Samuel was very active in establishing the State of Franklin, and he was Sevier County's State Representative and Chairman of Sevier County Court. In 1796, Samuel was Sevier County's delegate to the convention that drafted the State of Tennessee's Constitution and later represented Sevier County in the first Tennessee Legislature. (2) A historical marker located in Seymour designates the location of Newell Station.

Samuel and Jane left Sevier County in the early 1800s and followed their daughter Susannah and her husband, Andrew Evans, to Indiana. Samuel died 21 September 1841 in Owen, Indiana, and Jane died 11 February 1843, also in Owen, Indiana.

Samuel and Jane's children:
- Esther was born 20 September 1783 in Virginia, married Jesse Evans in 1810 in Indiana, and died 27 January 1851 in Indiana.

- Samuel B. was born 24 March 1786 in Augusta, Virginia, married Nancy Owens, and died 2 October 1849 in Kentucky.
- Margaret was born 3 June 1788 Augusta, Virginia married William Owens on 9 March 1814 in Shenandoah Valley, Virginia, and died 28 March 1851 in Pulaski, Kentucky.
- John Montgomery was born 20 September 1790 in Augusta, Virginia, married Margaret Beatie on 31 January 1820 in Pulaski, Kentucky, and died 22 October 1871.
- Susannah was born 4 November 1792 in Washington County, Tennessee, married Andrew Evans in 1814, and died 1864 in Jefferson Township, Indiana.
- Dorcas was born 1795 in Augusta, Virginia, and died 7 September 1824.
- Elizabeth was born 27 August 1797 in Augusta, Virginia, and died 7 August 1831.
- Joseph B. was born 1800 in Washington County, Virginia, married Jane Kinkead on 24 January 1824, and died in 1880.
- William was born 7 May 1801 in Kentucky, married Paulina Faine, and died 21 September 1851 in Adams, Indiana.
- Jane was born 13 March 1806 in Kentucky and married James Evans on 20 April 1837 in Owens, Indiana. (3)

Historical Fact: Andrew, James, and Jesse Evans are sons of Patriot Andrew Evans, and Samuel's half-sister, Martha Blackburn, married Patriot John B. Cusick.

Sources: (1) Montgomery and Rowntree Families and Genealogy, maintained by Keith Montgomery, (2)Sevier County, Tennessee, and Its Heritage, pp 18- 21, 1994, Don Mills, (3) Family Search, Church of Jesus Christ of the Latter-day Saints.

Nichols, Flayl (Flail Nicholes)

Flayl served both Sevier and Blount counties in the Tennessee government. Flayl was born 4 January 1747 in Bedford County, Virginia, to Lieutenant John, Sr., and Martha Payne Nichols. Flayl is recorded on the muster rolls of Captain Adam Clement's Bedford County Militia Company, serving as a wagon master. He also served under Colonel William Campbell and General Nathaneal Greene at the Battle of Kings Mountain. [1]

Flayl married Nancy Ann Hatcher, the daughter of Edward and Sarah Susannah Farley Hatcher, on 7 January 1780 in Bedford County, Virginia. Flayl and Nancy sold their Bedford County land in the late 1780s and moved to Sevier County about 1790. According to family legend, Flayl and his family first resided in Wear's Fort after their arrival from Virginia.

Flayl was a state senator for Sevier and Blount Counties in the Tennessee legislature in 1803-04. In 1808, Flayl received a Tennessee Land Grant for 331 acres located on the West Fork of the Little Pigeon River near the mouth of Walden's Creek. His land adjoined the land of Stephen Winton, George Green, John Mahan, and Alexander Montgomery. Flayl died on 7 September 1823 in Pigeon Forge and is buried in Shiloh Memorial Cemetery in Pigeon Forge, and Nancy died about 1830. In 1950, a granite headstone showing Flayl's Revolutionary War service was placed on his grave in Shiloh Memorial Cemetery. (2), (5), (6)

Flayl and Nancy's children:
- Sarah was born 1 November 1780 in Bedford, Virginia, married John Matson on 28 August 1802, and died 22 August 1857 in Talladega, Alabama.
- Martha was born 25 June 1784 in Bedford, Virginia, married Robert Lawson in Sevier County in 1803, and died in Talladega, Alabama, about 1851.
- Rhoda was born 26 March 1785 in Bedford, Virginia.
- John J. was born 4 March 1787 in Virginia, married Esther Black on 13 January 1814 in Tennessee, and died 16 March 1865 in Sevier County.
- Jesse was born 13 December 1788 in Bedford, Virginia, and died about 1841 in Marshall County, Alabama.
- Edward was born about 1791 in Sevier County and died in Fort Bend, Texas, on 12 May 1860.
- Simon was born 25 August 1785 in Sevier County and died about 1849 in Marshall County, Alabama.
- William was born 6 October 1797 in Sevier County, married Martha Susan Cannon in 1821 in Sevier County, and died 10 June 1884 in Randolph County, Missouri.

- Robert was born 23 March 1880 in Sevier County, married Rebecca Cannon, and died 30 June 1873 in Macon, Missouri.

Historical Fact: Nancy Ann Hatcher is a member of the Hatcher Family of Sevier and Blount Counties.

Sources: (1) History of Virginians in the Revolution, John Gwathney, pp 157, 565, (2) Sevier County, Tennessee, and Its Heritage, 1994, Don Mills, P. 18, (3) Family Search, Church of Jesus Christ of Latter-day Saints, (4) Smoky Mountain Ancestral Quest, smokykin.com, maintained by David L. Beckwith, (5) In The Shadow of the Smokies, Smoky Mountain Historical Society, 1993, p.362.

Norton, David Jr.

At the age of seventeen, David entered service as a substitute and fought for his country for eighteen months. David was born about 1763 in Fluvanna, Virginia, to Reverend John and Mary Norton. His occupation before entering the war is listed as a planter. He entered the military on 18 May 1780 in Amherst County, Virginia, at the age of seventeen as a private and served eighteen months as a substitute. (1)

David is listed on the tax rolls of Washington County, Virginia, in 1782 as owning five horses and four head of cattle. His land was near the Cumberland Gap and the only route into Kentucky. It is believed that David was engaged in transporting settlers by horseback into Kentucky since the trail at that time was too rugged and narrow to allow travel by wagons. (2)

David married Sophia Fancher about 1783 in Virginia and moved to Fancher (now Pigeon Forge), Sevier County. Several members of the Fancher family already lived in the area. Also, Norton Branch connected to the Little Pigeon River near the Fancher's home. David and Sophia lived in Pigeon Forge for seven to eight years before rejoining the rest of their family in Bourbon, Kentucky, in 1791. David died 1818 in Pendleton, Kentucky and Sophia died 1823 in Grant, Kentucky. (3)

David and Sophia's children:
- Samuel was born 1785 in Sevier County, married Nancy Jones in 1808 in Bourbon, Kentucky, and died 1819 in Bourbon.
- John H. was born 1786 in Sevier County, married Mary "Polly" Benefield in 1805 in Ohio.

- Mary was born 1788 in Sevier County.
- Sophia was born 1789 in Sevier County.
- Henry was born in 1791 in Bourbon, Kentucky, married Betsy Ann Wright in Pendleton, Kentucky, in 1812, and died in 1831.
- Sally was born 1793 in Ohio and married Jacob Ashcraft in Pendleton, Kentucky, in 1817.
- Rachel was born in 1795.
- David, Jr., was born 23 October 1796 in Pendleton, Kentucky, married Elizabeth Benefield on 10 February 1820 in Wayne, Indiana, and died 2 June 1860 in Lehi, Utah.
- Hiram was born 1803 in Ohio and married Lydia Ashcraft in Pendleton, Kentucky, in 1833.
- James was born 8 October 1808 in Pendleton, Kentucky. [2]

Sources: (1) Historical Registry of Virginians in the Revolution, Soldiers, Sailors and Marines. 1775-1783, by John Gwathney, Richmond, VA 1938, Vol. 126, P 126, (2) nortonfamily.net, (3) nortonfamily.net/fluvanna-ky-utah-davidjr.htm

Nucum (Newcomb), Solomon

Information on Solomon's exact date of birth, location of his birth, and names of his parents is not known. All the information we have is based on his application for a war pension. On 4 March 1828, at the age of seventy-nine, Solomon appeared in Sevier County Court to make application for a Revolutionary War Pension #973. In the application, he stated that he was born about 1749 in Virginia. He further stated that he enlisted in the Virginia Line on 25 December 1777 under Captain Fleming, Major Ball, and Colonel Russell and continued to serve until the end of the war when he was honorably discharged in Richmond, Virginia. He further stated that he did not have a family, was a cooper by trade, and because of old age and other bodily infirmities was unable to work. He did not apply for a pension sooner because he considered himself to be a man of good worth, and as long as that was the case, he never thought of asking for charity from this country. Solomon received a pension beginning on 17 June 1828.

On January 14 1850, Susannah Nukum appeared in Bradley County, Tennessee Court to file for a widow's pension. In her application, she stated that she was the widow of Solomon Nukum and that she married him in August 1798 in Wilkes County, North Carolina. Susannah also said Solomon died 18 February 1834. Neither pension application gives the date Solomon and Susannah arrived in Sevier County or exactly where they lived, but he is believed to have owned 100 acres in the East Fork of the Little Pigeon River area of the county. (1), (2)

Also appearing in court with Susannah was eighty-three year old Alan Morgan, who testified that he was well acquainted with both Solomon and Susannah and that he personally knew of the marriage between Solomon and Susannah Waits Nukum in Wilkes County. Susannah received pension #W973 beginning 4 March 1848. (1), (2)

No children have been identified.

Sources: (1) Revolutionary War Gravesite's of Knox and Surrounding Counties, Stephen Holston Chapter, SAR, (2) Southern Campaign American Revolution Pension Statements and Rosters, transcribed by Will Graves.

Ogle, William, "Billy"

William was determined to provide a better life for his family in the fertile valleys and hills of Sevier County. However, his untimely death prevented him from completing this task, but the strong will and determination of his widow and children became legendary and are still remembered to this day.

William was born about 1751 in New Castle County, Delaware, to Thomas (1721-1803) and Elizabeth Robeson Ogle (about 1721-?). According to family legend, William served in the Revolutionary War. [1] Military records list a soldier by the name of William Ogle serving as a private in the 2nd Battalion of the Delaware Militia during the Revolutionary War. [2] In the late 1770s, William married Martha Jane Huskey and moved to South Carolina. Martha Jane was born 9 December 1756 in Wake County, North Carolina, the daughter of John Frederick and Rebecca Washington Huskey of Rowan County, North Carolina.

Martha Jane was thought to be part Indian, and it was believed William hunted with the Indians in the Great Smoky Mountains. William decided to build a log cabin in "The Land of Paradise" (Gatlinburg, Tennessee), where the water ran clear and there was plenty of game and fish. He selected a house site, (near the Arrowmont School of Arts and Crafts), cut and hewed the logs, left them to dry, and returned home to South Carolina to grow a crop and then bring his family to their new cabin. While at home, an epidemic broke out. William caught the disease and died in 1803. Martha brought her five sons, two daughters, her brother, Peter Huskey, and his family to "The Land of Paradise" to establish a new home. By 1807, Martha Jane, with the help of her children and brother, finished building the cabin. Martha died in Gatlinburg before July 1826 and is buried at White Oak Flats Cemetery in Gatlinburg. She became a legend in "The Land of Paradise" for her remarkable hard work and determination to succeed. William and Martha Jane's cabin was officially donated to the city of Gatlinburg and is located at the Gatlinburg Welcome Center. (3) (4)

William and Martha Jane's children:
- Hercules "Hike" was born 1780 in South Carolina and first married Elizabeth Haggard about 1800 and, secondly, Rebecca Huskey in 1845/50. He died about 1854 in Gatlinburg and is buried in the White Oak Flats Cemetery in Gatlinburg.
- Rebecca was born 1782 in North Carolina, first married James McCarter about 1800 and, secondly, Middleton Whaley about 1818, and died about 1870/80 and is buried in the P. A. Proffitt Cemetery in Sevier County.
- Thomas was born 1784 in Wilkes County, Georgia, married Sophia Bosley about 1804, and died 1862 in Gatlinburg and is buried in the White Oak Flats Cemetery in Gatlinburg.
- John "Johnny" was born 1786 in Edgefield County, married Elizabeth McBryant in 1808, and died 1841 in Blount County, Tennessee.
- Isaac "Shucky" was born 1788 in Edgefield County, married Susannah Bohannon about 1809, and died 2 September 1881 and is buried in Banner Cemetery in Gatlinburg.

- William "Black Bill" was born 1790 in Edgefield County, married Nancy Bohannon about 1810, and died 25 August 1855 and is buried in Cole Cemetery in Sevier County.
- Mary Ann was born 1793 in Edgefield County, married William M. Whaley on 26 December 1811 in Sevier County, and died 1872/1880 and is buried in Plemons Cemetery in Sevier County. (1)

Historical Fact: Susannah and Nancy Bohannon are daughters of Patriot Henry Bohannon.

Sources: (1) Smoky Mountain Ancestral Quest, smokykin.com, David L. Beckwith, administrator, (2) ancestry.com, search, William Ogle, (3) In the Shadow of the Smokies, Smoky Mountain Historical Society, 1993, p. 575, (4) Carroll McMahan, The Mountain Press, 8 May 2016.

Oldham, James

James became an active member in the formation of Sevier County and Oldham's Creek, named in his honor, remains on Sevier County's maps as a testament to his place in this county's history. James is listed on the Virginia 5th Regiment payroll muster roll for August 1776, December 1776, and May 1777. James married Leah Stephens, daughter of William and Mary Sampson Stephens, on 2 January 1774 in Loudoun County, Virginia.

In 1788, James and Leah are living in Sevier County. James and his father-in-law, William Stephens, signed the 1788 and 1799 "Territory South of the French Broad and Holston River" petitions. They are believed to have settled east of Pigeon Forge in a community named Oldham's Creek. This area was possibly named for James and Leah Oldham who settled there between 1789 and 1795. James also signed the "Sundry Inhabitants South of the French Broad" petition requesting that land prices be based according to its value as tillable farmland. James bought 225 acres on the East Fork of the Little Pigeon River that joined land belonging to his son, John Oldham, Hugh Duggan, and Henry Bohannon.

In 1815, three of James and Leah's sons, Stephen, James, and John were granted land in Union and Fayette Counties, Indiana. James and Leah followed a few years later. Leah died in 1827 in Fayette County, Indiana, and James died on 15 May 1827, also in Fayette County.

James and Leah's children:
- Stephen was born 4 November 1774 in Loudoun County, Virginia, married Rebecca Potts about 1800 in Sevier

County, and died 14 May 1834 in Fayette County.
- Moses was born about 1776 in Virginia, first married Jean Unknown and, secondly, married Elizabeth McDaniel, and died June 1853 in Union County, Indiana.
- George was born 7 June 1779 in Virginia, married first Catherine Caty Hill and, secondly, Sarah Maples, and died 7 September 1828 in Shelby County, Indiana.
- William was born 5 June 1783 in Pittsylvania County, Virginia, first married Anne (Anna) White (1785-1821) in Sevier County on 19 July 1804 and married, secondly, Naoma Morphew on 7 July 1822 in Union County, Indiana, and died 23 October 1854 in Wapello County, Iowa.
- John was born 1785 in Henry County, Virginia, married Nancy Keeney, and died in Howard County, Indiana.
- Nancy was born about 1786 in Sevier County and married James Sewell in 1812 in Sevier County.
- Sarah was born about 1791 in Sevier County, married Andrew Jonathon Longley on 28 August 1810 in Sevier County, and died 1872 in Polk County, Tennessee.
- James, Jr., was born 7 December 1794 in Sevier County, married Mary Fansher on 5 November 1817 in Sevier County, and died 22 May 1853 in Rush County, Indiana.

- Mary was born about 1800 in Sevier County, married Unknown Adams, and died before 1827 in Lauderdale County, Alabama. (1)

Historical Fact: Reverend Samuel Oldham was a trustee of Sevierville's historic Nancy Academy. Andrew Jonathon Longley is the son of Patriot William Longley.

Sources: (1) Oldham Family History, Oldham.one-name.net, maintained by Jan Oldham

Parsons, George

George fought in many battles during the Revolutionary War, during which he was wounded and taken prisoner. The debilitating injuries he received during his fight for our freedom and independence resulted in a lifelong struggle to adequately provide for his family.

George enlisted on 22 December 1777 for three years in Culpeper County, Virginia's 10th Regiment under Captain John Gillison and commanded by Edward Stevens. During this time, George was at the Battle of Brandywine on 11 September 1777, the Battle of Germantown on 4 October 1777, the Storming of Stony Point on 15 July 1779, and the Battle of Monmouth on 28 June 1778.

Later, George enlisted in the Hillsborough, North Carolina Cavalry under Colonel William Washington in the 3rd Regiment of Light Dragoons. He was in the Battle of Cowpens on 7 January 1781, the Battle of Guilford Courthouse on 15 March 1781, and lastly at the Battle of Hobkirk Hill near Camden, South Carolina, on 25 April 1781, at which time he was wounded, taken prisoner, and remained a prisoner until the end of the war. George's wife is listed as Rachel, and no other information concerning her is available.

On 13 June 1818, George appeared in Greene County, Tennessee Court to apply for a Revolutionary War Pension # 15238 that began on the date of the application. George appeared in Sevier County Court of Pleas and Quarter Sessions on 19 September 1820 and stated he was now a resident of Sevier County, and his need for financial assistance continued because of the wound suffered at the Battle of Hobkirk. (1), (2) It is believed George lived in the area known today as New Era near Gist's Creek. (3)

George and Rachel's children:
- George was born about 1805.
- David was born about 1811.
- Susanna was born about 1813.
- Robert was born about 1815.
- Evalina was born about 1818. (1), (2)

Sources: (1) Southern Campaign American Revolution Pension Statements & Rosters, transcribed by C. Leon Harris. Revised 7 September 2012, (2) Joseph A. Sharp Collection, McClung Historical Collection , (3) Roster of Soldiers and Patriots of the American Revolution Buried in Tennessee, DAR, 1974, p. 312.

Pierce (Pearce), Captain- James George, Jr.

James was a close friend of John Sevier and the ancestor of a large Pierce family in Sevier County. He was born March 24, 1748 in Berkeley County, Virginia, to James George, Sr., (1720-1756) and Mary Moore Pierce (1729-1789). In the late 1770s, James, along with his wife, Margaret, their children and his in-laws, Jeremiah and Rebecca Dungan, moved from Virginia to Washington County, North Carolina (now Washington County, Tennessee).

In the summer of 1779, James received an order from Colonel John Sevier to raise a company of volunteers and march to the French Broad River to prevent the Cherokee Indians from crossing the river and entering frontier settlements. James was named Captain of this company. Again, in the spring of 1780, he raised a company of volunteers and marched against the Indians at Beaver Dam on Lick Creek, where the Indians were attacking and killing settlers. James remained in the frontier for two weeks and then returned home.

Early in the fall of 1780, James and his company volunteered under Colonel Sevier, marched to Gap Creek in Carter County, Tennessee, and joined Colonel William Campbell's Virginia Regiment. These two companies were later joined by Colonel Isaac Shelby's Sullivan County Regiment. The frontiersmen, or as they are more commonly known "Over the Mountain Men," marched on to Kings Mountain, South Carolina, and soundly defeated the British, killing their commander, Major Patrick Ferguson, in the Battle of Kings Mountain, which lasted a little over sixty minutes. Every single British soldier was either killed or captured.

Shortly after returning home from Kings Mountain, James again received orders from Colonel Sevier to guard the frontier against the Indians. He marched his company to Lacy Creek, now in Jefferson County, and joined Colonel Sevier's Regiment. From Lacy Creek, they marched over the French Broad River and camped at Boyd's Creek. The next morning, they marched ten miles and were attacked by Chicamauga Indians and fought the Battle of Boyd's Creek. The Indians, under the leadership of Dragging Canoe, were defeated, with eleven captured, but none of the soldiers were killed. Shortly thereafter, reinforcements arrived, and all the companies marched south into Indian towns, which were either burned or destroyed. (1) (2)

James married Margaret Dungan, the daughter of Jeremiah and Rebecca Hendry Dungan, in 1771 in Berkeley, Virginia. Margaret was born 4 February 1755 in Frederick, Virginia. The date of James and Margaret's arrival in Sevier County is not known, but apparently it was later in life. They lived north of Sevierville near the head of Gist's Creek. James applied for a Revolutionary War pension in 1832. James died 1 April 1833 in Sevier County and is buried in an unmarked grave near his home. Margaret died 20 February 1837 in Washington County, Tennessee, at the home of her daughter Sarah and is buried in Washington County. (3), (4)

James and Margaret's children:
- George was born 10 March 1772, married Agnes Nancy Robertson on 7 October 1794 in Greene County, and died 22 May 1842 in Sangamon, Illinois.
- Elizabeth was born 17 June 1774, married Adam Miller 23 March 1801 in Greene County, and died 18 September 1854 in Roane County, Tennessee.

- John was born 15 May 1776, married Mary Fain on 19 November 1801 in Greene County, and died 24 February 1818 in Washington County, Tennessee.
- Mary was born 20 April 1778 in Washington County, married John Fain about 1795 in Greene County, and died February 1842 in Jackson, Mississippi.
- Sarah was born 20 April 1780 in Greene County, married Thomas Gibson on 20 September 1806 in Greene County, and died 2 May 1852.
- Rebecca was born 2 March 1783 in Greene County, married Henry Pleasant Collins on 3 March 1807 in Greene County, and died 1847 in DeKalb, Alabama.
- Margaret was born 19 April 1785 in Greene County.
- Solomon was born 14 February 1787 in Greene County, married Mary Bartlett in 1812, and died November 1836 in Sangamon, Illinois.
- James was born 14 May 1789 in Greene County, married Rachel King Dinsmore on 21 March 1814 in Greene County, and died 6 October 1863.
- Orpah was born 20 September 1791 in Greene County, married Atlas Gibson on 3 September 1822 in Blount County, and died 1827.
- Jeremiah was born 26 December 1793 in Greene County, married Salley Parker on 19 November 1813, and died 19

November 1861 in Dyer County, Tennessee.
- Thomas was born 2 March 1796 in Greene County, married Elizabeth McKhen in 1833 in Sangamon, Illinois, and died in Sangamon, Illinois.
- Charlotte was born 10 April 1800 in Greene County, married John Renfrow in 1820 in Greene County, and died 25 April 1882 in Pettis, Missouri. (3)

Interesting Fact: James is the ancestor of a large Pierce family in Sevier County. His grandson, Pleasant Pierce, donated land for the building of Pleasant Hill United Methodist Church and the cemetery.

Sources: (1) Some Tennessee Heroes of the Revolution, Pamphlet III, by Zella Armstrong, (2) *The Over the Mountain Men* by Pat Alderman, Over the Mountain Press, Johnson City, TN 1970, (3) Revolutionary War Claim Abstracted, TNGenWeb Project, C. Hammett, 2001, (4) Family Search, Church of Jesus Christ of Latter-day Saints.

Porter, Mitchell

Mitchell was a devout Methodist and a good friend of Bishop Francis Asbury, the first Bishop of the Methodist Church in America. Bishop Asbury wrote in his journals of visiting the Porter home in 1802, 1808, and 1810. Bishop Asbury preached in Mitchell's home in 1802, and he also preached in an old log church situated at present day Shiloh Cemetery in 1808. (1), (2)

Mitchell was born 17 April 1759 in Lancaster County, Pennsylvania, to John and Elizabeth Porter. He was living in Winchester County, Virginia, when he entered service for a term of three months and two weeks in Captain Thurston's Virginia Company and fought in a skirmish at Quibbletown, New Jersey. He moved to Botetourt County, Virginia, in 1780, and in that year, he served three months in Captain William Handley's Company under Major Campbell and was in a skirmish near Salisbury, North Carolina. Later, he served two months in Captain Arbuckle's company and was in a skirmish against the Indians at Point Pleasant. (3), (4)

Mitchell married Penelope West on 25 January 1785 in Greenbrier County, Virginia, and moved to Sevier County in 1800. He was approved for Revolutionary War Pension # S1477 in February 1832. Mitchell died 3 April 1836 in Sevier County and is buried in Shiloh Cemetery. A Revolutionary War headstone was placed in Shiloh Cemetery in the fall of 1931 in memory of Mitchell. (5), (6)

Mitchell and Penelope's children:
- Alexander was born in 26 January 1786 in Botetourt, Virginia, and died about 1867 in Talladega, Alabama.

- William was born 12 September 1787 in Virginia, married Jinny Semore on 12 March 1808, and died in Smith County, Tennessee, in 1854.
- Elizabeth was born in 1790.
- Ester was born 19 November 1791 in Botetourt County, Virginia, married Aaron Alexander Runyan in 1808, and died 31 July 1865.
- John W. was born in 1793.
- Mary Caroline was born 11 December 1795 in Botetourt County, Virginia, married George McCown on 24 July 1812, and died 28 September 1837 in Sevier County.
- Mitchell, Jr., was born 29 November 1796 in Botetourt County, Virginia, married Mary Margaret Wade in 1823, and died 4 February 1826 in Shelby County, Alabama.
- Joshua was born in 29 November 1796 in Botetourt County, Virginia, and died 20 June 1803.
- Nancy was born 24 December 1799 in Sevier County, married Ashley Wynn in 1830, and died 11 July 1889 in Pigeon Forge, Tennessee.
- Sarah was born on 14 December 1802 in Sevier County, married Henry Massengill Thomas, and died 27 December 1884 in Sevier County.
- James was born 21 April 1805.
- McKindra B. was born 9 February 1807.

(5)

Historical Fact: Henry Massengill Thomas is the son of Patriot Isaac Thomas, and Aaron Alexander Runyan is the son of Isaac Barefoot Runyan.

Sources: (l) GEDCOM, Joe Chilton 1994, (2) Sevier County, Tennessee, and Its Heritage, Don Mills, 1994, (3) Joseph Sharp Collection, McClung Museum, (4) Some Heroes of the Revolution, Second Pamphlet, Zella Armstrong, (5) Smoky Mountain Ancestral Quest, smokykin.com, maintained by David L. Beckwith, (6) In the Shadow of the Smokies, 1994, Smoky Mountain Historical Society, 1993 p. 365.

Rains, John Captain

John was captured by the Tories but escaped and continued to fight in the war for several years. He was born 2 August 1759 in Raines Corner, Caroline County, Virginia, to John Henry Rains (1725-1785) and an unknown mother. While still a young boy, John's family moved to Randolph County, North Carolina. On 1 December 1779, he was drafted into the Randolph County Militia in the company commanded by Captain James Robertson, Lieutenant William Arnett, and Ensign William Rainey. He was in a skirmish with both the British and the Tories near Cheraw Hills, South Carolina, and he was discharged in March 1790 by Captain Robertson after serving three months. In June or July of 1790, John was captured by the Tories, taken to Wilmington, North Carolina, and held for three or four weeks before he escaped and returned home.

In April 1781, John received the commission of Captain by Colonel John Collie in a company of Rangers and ordered to patrol the counties of Randolph, Chatham, Moore, and Cumberland, Virginia, in search of British and Tories. He continued in the service of his country and was discharged in 1783. (1)

When the war ended, John returned to Virginia and married Letitia Gower on March 8, 1787. She was born in 1769 in Powhatan, Virginia, and is believed to be a member of the Rappahannock Tribe of the Powhatan Indian Nation. (2) John and Letitia moved to Sevier County, Tennessee, about 1787, lived in the county for nearly twenty years before moving to Overton County, Tennessee, and then three years later to Bledsoe County, Tennessee.

John appeared in Bledsoe County Court of Pleas and Quarter Sessions on 13 November 1832 to apply for a Revolutionary War pension. On 3 June 1839, Letitia appeared in Bledsoe County court to file for a widow's pension #W982. She stated John died 28 January 1835 in Bledsoe County, and Letitia died after 1847. (1), (3)

John and Letitia's children:
- John was born about 1788 in Virginia.
- Robert was born 1792 in Sevier County, married Polly Moore in 1815, and died in 1880 in Carroll County, Arkansas.
- James was born 1795 in Sevier County, married Elizabeth Jackson, and died 1870 in Bledsoe County.
- Charles B. was born 1798 in Sevier County.
- Josiah was born 1800 in Sevier County, married Mary Elizabeth Swafford on 13 March 1822, and died 4 June 1880 in Bledsoe County, Tennessee.
- Samuel was born 19 July 1803 in Sevier County, married Margaret Jane Campbell on 30 January 1823, and died 24 May 1843 in Carroll County, Arkansas.
- Elizabeth was born about 1807 in Sevier County.
- Letitia was born 1807 in Sevier County.

(2)

Sources: (1) Southern Campaign American Revolution Pension Statements & Rosters, transcribed by Will Graves; (2) rootsweb: Rains Family from Bledsoe County, Tennessee, owner, Kirk Rains; (3) Some Tennessee Heroes of the Revolution, Pamphlet No. II, compiled by Zella Armstrong.

Reagan, Timothy

Timothy has indeed left an immeasurable imprint on Sevier County. His descendants are numerous, with countless books and articles having been written about their contributions to this county. The Reagan name is synonymous with Sevier County, and when you hear the name Reagan, you automatically know there is a Sevier County connection.

Timothy was born 1750, probably in the Elk Ridge Community of Anne Arundel County, Maryland, to Timothy and Rachel Nelson Reagan. (1) Records show Timothy enlisted for three years as a private in Captain John Eccleston's Company, 2nd Regiment of the Maryland Continental Troops, in early 1777. This regiment was commanded by Colonel Thomas Price under General George Washington. Timothy fought in the Battle of Brandywine and was seriously wounded. He was hospitalized in Chester County, Pennsylvania, for six months. He recovered and served out his three year enlistment. According to family legend, Timothy carried horrible scars and three buckshots in his body for the rest of his life. (2)

Timothy married Elizabeth Trigg in 1776 in Prince Georges County, Maryland. She was born in 1760 in Prince Georges County, Maryland, the daughter of Clement and Mary Ann Fouracres Trigg. In late 1778, Timothy and his family moved from Prince Georges County, Maryland, to Caswell County, North Carolina. Land records in Raleigh and Caswell County, North Carolina, show that Timothy made two entries of land, one for 150 acres and another for 200 acres.

After selling this land, Timothy and his family moved to Sevier County, and it is said that he joined a group of pioneers who built a settlement around Shields Fort in the Middle Creek of Sevier County. (2) Timothy, one the first settlers in White Oak Flats (present day Gatlinburg), was a blacksmith, farmer, and carpenter. Timothy died in 1827, and Elizabeth died in 1830 in Gatlinburg, and both are buried in White Oak Flats Cemetery. (1), (2), (3)

Timothy and Elizabeth's children:
- Richard was born in 1776 in Prince Georges County, Maryland, married Julia Ann Shultz, and died 1829 in Sevier County.
- Robert was born in 1779 in Pittsylvania County, Virginia, and married Louise Emmert.
- Rachel was born in 1781 in Pittsylvania County, Virginia, married Edward Mahan, and died in 1826 in Bibb County, Alabama.
- Reason was born 1783 in Pittsylvania County, Virginia, married Rachel Thomas, and died 1814 in Madison County, Illinois.
- Elizabeth was born 1785 in Caswell County, North Carolina, married Phillip Emmert, and died in 1838 in Sevier County.
- Sarah was born 16 October 1787 in Caswell County, married Daniel Emmert, and died 6 June 1855 in Sevier County.
- Mary Jane was born 1789 in Caswell County, never married, and died 4 March 1844 in Macoupin County, Illinois.
- Celia Drucilla was born 15 February 1792 in Caswell County, married

Frederick Emmert, and died 29 August 1869 in Blount County, Tennessee.
- Catherine was born 1794 in Caswell County, married Davis Carter, and died 1844 in Greene County, Illinois.
- Rhoda was born 20 March 1796 in Sevier County, married James Huskey, and died 10 October 1855 in Macoupin County, Illinois.
- Jeremiah was born 1798 in Sevier County, first married Mary Huskey and, secondly, Eliza Powell, and died in late 1880s in Bartow County, Georgia.
- Timothy, Jr., was born 1 July 1800 in Sevier County, first married Barbara Shultz and, secondly, married Martha Moore, and died 21 August 1883 in Bollinger County, Missouri.
- Joshua was born 1804 in Sevier County, married Jane Huskey, and died 13 October 1874 in Macoupin County. (2)

Historical Fact: Edward is the son of Patriot John Mahan. Celia Drucilla, Elizabeth, Robert, and Sarah married the children of Patriot Frederick and his wife, Barbara Ann, Emert (Emmert). (1), (2)

Sources: (1) Smoky Mountain Ancestral Quest, smokykin.com, maintained by David L Beckwith, (2) The Book of Ragan/Reagan,1993, p. 15, 16 Donald B. Reagan, (3) In the Shadow of the Smokies, p. 578, Smoky Mountain Historical Society, 1993.

Richardson, William

Richardson's Cove is one of the most beautiful, scenic, and serene valleys in Sevier County. However, on 22 December 1792, this peaceful cove was the scene of one of the most brutal incidents in Sevier County history. William was born 1746 in Virginia to unknown parents. He entered service under Colonel William Christian, Captain Shelby, and Lieutenant Joseph Drake, rendezvoused at Kings Salt Works in Virginia and marched to Staunton, Virginia, where he remained for some time, and was discharged and returned home. William reentered service under Captain John Renfro and Lieutenant E. Drake, and the company marched to North Carolina to spy on the Indians, who were committing acts of cruelty against the settlers in North Carolina. William and the company were soon discharged and returned home. [1]

Shortly after the war, William moved his family to the part of North Carolina that would later become Sevier County. He was accompanied by his wife, Mary, their daughter, Leah, and her husband, Obedieh Matthews. The family built a cabin beside a spring in an area that would become known as Richardson's Cove. There was much unrest between the settlers and Indians in this area, and William was involved in many actions with both the Army and Militia. He served with Colonel John Sevier at Southwest Point and with Colonel John McNabb in Greene County. Altogether, William fought the Indians for eight or nine years. [2]

On 22 December 1792, a party of Indians led by Tawakka laid in wait atop a hill that overlooked the Richardson's cabin until William left home. Then, they entered the house attacked and killed William's wife, two of his children, and his wife's sister, Nancy Schull.

All the livestock and family belongings were taken. A search was mounted against the Indians, and William received a serious facial wound during a skirmish. It is believed William never returned to the cabin and instead lived with Leah and Obedieh for the rest of his life.

The area where William and his wife settled is still known today as Richardson's Cove. It is located nine miles east of Sevierville in a beautiful valley on the Middle Prong of the Little Pigeon River. Many early settlers moved into this area because the nearby river and springs were a vital source of water. At least two other places in Sevier County, besides Richardson's Cove, are named for members of the Richardson family. Obedieh settled on a branch of the East Fork of the Little Pigeon River now called Obies Branch. Obedieh's son, Robert, settled on a creek in the same area that is known as Matthew's Creek.

William appeared in Sevier County Court on 1 September 1832 to apply for a Revolutionary War Pension, #R8779 . (1) The date of William's death is not known, but family members believe he was buried alongside his wife and children in Richardson's Cove. (2)

William and Mary's children:
- Leah married Obedieh Matthews.
- Second child died 22 December 1792 and was buried in Richardson's Cove in Sevier County.
- Third child died 22 December 1792 and was buried in Richardson's Cove in Sevier County. (2)

Sources: (1) Southern Campaign American Revolution Pension Statements & Rosters, transcribed by Will Graves, (2) Sevier County, Tennessee, and Its

Heritage, Don Mills, 1994, pp. 19, 20, 272, (3) In the Shadow of the Smokies, Smoky Mountain Historical Society, 1993, p. 429.

Riggin, James

James moved to Sevier County, became active in the county government, and was appointed Justice of the Peace. He was born 21 May 1756 in Somerset, Maryland, to Tigue (Teague) (1730-1773) and Hannah Harris Riggin (1732-1787). He is listed as serving under Captain Adams in Smith County's 4th Regiment of the Continental Line. (2), (3) James is listed as having a Revolutionary War pension by the East Tennessee General Accounting Office. James married Mary Howard on 27 January 1791 in Washington County, Virginia. Mary was born on 25 June 1765 to Ignatius (1725-1777) and Sarah Simms Howard (1726-1789). Ignatius was born in St. Mary's City, Maryland, and Sarah was born in St. Peter's, Virginia, and they married in 1745 in Virginia. (1)

James was a Methodist Church Circuit Rider in Virginia and North Carolina. He and Mary moved to Sevier County and bought twelve acres on the Little Pigeon River and lived there for several years. In 1807, James received Land Grant # 240 for 50 acres on Walden's Creek, and in 1808, he received another Land Grant # 241 for 284 acres, also on Walden's Creek. He sold the twelve acres on the Little Pigeon River and moved his family to the Walden's Creek property. (2), (5)

James was elected the first Justice of the Peace in Sevier County under the new State of Tennessee. (6) He died 1 April 1826 and is buried in Shiloh Methodist Memorial Cemetery in Pigeon Forge. (7) Mary was living with her daughter, Sarah, at the time of her death on 21 November 1830 and is buried in Bradley County, Tennessee.

James and Mary's children:

- Harry was born 2 September 1793 in Sevier County, married Miriam Lee Rogers on 2 March 1820, and died 23 March 1875 in Menard County, Illinois.
- James, Jr., was born 2 December 1794 in Sevier County, married Elizabeth Rogers in 1826 in Menard County, Illinois, and died in 1858.
- Mary "Polly" B. was born 23 June 1796 in Sevier County, married Charles R. Benson, and died 26 December 1838.
- Sarah was born 21 March 1798 in Sevier County, married Isaac Huffaker on 1 August 1816 in Tennessee, and died 21 October 1881 in Tunnel Hill, Georgia.
- John C. was born 3 February 1801 in Sevier County, married Elizabeth Reid on 26 August 1824 in Madison, Illinois, and died 1839 in Madison, Illinois.
- Ignatius was born 7 March 1803 in Sevier County, married Matilda Langford Rogers on 10 January 1828 in Sevier County, and died 1837.
- Elizabeth Ann was born 15 December 1803 in Sevier County, married Joseph Speer on 28 December 1820 in Jasper, Georgia, and died 4 March 1868 in Fayette, Georgia.

Historical Fact: Elizabeth and Miriam Lee Rogers are sisters and daughters of Matthew and Susanna Morse Rogers of Burlington, New York. Matilda is the daughter of Reverend Elijah Rogers, one of Sevier County's first preachers. However, she is not related to Elizabeth or Miriam. Isaac is the son of George Michael

Huffaker, of Seven Islands, who is the progenitor of the Huffaker Family of Sevier and Knox Counties.

Sources: (1) Family Search, Church of Jesus Christ of the Latter-day Saints, (2) Teague Riggen and His Riggen, Riggan, Riggins Descendants, Sharol Riggin, Gateway Press, Baltimore, 1987, p. 470-472, (3) Ancestry.com. U. S., Revolutionary War Pensioners, 1801-1815, 1818-1872, Record Group Number: 217; Series Number: 7718, Roll Number 8, (4) Ancestry.com. U. S., Revolutionary War Pensioners, 1801-1815, 1818- 1872, Record Group Number: 217; Series Number: 7718, Roll Number 8, (5) East Tennessee land Grants, Roll 56, Book 1, Family Search, Church of Jesus Christ of the Latter-day Saints, (6) Sevier County, Tennessee, and Its Heritage, 1994, Don Mills, p. 8, (7) In the Shadow of the Smokies, Smoky Mountain Historical Society 1993, p. 367.

Robertson, William

William was born into a well-to-do English family, but the tragic death of his father and the resulting family turmoil led him to leave his home country and travel to America. A few years later, he made another major decision to take up arms against the land of his birth and fight for his new homeland. William was born 25 May 1759 in London, England, to John and Elizabeth Robertson. His parents owned a silk mill; however, his father died before William turned four years old. His mother remarried three months later in April 1763, but she died in 1769, and since William did not get along well with his step-father, he stowed away on a ship bound for American. He arrived in America in 1773 at the age of fifteen, landed not far from Richmond, Virginia, and settled in Greenbrier County, Virginia.

In 1780, William enlisted in the Continental Army for eighteen months under Captain Andrew Wallace, Major Ridley, and Colonel Bluford. He and his company marched to Hillsboro, North Carolina, where they joined a main regiment and then marched on to Charlotte, North Carolina, where General Nathaneal Green took command and marched to Cheraw Hills, South Carolina.

Later, William transferred to Colonel Henry Lee's Regiment of Light Infantry, marched to the Pee Dee River and went by boats to Georgetown. After arriving, the troops hid out in a cane break for the night, and at daybreak, William's unit raided the quarters of British commander, Colonel Campbell. The colonel was reluctant to surrender and was informed by Colonel Michael Rudolph that he had 500 of the best men America afforded, after which Colonel Campbell surrendered. With Colonel Campbell safely in the hands of the patriots, William and his company marched to Guilford Court House, North Carolina, and during this battle, he was assigned near the front line to care for the wounded. This five-hour battle led to the defeat of British General Cornwallis in the Carolinas. Later, William was assigned as a body guard for General Green and acted in that capacity for several months and was discharged in December 1781 in Charlotte, North Carolina. (1)

After the war, William, along with his wife, Delilah Ritchie Robertson, moved from Virginia to Lancaster, South Carolina, and remained there until moving to Sevier County in 1829. They settled in the Shady Grove community, where he crafted saddles and leather goods for as long as he lived. William married Nancy Breeden Shepherd on 10 December 1837, and they did not have any children. He died 15 January 1847 and is buried in Eslinger Cemetery. (2)

William and Delilah's children:
- William "Dr. Billie" was born 1789 in Greenbrier County, Virginia, married Hannah Hutchinson, and died May 3, 1880 in Wise County, Virginia.

- Delilah "Lillie" was born 1800 near Natural Bridge, Virginia. (2)

Sources: (1) Joseph A. Sharp Collection, McClung Historical Collection, (2) A Short Biography of William Robertson, Smoky Mountain Historical Society Newsletter, autumn, 1998, p. 3, Debra Pack Gilberstadt.

Rogers, Henry

Henry and his children were some of the most influential early settlers in Sevier County. His son Reverend Elijah Rogers was the pastor of present-day First Baptist Church of Sevierville for years. His daughters married into the family of Spencer Clack, another Revolutionary War patriot who helped establish the town of Sevierville and the county of Sevier.

Henry was born in 1741 in Prince William County, Virginia, to George and Ann Lee Rogers. (1) He married Elizabeth Langford about 1760 in Fauquier, Virginia. She was the daughter of Thomas and Mary Collier Langford. According to the Roger's family legend, Henry served in Captain Francis Triplett's Virginia Troops. The Navy report book states that Henry was paid for services rendered aboard a Brigade Schooner on or near the Potomac River. (2) The Bulletin of Fauquier County Historical Society stated Henry furnished the Army with 370 pounds of beef. (3) He left Fauquier County after the war and moved to Franklin County, Virginia, lived there for a short period of time, and then waited in Chatham County, Virginia, to join a large group of Virginians moving to Sevier County. (4) Henry died in 1794 in Sevier County and is buried in the Forks of the Little Pigeon Cemetery.

Henry and Elizabeth's children:
- George was born 6 February 1764 in Fauquier County, Virginia, married Elizabeth Randall on 17 October 1791, and died 28 November 1858 in Wayne County, Kentucky.
- Bashaba was born 1765 in Virginia.
- Josiah was born 1766 in Fauquier County, Virginia, married Martha Clack on 22 January 1786 in Franklin,

Virginia, and died 12 August 1834 in Sevier County and is buried in Forks of Little Pigeon Cemetery.
- Henry, Jr., was born 1767 in Fauquier, Virginia, and died in 1820 in Virginia.
- Mary was born 15 April 1769 in Virginia, married James Cannon, and died 19 April 1852 in Grayson, Kentucky.
- Elijah was born in May 1774 in Washington, County, North Carolina (now Tennessee), married Catherine Clack in 1794, and died 11 May 1841 in Sevier County. (1)

Historical Fact: Catherine and Martha Clack are the daughters of Patriot Spencer Clack.

Sources: (1) Family Search, Church of Jesus Christ of Latter-day Saints, (2) Ancestry.com, The Navy Report Book # 8, page 6, (3) Bulletin of Fauquier Historical Society 1921-1924, p. 367, (4) Sons of the American Revolution Application, #53296.

Rudd, Burlingham

The only documents showing Burlingham's presence in Sevier County is the 1830 Sevier County Census and the U.S. Revolutionary War, Pension Roll #1835. Burlingham was born 25 December 1760 in Anson County, North Carolina, to Burlingham, Jr. (1733-1836) and Sarah Whaley Rudd (1740-1827). In 1782, Burlingham was drafted in Anson County and mustered into service at Wadesboro under the command of Captain Patrick Bogan in the regiment of Colonel Thomas Wade and marched to Drowning Creek, North Carolina, under General Harrington. He was in a scrimmage at Drowning Creek at Beattie's Bridge against the Tories and the British. The patriots were defeated even though several British and Tories were killed. The Regiment marched on to Black River, and Burlingham was discharged in May by General Harrington after serving three months.

Burlingham was drafted again for a six-month tour, marched toward Wilmington, North Carolina, and was stationed for a while at Fayetteville, North Carolina. Later, he marched to the Little Pee Dee River toward Georgetown to scout the countryside for British and Tories and was involved in several scrimmages during the six months. He marched on to Cheraw Hills and was discharged. Just before the end of the war, Burlingham volunteered under the command of Captain Patrick Bogin and assigned to guard General Harrington at his house for three months. (1)

After the war, Burlingham moved to Tennessee, and he is listed on the 1830 Census records of Sevier County. Burlingham married Mary Vaughn (1790-1865), the daughter of William Vaughn, about 1800 in Anson, North Carolina. He applied for a Revolutionary

War pension on 8 February 1833 in Blount County. Burlingham died 29 July 1853 and is buried in Six Mile Baptist Cemetery in Blount County. Mary filed for a widow's pension in Blount County, # W20038 on 30 September 1853, and she died before August 1865 and is also buried in Blount County. (1), (2)

Burlingham and Mary's children:
- Stephen was born after 1805 in Blount County, married Elizabeth Stallions on 12 April 1849 in Blount County, and they lived in the Montvale Springs area of Blount County.
- David was born about 1809 in Tennessee and married Charlotte Unknown about 1834.
- Andrew Jackson was born 1812, married Margaret Ann Frye, daughter of George and Margaret Harper Frye, and died between 1880 and 1900.
- George was born about 1819 and first married Rebecca J. Maxwell on 16 February 1842 in Blount County; secondly, married Barbara Unknown before 1842; thirdly, Sarah Stallions on 04 January 1844 in Blount County, and then Ellen Teffeteller on 14 September 1845 in Blount County.
- Absela was born 1822.
- William Vaughn was born 1825 in Tennessee and first married Abiline S. Costner on 24 January 1870 in Blount County and, secondly, married Martha Elizabeth Ragan on 29 November 1851 in Blount County.
- St. Clair was born 1833 in Tennessee, married Loucinday Watts on 22

September 1859 in Blount County, and died about 1889. (2)

Sources: (1) Southern Campaign American Revolution Pension Statements & Rosters, transcribed by Will Graves, (2) Ancestry.com. U. S., The Pension Roll of 1835 (2) genealogy.com, Ancestors in Middle Tennessee and Smoky Mountains: Information about Burlington Rudd III, Jim Beasley.

Runyan, Isaac Barefoot

On 27 July 1808, Isaac received an occupancy grant for 168 acres located on the West Fork of the Little Pigeon River. This land is now the heart of present day Pigeon Forge and near the town's most popular tourist attraction: the Mill Creek Dam.

Isaac was born about 1757 in Rockingham County, Virginia, to John (1705-1797) and Anna Barefoot Runyan. They were married about 1757 in Brocks Gap, Virginia. (1) Isaac is listed in Revolutionary War Militia Records of Shenandoah County as receiving thirteen shillings and six pence in pay. He is also listed as serving in General Sullivan's Brock's Gap Regiment in the Battle of Kings Mountain. (2)

Isaac married Margaret Rambo on 19 May 1777 in Brock's Gap Baptist Church, Rockingham County, Virginia. Margaret was born 1755 in Botetourt, Virginia, to Jacob Swanson and Deborah Allen Rambo. After the Revolutionary War, Isaac's family lived in Shenandoah Valley for several years, and in 1792, they settled on the West Fork of the Little Pigeon River in Jefferson County (now Sevier County). In 1808, Isaac was granted 168 acres on the Little Pigeon River, and again on 28 July 1898, he received 151 acres. (3) Isaac's land was near the "Old Mill" in Pigeon Forge, and Patriot Marshall Lovelady was a neighbor.

Margaret died 1802 while giving birth to Loami Wesley, and she is buried in Shiloh Cemetery in Pigeon Forge. Isaac and Margaret's son Tavenor was ambushed and killed by Indians at the age of fifteen in 1802. Isaac and several members of his family moved to the counties of Shelby and Talladega in Alabama, and Isaac died in Talladega County about 1867 at the age of one hundred plus.

Isaac and Margaret's children:
- John Wesley was born 1778 in Shenandoah, Virginia, married Nancy Mullendore on 2 November 1802, and died 23 November 1851 in Hamilton County, Tennessee.
- Aaron Alexander was born about 1786 in Shenandoah, Virginia, married Esther Porter, and died 6 June 1869 in Sevier County and is buried in Shiloh Cemetery.
- Tavenor was born about 1787 and died 1802 in Sevier County as a result of being attacked by Indians.
- Ware was born 1791 in Jefferson County (now Sevier County), married Mary Unknown, and died 23 October 1837 in Alabama.
- Isaac II was born 17 March 1793 in Jefferson County (now Sevier County), married Mary Lowery, and died 13 August 1873 in Clark County, Arkansas.
- Loami Wesley was born 1802 in Sevier County and married Nancy White on 30 June 1843. (1)

Historical Fact: Esther Porter was the daughter of Patriot Mitchell Porter.

Sources: (1) Smoky Mountain Ancestral Quest, smokykin.com, maintained by David L. Beckwith. (2) *King's Mountain Men*, Pat Alderman, p. 38. (3) wikitree, Isaac Barefoot Runyan, 1757-abt. 1867.

Sharp, John, Jr.

John's decision to enjoy a short visit with his sister in Blount County, Tennessee, while traveling from Lancaster, Pennsylvania, to Savannah, Georgia, resulted in a dramatic, life-changing experience. John was born 11 November 1762 in Lancaster County Pennsylvania to John, Sr., and Ann Boyd Sharp. In 1778, John decided to join his older brother, James, in Savannah, Georgia, to study medicine and prepare himself to be a physician. On the way south, John stopped to visit his sister Margaret Wear in Maryville, Tennessee. While there, the Indians attacked and burned the Wear's house to the ground, leaving John and his sister's family without a home, clothes, or any possessions. In nearby Greeneville, Tennessee, a company of men was being recruited to guard the frontier settlements. John decided he could get some clothes and settle his score with the Indians by joining the group. John served in the Revolutionary War for two years and seven months with Colonel John Sevier and as a spy under James Cunningham.

After the war, John settled on a farm between Maryville and Sevierville, in present day Seymour. John's vocation was buying and selling. He bought horses from the Indians, took them to eastern Virginia to sell, and then bought farm and household goods in Richmond, Virginia, to bring back to Seymour to sell. He engaged in traveling, trading horses, furs, and goods for eleven years.

John married Isabella McChesney on 23 August 1796. She was born 1773 in Ireland to James and Sarah Mary Patterson McChesney, and after the marriage, John settled down on the farm. He received land grants in 1806 and 1807 for an additional 393 acres. This land was located at Trundles Crossroads and is the present day location of the historic Keener House and Van Gilder farm. Isabella died 8 September 1810 and is buried in Blount County, Tennessee. In 1812, John married Jean Ann Johnston, who was born in 1783 and was the daughter of Zachariah and Ann Johnston. John died 16 July 1844 and was buried in Eusebia Cemetery in Blount County. A bronze marker at Eusebia Cemetery commemorates John's service in the Revolutionary War. Jean Ann died in 1822 and is buried in Eusebia Cemetery. (1)

John and Isabella's children:
- Mary McChesney was born 28 July 1798 in Seymour, married Robert Scott McCroskey in 1811, and died 21 December 1884 in Sevier County and is buried at Eusebia Cemetery in Blount County.
- Amy was born December 1800 and died 2 December 1802.
- Martha Montgomery was born 16 March 1806 and married Dr. Samuel Pride.
- Narcissa was born 8 January 1807 in Blount County, married William Cowan Gillespie, and died 27 July 1844.
- Sally was born on 12 April 1808 and died 17 August 1809.

John and Jean Ann's children:
- Ann married Caswell Lea
- James Madison was born 8 July 1816, married Rebecca Cannon on 3 December 1846, and died 30 August 1905 and is buried at Eusebia Cemetery in Blount County. (2)

Historical Fact: Robert Scott McCroskey is

A Portrait of Patriots and Pioneers in Sevier County

the son of Patriot John Blair McCroskey.

Sources: (1) Sevier County, Tennessee, and Its Heritage, pp. 336-337, Don Mills, 1994, (2) Family Search, Church of Jesus Christ of the Latter-day Saints.

Shields, Robert Perry

The name Shields is embedded in Sevier County history. Shields Fort was one of the first structures to be built in this yet to be named county. Shields Mountain is on the county's map. Robert's descendants became leaders not only in this county, but famous members of a legendary expedition. Robert was born about 1740 in Albemarle, Virginia, to John S. (1709-1772) and Margaret Perry Shields (1710-?). Robert is recorded as being an ensign in Captain Manson's Company of the York Militia on 21 July 1777 He was recorded as a 2nd Lieutenant in both Captain Lang's and Captain Manson's Company on 18 September 1780. (1)

Robert married Nancy Stockton (1744-1805) in 1761 in Virginia, and she is the daughter of Richard and Agnes Ann Anthony Stockton. At the end of the Revolutionary War, the Shields family was living in Botetourt County, Virginia. After the war, Thomas, the oldest son, spent many months exploring the Great Smoky Mountains. He returned home and convinced his father to move to the area. Robert and his five oldest sons came about 1784 to build a cabin, and then the remaining members of the family joined them around 1785 but only after Jennet's marriage to Joshua Tipton in Botetourt County on 10 August 1785.
(1)

Robert bought a tract of land on Middle Creek somewhere in the vicinity of present day Middle Creek Methodist Church. Family legend tells that Robert and his sons cleared the land, built a cabin, and erected "Shields Fort" at the foot of Shields Mountain. This fort became a safe haven for the Shields family and other settlers for many years. Robert died on 18

January 1802, Nancy died in 1805, and both are buried in Middle Creek Methodist Church Cemetery in Sevier County. (1)

Robert and Nancy's children:
- Jennet was born 7 March 1762 in Botetourt County, Virginia, married Joshua Tipton on 10 August 1785, and died 17 February 1827 in Jackson, Indiana. Joshua was killed by Indians in 1793 in Jefferson County (now Sevier County).
- Thomas was born 4 March 1763 in Augusta County, Virginia, married Rhoda Brown in 1783 in Sevier County, was killed by Indians on 4 March 1797, and was buried in Shields Fort.
- Richard Stockton was born 4 July 1764 in Augusta County, married Matilda Maud Arnett in 1781 in Augusta, Virginia, and died in 1825 and was buried in Sevier County.
- David was born 1766 in Rockingham, Virginia, married Sarah Deer 1784 in Sevier County, and died 28 May 1847 in Corydon, Indiana.
- William was born 13 October 1768 in Augusta County, first married Margaret Wilson in 1789 and, secondly, married Amanda Logan 20 February 1813 in Harrison County, Indiana, and died 2 February 1846 in Jackson, Indiana.
- John Page was born 1769 in Augusta County, married Nancy White in 1790 in Sevier County, and died December 1809 in Corydon, Indiana. John was the

blacksmith for the famous Lewis and Clark Expedition.
- James was born 10 August 1700 in Augusta County, married Penelope White in 1791 in Sevier County, and died 2 February 1848 in Jackson, Indiana.
- Robert Perry, Jr., was born 1772 in Charlotte, Virginia, married Sabra Ellen White, and died 21 September 1835 in Sevier County.
- Joseph was born 17 March 1773 in Virginia, married Martha Veach in 1820 in Harrison County, Indiana, and died 28 May 1847 in Harrison County.
- Benjamin was born 1780 in Augusta County, married Mary Elizabeth "Polly" Veatch, and died 10 May 1819 in Harrison County.
- Jesse was born 10 March 1782 in Rockingham, married Catherine Fox in 1799 in Tennessee, and died 16 September 1847 in Harrison County. (2)

Historical Fact: Thomas is also a Revolutionary War patriot, and Sabra, Penelope and Nancy White are the daughters of Patriot Meady White.

Sources: (1) Sevier County, Tennessee, and Its Heritage, 1994, Don Mills, p. 339-340, (2) Family Search, Church of Jesus Christ of Latter-day Saints.

Shields, Thomas

Thomas' life was cut short by a surprise Indian attack while providing for his young family. Rhoda, his widow, and two young sons remained strong, and shortly thereafter moved to Indiana. Thomas was born 3 March 1763 to Robert Perry and Nancy Stockton Shields in Augusta County, Virginia. In 1780, Thomas visited his cousins in Yadkin, North Carolina, and while there he enlisted in the Revolutionary War Army under Colonel John Sevier and fought in the Battle of Kings Mountain. After the war, he spent the next two years exploring the Smoky Mountains, including the area around the Little Pigeon River. He returned home to Botetourt County, Virginia, with reports of the fertile soil, abundant game, and the beauty of the countryside and convinced his father to move into the area. His father, Robert, and several older brothers came to Sevier County to build a cabin, and then the remaining members of the family made the trip via North Carolina sometime around 1785. The family settled on Middle Creek, a tributary of the Little Pigeon River. (1)

Thomas married Rhoda Brown in 1786 in Pigeon Forge, Tennessee. In 1795, Thomas and his two small sons were in an orchard boiling sugar maple sap when Thomas was ambushed by Indians. After ordering his two sons to run, he rolled behind a log within reach of his rifle and shot one of the Indians before he was killed. The two sons and their blind horse fled for six miles and safely reached Shields Fort, just ahead of the Indians' pursuit.

Thomas and Rhoda's children:
- John Tipton was born 14 August 1786 in Pigeon Forge and died 5 April 1839 in Indiana.

- Joshua Tipton was born 10 April 1788 in Pigeon Forge, married Rhoda Tipton in 1804 in Sevier County, and died 20 January 1852 in Cass County, Indiana. (2)

Historical Fact: Thomas is the son of Patriot Robert Shields.

Sources: (1) Sevier County, Tennessee, and Its Heritage, 1994, Don Mills, p. 339-340, (2) Family Search, Church of Jesus Christ of the Latter-day Saints.

Smallwood, William

William answered his country's call to service and served honorably for months. He was born 20 November 1760 in Lancaster, Pennsylvania, to unknown parents. William was living in Botetourt County, Virginia, when called into service for a six-month tour in September 1780 under Major David Campbell's Regiment of Militia. William, along with the militia, marched through the Moravian towns then on to Salisbury, North Carolina, and to the Catawba River and Charlotte. The Regiment met General Morgan the second night after the Battle of Cowpens, and then the Regiment marched back across the Catawba River at Island Ford to keep the British from crossing the river at the forts. However, the British crossed the river and killed General William Davidson on 1 February 1781 at Cowan's Fort. The regiment retreated to Salisbury and then across the Yadkin River and Dan Rivers, where he was honorably discharged by Major Campbell on 1 March 1781 after serving the six months.

William lived in Botetourt County, Virginia, about three years after the war, and then he moved to Sullivan County, North Carolina (now Tennessee), and lived there for two years and moved to Sevier County. William appeared in Sevier County Court of Pleas and Quarter Sessions on 5 December 1832 to apply for Revolutionary War Pension #S3946. He stated that he had lived in Sevier County for more than forty years and his actual service in the war could be verified by Patriots Mitchell Porter and Jeremiah Compton, and both of these men provided the court with supporting affidavits.

William was listed on the 1830 Sevier County

Census, and he died after 1832, probably in Blount County, Tennessee, and no additional information is available. (1), (2)

William and unknown wife's child:
- George was born in Tennessee and married Rosana, or Rosie, Dims.

Sources: (1) Joseph Sharp Collection, McClung Collection, (2) Family Search, Church of Jesus Christ of Latter-day Saints

Stanfield, James

James served his country for twelve months as an orderly sergeant and fought in several battles and skirmishes in North and South Carolina. He was born 2 February 1753 in Edgecombe, North Carolina, to Thomas (1732-1796) and Elizabeth Banks Stanfield (1732-1797). James was drafted in the service as a militia man on 18 July 1782 under Captain Benjamin Carter. James was based at Forhock's Mills in Rowan County, North Carolina, and marched into Camden, South Carolina, to the Santee and joined General Nathaneal Greene's Army and took the main road to Charleston and fought the British at Eutaw Springs. After the battle of Eutaw Springs, the patriots chased the British for several miles but did not overtake them. The troops then marched to Orangeburg and to Bacon's Ridge, South Carolina. James was discharged at Bacon's Bridge, South Carolina, by Colonel Murphree on 10 July 1783.

James states in his application for Revolutionary War Pension #158 that he moved to Buncombe County, North Carolina, after the war and from there to Sevier County and then to Bedford County, Tennessee, and he finally settled in McMinn County, Tennessee. James married Fanny Gwinn (1753-1842) in 1774. James died 3 November 1840, and Fanny died 18 December 1842 in Bradley County, Tennessee. (1)

James and Fanny's children:
- Delphia was born 1795 in Alabama, married David Price in November 1814 in Warren County, Tennessee, and died 1850 in Crawford County, Arkansas.
- Cornelius (no additional information).

- James (no additional information).
- Mary Ann was born in 1796 and married William Brittain in 1815. (2)

Sources: (1) Southern Campaign American Revolution Pension Statements, transcribed by Will Graves, (2) Ancestry.com, search James Stanfield.

Stone, Ezekial

Ezekial's devotion to American independence and his longevity are nothing short of remarkable. He entered into the service of the United States at the age of nineteen in 1774, one year before the beginning of the Revolutionary War, and served until the war was over. What is even more unbelievable is that he lived to the ripe old age of ninety-nine years. It is rare for someone to live to the age of ninety-nine in the twenty-first century but almost unheard of in the nineteenth century.

Ezekial was born 24 November 1756 to David and Elizabeth Jenifer Stone in Charles County, Maryland. However, he was living in Surry County, North Carolina, when he entered service as a volunteer against the Tories under Major Joseph Winston and Captain Richard Good and served a tour of three weeks. In 1776, he volunteered as an orderly sergeant in Captain William Dobson's Company, commanded by Colonel Joseph Williams and Major Winston. The Company marched from Surry County to the Chiswell's lead mines in Virginia and then down the Holston, French Broad, and Tennessee Rivers into the Cherokee Nation and destroyed several Indian Towns along the Tennessee River. He served three months and returned home. (1), (2)

In 1781, he was drafted for a period of about two weeks under Captain William Bostic and Major Joseph Winston to fight against the British. Again, in 1781, he was drafted as a private to serve three months under Captain Humphreys and marched from Surry County to Wilmington, North Carolina, to fight against the British. There was no engagement or battle, as the capture of Cornwallis at the Battle of York Town had taken place and the enemy withdrew from Wilmington.

After the war, Ezekial continued to live in Surry County until 1784, when he moved to Union, South Carolina. In 1795, he moved to Sevier County and lived there until moving to Bledsoe County, Tennessee, in 1816 and then to Marion County, Tennessee, in 1819. He applied for Revolutionary War Pension #S1933 on 21 August 1832 in Marion County at the age of seventy-six. (1), (2)

Ezekial married Jane Wood in 1779 in North Carolina, and she died 1837 in Marion County and is buried in Marion County. Ezekial died in 1855 in Marion County and is buried in Mount Zion Cemetery in Marion, County.

Ezekial and Jane's children:
- Rebecca was born 12 October 1782 in Surry County, married John Nelson Baird on 16 June 1803 in Sevier County, and died 18 February 1848 in Lamar, Texas.
- Catharine Elizabeth was born in 1783 Surry County, married Thomas Blair on 5 May 1802 in Tennessee, and died 16 January 1857 in Hamilton County, Tennessee.
- Hannah was born 14 August 1786 in Surry County, married Thomas Blair, and died 18 January 1857 in Hamilton County, Tennessee.
- Mary was born 1788 in Surry County.
- William was born 26 January 1791 in Surry County, married Mary Randall on 30 November 1809 in Tennessee, and died 18 February 1853 in Marion County.
- John was born in 1796 in Sevier County,

married Susannah H. Kelly about 1818, and died 1861.
- Richard was born 19 May 1800 in Sevier County, married Anne Kelly on 2 December 1822, and died 1 December 1884 in Rayville, Missouri.
- Thomas was born 20 January 1803 in Sevier County, married Winnie Simmons Bell, and died 26 May 1881. (3)

Sources: (1) Southern Campaign American Revolution Pension Statements & Rosters, transcribed by Will Graves, (2) Some Heroes of the American Revolution, Pamphlet No.1, Zella Armstrong, (3) Family Search, Church of Jesus Christ of Latter-day Saints.

Thomas, Isaac

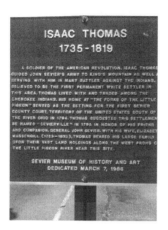

Isaac's friendship with the Cherokee Indians was a blessing in 1755 when a band of Cherokee Indians attacked Fort Loudon, a British Fort, on the Tennessee River and massacred men, women, and children. Isaac's life was saved because he was a friend of their Chief, Little Carpenter. Isaac was a remarkable man! He was a Cherokee Indian scout and trader who had a trading post at Chota, the Cherokee's capital, by 1755 and he also had a Cherokee wife, Ah-Lee-sss-kway-lee. Isaac was revered by the Cherokees and well respected by the white settlers. He was well versed in knowing how to live and succeed in both worlds. Nancy Ward, the beloved Princess of the Cherokee Nation, was a trusted friend and confidant. Her friendship with Isaac saved the lives of many settlers. (1), (2) Isaac was born in 1735 in Frederick, Virginia, to an unknown father and Lucretia Hart Thomas. Isaac fought in the Battle of Kings Mountain, and he was an Indian scout for Colonel John Sevier during the Battle of Boyd's Creek. In July 1776, Nancy Ward, the Cherokee

Princess, warned Isaac that the Chickamauga Indians, led by her nephew, Dragging Canoe, were planning to go on a warpath and attack the white settlers. Isaac traveled 150 miles in 3 days to warn the settlers along the Tennessee River, and when he finally arrived at the Watauga Settlement, he relayed the news to John Sevier. Isaac's actions enabled the inhabitants to prepare themselves for the impending attack and saved hundreds of lives.

After the war, Isaac returned to Virginia for a short time and then moved into East Tennessee by traveling through the Cumberland Gap. Isaac married Elizabeth Isabella Massengill on 11 June 1789 in Washington County, Tennessee. Elizabeth was born in 1759 at Watauga Settlement, North Carolina (now Tennessee), the daughter of Henry and Mary Cobb Massengill. He settled in the area that would later become Sevier County and established a trading post on the bank of the Little Pigeon River. He was the first white settler in the area and the founder of Sevierville, which he named for his good friend, John Sevier. In 1794, the first Sevier County Court in the new State of Tennessee met at Isaac's house at the Forks of the Little Pigeon River. His house also served as a tavern and hotel. [1], [2]

Isaac died 30 October 1818 in Sevier County and was buried in the Forks of the Little Pigeon Cemetery in Sevier County. Elizabeth died 15 September 1830 and is also buried in the Forks of the Little Pigeon Cemetery. [3]

Isaac and Ah-Lee-sss-kway-tee's children:
- Jesse Jaysee was born about 1755/1757.
- John was born about 1755/1757.

Isaac and Elizabeth's children:
- Mary Ann was born 28 April 1782 in Tennessee, married Samuel Douthit, and

died 19 October 1839 in Monroe County, Tennessee.
- Lucretia was born 1 August 1784 in Sevier County, married Captain Robert Wear on 30 December 1802 in Sevier County, and died 21 February 1830 in Greenback, Tennessee.
- Isaac, Jr., was born 4 November 1784 in Sevier County, married Anne Pryor in 1816 in Williamson County, Tennessee, and died 2 February 1859 in Louisiana.
- Elsie was born 15 April 1788 in Sevier County, married Jonathan Eppler on 16 February 1805 in Sevier County, and died 10 October 1836 in De Witt, Missouri.
- Ellis was born 1790 in Sevier County, married Unknown in 1810 in Sevier County, and died January 1820 in Blount County, Tennessee.
- John Henry was born 24 January 1794 in Sevier County, married Hannah Andes 12 December 1815 in Sevier County, and died 11 April 1875 in Dallas, Texas.
- Elizabeth was born 26 October 1795 in Sevier County, married Jeremiah M. Ellis in 1810, and died 31 August 1831.
- Henry Massengill was born 28 October 1798 in Sevier County, married Sarah R. Porter in 1823 in Sevier County, and died 3 June 1871 in Sevier County.
- Dennis Masssengill was born 31 August 1800 in Sevier County, married Jerusha Henderson in 1828 in Sevier County, and died 17 February 1873 in Pigeon Forge, Tennessee. (4)

Historical Fact: Sarah Porter is the daughter of Patriot Mitchell Porter, and Robert Wear is the son of Patriot Samuel Wear.

Sources: (1) Sevier County, Tennessee and Its Heritage, 1994, Don Mills, pp. 21, 22, 355, 356, (2) Smoky Mountain Ancestral Quest, smokykin.com, maintained by David L. Beckwith, (3) Forks of the Little Pigeon Cemetery and Park History, Theresa Williams, genealogist Sevier county Public Library System, (4) Family Search, Church of Jesus Christ of Latter-day Saints.

Thurman, John Thomas

John fulfilled his patriotic duty immediately after the war began and served until the British surrendered at Yorktown. He was a young single man when the war started, but a few years later he married and became a father. However, John remained a true patriot and continued to risk all for the future of his country.

John was born 3 December 1757 in Prince Edward County, Virginia, to Richard Thomas, Jr., and Sarah Farmer Thurman. While living in Albemarle County, Virginia, John volunteered between the years of 1776 and 1781 to serve as a private in the Virginia Line under Captains John Miller, John Key, Christopher Clark, Epperson, Brown, and Benjamin Harris and Colonel Lindsey. John was in several engagements, including one near Charlottesville, Virginia, and also he was at the Battle of Yorktown when British General Cornwallis surrendered. John was honorably discharged soon afterwards in October 1781, and the length of his service amounted to three years. (1)

John married Nancy Anne Graves Sandbridge on 10 December 1780 in Albemarle County. Nancy was born 4 February 1759 in Albemarle County to William and Elizabeth Graves Sandbridge. John and Nancy lived in Albemarle County for twenty years before moving to Sevier County around the early 1800s. John died 6 October 1827 and is buried in Stafford Cemetery in Sevier County. Nancy applied for Revolutionary War Widow's benefits #W28009 on 25 October 1843 in Blount County, Tennessee. Nancy died about 1854 and was buried in the Stafford Cemetery. (1), (2)

John and Nancy's children:
- Sarah was born in 1781 in Albemarle

- County, Virginia, married Edmond Boaz on 3 October 1795, and died 1837 in Blount County, Tennessee.
- Lucy was born 31 May 1783 in Albemarle County, Virginia, married Unknown Tunes in about 1805, and lived in Sevier County.
- Samuel was born about 1787 in Albemarle County, Virginia.
- Graves was born 1788 in Albemarle County, Virginia, married Christina Terry on 8 October 1812 in Williamson County, Tennessee, and died in Tennessee.
- Ailsey was born 1791 in Albemarle County, Virginia, and married William Richardson on 15 November 1806 in Pittsylvania County, Virginia.
- Barnabas was born about 1793 in Albemarle County, Virginia, married Sarah Moon in 1821 in Virginia, and died 1839 in Sevier County and was buried in the Stafford Cemetery.
- Jabez was born 24 December 1795 in Virginia, married Elizabeth "Betsy" White in 1827 in Knox County, Tennessee, and died 24 February 1891 in Knox County, Tennessee.
- Martha was born 6 July 1796, married Randolph James, and died in Sevier County about 1860.
- John F. was born 1800 in Albemarle County, Virginia, married Martha Thomas on 6 August 1832 in Albemarle County, Virginia, and died 9 May 1896.

- Susannah was born 12 March 1801 in Sevier County, married R. S. Shields in 1814, and died 1841 in Sevier County.
- William T. was born about 1804 in Sevier County, married Elizabeth Snider on 11 May 1829 in Blount County, Tennessee, and died 1879 in McMinn County, Tennessee. (3)

Sources: (1) Southern Campaign American Revolution Pension Statements & Rosters, transcribed by Will Graves, {2} In the Shadows of the Smokies, Smoky Mountain Historical Society, 1993, p.176, (3) Smoky Mountain Ancestral Quest, smokykin.com, maintained by David L Beckwith.

Tipton, Joshua

Joshua is known as the "Forgotten Revolutionary War Soldier." Somewhere along the waters of the East Fork of the Little Pigeon River or near the site of Shields Fort is the unmarked grave of Joshua Tipton, who was killed by the Cherokee Indians. According to family legend, on 18 April 1793, Joshua and his brother-in-law, Joseph Shields, were on their way to join the militia after being summoned to help repel hostile Indians. Two shots rang out from a thicket, and both men fell to the ground. Joshua was killed and Joseph was severely wounded. Joseph's gun had fallen a few feet away from where he fell, but he was afraid to move for fear the Indians would shoot him again. The Indians, thinking the two were dead, rushed in with scalping knives. Joseph sprang up and killed the Indian who was about to scalp him and then shot the other Indian before he could escape. (1)

Joshua was born in 1760 in Maryland to Mordecai (1724-after 1799) and Sarah Tipton. The family moved from Maryland to Frederick County, Virginia, and then to Botetourt County, Virginia. It is believed Mordecai and his sons moved to Sevier County in 1786. Mordecai's signature is on a petition to the Tennessee General Assembly dated 1799.

Jennet Shields and Joshua were married on 10 August 1785 in Botetourt, Virginia. She was born 7 March 1762 in Botetourt, Virginia, to Robert Perry and Nancy Stockton Shields. Jennet filed for a Revolutionary War Pension on her husband's service. She was granted a pension as a half-pay pensioner, which was started on 20 April 1815.

Jennet moved her family to Indiana in the fall of 1807. They settled at Brinley's Ferry in Harrison

County, Indiana. In later years, she moved to Seymour, Indiana, to a fort commanded by her brother, James Shields. She lived there until her death on 17 February 1827. (1)

Joshua and Jennet's children:
- John was born 14 August 1876 at Shields Fort in Sevier County. He married Martha Shields about 1801. Martha was a cousin and the daughter of John Shields, who was the blacksmith for the Lewis and Clark Expedition. The marriage ended in divorce in Harrison County, Indiana, in 1817. John Shields died 5 April 1839 and is buried in Mount Hope Cemetery in Logansport, Indiana.
- Rhoda was born 4 July 1788 at Shields Fort in Sevier County, married Joshua Tipton Shields, and died 24 July 1837 in Logansport, Indiana.
- Elizabeth was born 15 July 1791 at Shields Fort in Sevier County, married John Denbo on 28 March 1818 in Harrison, Indiana, and died 1845.
- Agnes was born 5 July 1793 in Pigeon Forge, Tennessee, married William Edwards on 10 October 1811, and died 24 July 1845 in Indiana. (2)

Historical Fact: Jennet is the daughter of Patriot Robert Shields.

Sources: (1) Joshua Tipton-Forgotten Revolutionary Soldier, Beulah d. Linn, Sevier County Historian, News Record, July 22, 1976, (2) Family Search, Church of Jesus Christ of Latter-day Saints.

Trotter, William

William Trotter's descendants are listed as some of the most prominent and influential citizens of this county. His children and grandchildren married the sons and daughter of other Revolutionary War patriots who moved to Sevier County. However, very little is known about William. In his application for a Revolutionary War Pension, William stated he did not know the date of his birth but does remember being told that he was born near Philadelphia, Pennsylvania, around Christmas time. Unfortunately, the names of his father and mother are unknown. William also stated that in the application that his family moved from Pennsylvania to Augusta County, Virginia.

William was living in Augusta County when he entered service in May 1781 for a term of six months as a substitute for Richard Trotter under Captain Thomas Smith and Colonel Samuel Lewis' Regiment and fought at the Battle of Yorktown, which resulted in the surrender of the British commander, General Cornwallis. William was honorably discharged at Williamsburg, Virginia.

William continued to live in Augusta County for twelve years after the war. He moved to Jefferson County, Tennessee, and lived there for about three years and then in 1797, moved to Sevier County. The name of William's wife is also unknown.

William appeared in Sevier County Court of Pleas and Quarter Sessions on 3 September 1832 to apply for a pension. William stated he was sixty-nine years old, which would place his birth at about 1763. He appeared before Justices of the Peace William C. Maples, Elijah Cate, and Randle Hill. The first application was denied due to lack of information, but a second application, #22288, was accepted and issued on 18 October 1833.

William died 16 August 1841, and the exact location of his grave is unknown, but it is somewhere near the waters of Flat Creek. Flat Creek was flooded by the headwaters of Tennessee Valley Authority's Douglas Dam in the early 1940s. His land on Flat Creek adjoined that of Daniel Atchley, Joseph Campbell, and the heirs of William Headrick, James Burdine, and Joseph Morrison. (1), (2)

William and Unknown's children:
- Mariah was born 1803 in Sevier County and married James Toomey in 1819 in Sevier County.
- Arminta was born 1805 in Sevier County, married Samuel Newman on 26 June 1838, and died 6 December 1842 in Sevier County.
- Clabourn was born 1805 in Sevier County.
- Diane was born about 1811 in Sevier County, married Seth Atchley about 1829, and died before 1831 in Sevier County.
- James was born 28 April 1813 in Sevier County, married Barsheba Stover on 10 September 1834 in Sevier County, and died 26 November 1886 in Sevier County.
- Angelia was born 24 August 1811 in Sevier County, married Amos Russell Atchley in 1831, and died 9 June 1856 in Grant, Arkansas. (1), (2)

A Portrait of Patriots and Pioneers in Sevier County

Sources: (1) Trotter-Revolutionary Soldier, Beulah D. Linn Sevier County Historian, Sevier County News Record, August 19, 1975, (2) Family Search, Church of Jesus Christ of the Latter-day Saints.

Troxel, Jacob

Jacob was born 18 January 1759 in Frederick County, Maryland, to David and Anna Elizabeth Saeger. The Troxels moved to Loudoun County, Virginia, about 1772. Jacob was drafted in Loudoun County, Virginia, in the winter of 1777 to guard and relocate British prisoners to the lower part of Virginia. After completing this tour, he was discharged and returned to Loudoun County. In the winter of 1778, he volunteered in the cavalry under Captain Ford and Colonel Crawford, marched to Fort McIntosh, and joined the regular Army commanded by Colonel Campbell and General McIntosh. These troops skirmished with the Shawnee and Delaware Indians. Jacob was discharged after serving six months. [1]

In the summer of 1781, he was again drafted in Loudoun County under Captain Lewis and Colonel West, then joined the troops under General Washington and marched to Yorktown. After the Battle of Yorktown and the surrender of British General Cornwallis, Jacob remained in Yorktown for several months and was discharged by Captain Lewis.

After the war, Jacob moved to Sullivan County, Tennessee, and shortly thereafter to Sevier County, where he lived for three years. He left Sevier County for Kentucky and lived there for about twenty-two years. Jacob married Elizabeth Blevins in 1810 in Kentucky. She was the daughter of Jonathan and Charlotte "Lottie" Muse Blevins. From Kentucky, he moved to Jackson County, Alabama, and then to Marion County, Tennessee. On 23 August 1832, Jacob appeared in Marion County, Tennessee Court of Pleas and Quarter Sessions to apply for Revolutionary War Pension #10717. [1] Jacob died 1 July 1843 in McCreary County, Kentucky, and Elizabeth died 1843 in DeKalb,

Alabama. (2), (3)

Jacob and Elizabeth's children
- Thomas was born 1787 in Maryland.
- Martin was born 9 June 1800 in Bedford, Pennsylvania, married Anna Unknown in 1827 in Chester Township, Ohio, and died 17 September 1872.
- Barbara was born and died 1801 in Pennsylvania.
- Jacob was born 1803 in Loudoun, Virginia, married Sarah Unknown, and died 13 November 1880 in Seneca, Ohio.
- Samuel was born 18 September 1806 in Pennsylvania and died 29 December 1835.
- Magdalena was born 18 November 1808 in Pennsylvania, married George Muckley 16 April 1833, and died 6 February 1882.
- William was born 13 December 1810 in Greensburg Township, Pennsylvania, married Sarah Pfeiffer, and died 3 September 1898 in Greensburg Township.
- Sarah was born 2 February 1811 in Wayne, Kentucky, married Abraham A. Tinker in 1830, and died about 19 October 1872 in Dade County, Georgia.
- Eliza was born 1830, married Samuel Thomas, and died about 1860 in Jackson, Alabama. (2), (3)

Sources: (1) Southern Campaign Ameriacan Revolution Pension Statements, transcribed by Will Graves, (2) Family Search, The Church of Jesus Christ of

Latter-day Saints, (3) find a grave.

Underwood, John

The Underwood Bend area of Kodak, now called the Bent Road Land, was originally settled by Revolutionary War Patriot John Underwood and his family. John, along with his parents, moved to Sevier County about 1797. By the late 1800s, Underwood Landing became a popular destination for steam boats on their way to and from Knoxville. The boats took area farmers' produce and animals to market, and on the return trip, brought the farmers items needed for farming. The landing was a popular swimming pool and fishing site and the name Underwood is still very prominent in this area, with roads and a school bearing this name. (1)

John was born on 13 September 1754 in Kent County, Delaware, to John Benjamin (1740-1811) and Mary Margaret Jackman Underwood (1740-1793). John enlisted as a private for a period of five months in the Continental Line in Kent County, Delaware, in July 1776. He served under Colonel Robert Hutcheson, Captain Joseph Caldwell, 1st Lieutenant Peter Loper, 2nd Lieutenant Jordon Coe, and Ensign William Dill. John and his company marched from Kent County to Philadelphia and from there to Trenton, New Jersey, then to Amboy and fought in the Battle of Staten Island on 22 August 1777. John returned to Philadelphia and was honorably discharged after serving for six months.

In the summer of 1778, John volunteered as a private in the Delaware Militia for a period of six weeks. His company was engaged in marching up and down the Delaware Bay for the purpose of protecting the country against the Tories, who were in the habit of plundering the inhabitants and giving these "spoils" to the enemy. Later, John substituted for his brothers

Joshua and Abraham, as they were married with families and John was single. Another brother, William, was also in the Revolutionary War. (2)

John and his parents moved from Orange County, Virginia, in 1779 and settled in Roaring Gap, North Carolina. John married Mary "Polly" Kirby in 1790 in Surry County, North Carolina. Mary was born in 1776 in Surry County and died 14 March 1858 in Sevier County. John and Mary had moved to Sevier County about 1797. John filed for a Revolutionary War Pension on 29 May 1833 in Orange County, #S9492. John also married Elizabeth Manifold (1782-1820) in 1802 and Mary "Polly" Evans (1785-1865) in 1850. Elizabeth Manifold Underwood filed for Revolutionary War Widow's Pension in Asheville, North Carolina. (3) John died 14 March 1858 in Sevier County and is buried in the Underwood Family Cemetery. (4)

John and Mary's children:
- George was born in 1791 in North Carolina, married Elizabeth Kimes on 16 September 1815 in Knox County, Tennessee, and died 12 March 1865 in Sevier County.
- Nancy was born 1792 in Sevier County, married Enoch Underwood in 1813 in Sevier County, and died 15 September 1872 in Sevier County.

John and Elizabeth's children:
- John was born in 1802 in Sevier County, married Jane Susan Guinn in 1821 in Knox County, Tennessee, and died 14 March 1858 in Sevier County.
- Thomas was born 4 August 1804 in Sevier County, married Elizabeth "Bettie" Johnson on 25 October 1834 in Knox County, and died 19 July 1888 in

Sevier County.
- Harvey was born in 1806 in Knox County and died 1858 in Knox County.
- Elizabeth was born 1810 in Knox County.
- Joel was born 2 February 1812 in Sevier County, married Rebecca Pettaway on 24 September 1831 in Wilson County, Tennessee, and died 23 December 1893.
- James Harvey was born 11 March 1815 in Sevier County, married Martha A. Newman in 1837 in Sevier County, and died 20 February 1892 in Dade, Missouri.
- Martha Angeline was born 1815 in Knox County, married George Fletcher Huffaker on 22 December 1843, and died 1850 in Knox County.
- Mary was born 1817 in Sevier County.
- Hugh was born 1821 in Sevier County.

(5)

Sources: (1) TN Gen Web, Sevier County, Tennessee, Genealogy & History, (2) Southern Campaigns American Revolution Pension Statements & Rosters transcribed by Will Graves, (3) Find a Grave, 45) In the Shadow of the Smokies, Smoky Mountain Historical Society, 1993, p. 69, (5) Family Search, Church of Jesus Christ of Latter-day Saints.

Varnell, Richard

Richard began life in England and migrated with his parents to America as a young man to become a patriot of the Revolutionary War and to help establish Sevier County. His Revolutionary War Pension was filed in 1779 in Henry County, Virginia, and later in Franklin County, Virginia. In 1787, Richard signed a deed of sale for his property in Franklin County and moved south into North Carolina and eventually ended up in Sevier County. Richard's neighbors in Franklin County, Spencer Clack and Elijah Rogers, also came to Tennessee in 1787 and they settled in the area of present-day Sevierville. They established the Forks of the River Baptist Church, and Elijah Rogers became the second pastor of the church. Forks of the River Baptist Church records show that Richard and his son, William, joined the church in 1813 and Richard became a deacon in 1817. (1) Three more Varnell families moved to Sevier County with Richard, and they are believed to be his sons, William, Richard, Jr., and Thomas. (2) Richard obtained several land grants on Gist's Creek. Many of Richard's descendants live in the Sevier County and, especially, the Gist's Creek area. Both Richard and William signed a petition in 1813 asking the state of Tennessee for leniency with state taxes.

Richard was born on 7 August 1730 in London, England, to William (1699-1779) and Louisa Grisham Varnell (1702-1780). He married Mary Ann Pitt, the daughter of William and Eliza Griffin Pitt. Mary Ann was also born in England, but it is not known when she came to America. Richard died 1 March 1829 in Sevier County, and Mary Ann died about 1807, also in Sevier County.

Richard and Mary Ann's children:

- Richard was born 1760 in Edgecombe County, North Carolina, and died 6 March 1829 in Sevier County.
- William was born 1764 in Virginia, married Lydia Sullins in 1790 in Sevier County, and died 18 November 1829 in Sevier County and is buried in the Old Boyd's Creek Cemetery.
- Joseph was born about 1773 in North Carolina, married Mary Cook about 1795 in Sevier County, and died about 1864 in Victoria, Texas.
- Jesse Varnell was born 1784 in Virginia, married Margaret Dixon about 1804 in Tennessee, and died 1871 in Whitfield County, Georgia.
- Sarah was born 1787 in Franklin, Virginia, married John Bryon Guinn about 1809, and died 27 October 1874 in Dade County, Georgia. (3)

Sources: (1) Forks of the Little Pigeon Church, Harold Ownby, 1989, p.10, (2) Richard Varnell Family, Virginia and Tennessee, Cheryl's Family Index, Cheryl Grubb, (3) Family Search, Church of Jesus Christ of Latter-day Saints.

Wall, Randolph

Randolph fought in a major battle shortly after being drafted. He was honorably discharged, returned home, and then volunteered almost immediately to again fight for this country's independence. Randolph was born in Dinwiddie County, Virginia, on 12 March 1761. He was living in Lunenburg County, Virginia, in July 1780 when drafted for a period of six months into the Virginia Militia in the company of Captain William Dawson and Lieutenant Abraham Maury. Randolph and the company marched from Lunenburg County across the mountains into North Carolina to join General Gates' Army. Upon arriving at their encampment on the Deep River, they were informed that General Gates had moved to South Carolina. The company marched on in that direction, and after advancing only a short distance, learned General Gates had been defeated by the British at Camden, South Carolina, on the 15th and 16th of August 1780. The company joined General Gates' retreating troops and marched back into North Carolina. Upon reaching Hillsboro, North Carolina, it was learned the Tories were causing havoc in many areas of North Carolina, and the Company of Captain Dawson was ordered to observe the movements of the Tories and keep them from assembling or communicating with the British. Randolph continued in this service until being discharged in the middle of January 1781 after having served six months.

Randolph had been at home only two weeks when a call went out for troops to join General Nathaneal Greene. He volunteered in February 1781 for a tour of three months and joined General Greene at the Dan River in Virginia. Randolph was in Captain Dawson's Company and Colonel Nathaniel Cooks'

Regiment when they crossed the Dan River and fought the Battle of Guilford Court House. Randolph was discharged at Ramsey's Mills on Deep River, North Carolina, by Captain Dawson on 7 April 1781. After the war, Randolph lived in the counties of Montgomery and Lincoln, North Carolina, and Union County in South Carolina. It is not known when Randolph came to Sevier County, but he appeared in Sevier County Open Court on 6 June 1836 at the age of seventy-five years to apply for a Revolutionary War Pension, #R11090. The Reverend Eli Roberts and Richard S. Shields provided the court with an affidavit supporting Randolph's claim of service as a soldier in the Revolutionary War. No additional information could be found on Randolph. [1]

Sources: (1) Southern Campaign American Revolution Pension Statements & Rosters, transcribed by Will Graves.

Wear (Weir), John

    Patriotism is the word that best describes the Wear family. Two brothers, John and his younger brother, Samuel, sacrificed their lives and fortunes fighting for our independence. After the war, both made their way to Sevier County and once again placed their lives in jeopardy to help establish a county that will be forever grateful for their accomplishments, and likewise, a grateful county will forever honor and remember the name Wear.

    John was born 17 January 1741 in Bucks County, Pennsylvania, to Robert, Jr., (1715-1790) and Rebecca Carrell (1725-1780) Weir. John volunteered in Greene County, North Carolina (now Tennessee), the first of January 1781 as a private under Captain John Sevier, marched to Abington, Virginia, in pursuit of Tories for three months, and then returned to Greene County and was honorably discharged around the first of April 1781.

    Later in August 1781, John took a wagon to Richmond, Virginia, for a load of salt, and on the trip home, he met Captain William Tate's Company on their way to join General George Washington's Army. He abandoned his wagon, borrowed a gun and volunteered. The troops marched to Yorktown, Pennsylvania, fought in the Battle of Yorktown, and were present at the surrender of Cornwallis. After the battle, John was honorably discharged and returned home.

Beginning the latter part of January 1782, he served four months in the companies of Captain Moses Moore and Captain Samuel Wear. The companies marched to Wear's Fort on the West Fork of the Little Pigeon River and established the fort as their headquarters. The troops scouted the countryside for Indians. Two Indians were killed in Wear's Cove, but the rest fled. The companies were verbally discharged the first of June 1782. (1)

John married Nancy Moore about 1765 in Augusta, Virginia, the daughter of Moses Moore and Jane Ewing. After the Revolutionary War, John and his family lived in Greene County until about 1800. He then moved to Cape Girardeau, Missouri, on the Mississippi River but lived there for only a few months. Unfortunately, Nancy died in October 1800 in Cape Girardeau. John then moved to Christian County, Kentucky, and lived there for a year before returning to Sevier County. John lived the rest of his life in Sevier County. He died 23 January 1835 and is buried in Shiloh Memorial Methodist Cemetery in Pigeon Forge, Tennessee.

John and Nancy's children:
- Samuel Moore was born 25 May 1766 in Bucks County, Pennsylvania, married Sarah Bean on 16 March 1789 in Washington County, Tennessee, and died 15 March 1852 in Jefferson County,

Alabama.
- Rebecca was born 1 February 1772 in Augusta, Virginia, married Nathan Wilkinson on 30 August 1792 in Washington County, and died 2 November 1854 in Lawrence, Missouri.
- Jane Elizabeth was born 1773 in Staunton, Virginia, married Thomas Loveday on 8 October 1792, and died January 1860 in Andrew, Missouri.
- John was born 1782 in Bucks County, Pennsylvania, and died 1800 in Cape Girardeau, Missouri. (2).

Historical Fact: John is the older brother of Patriot Colonel Samuel Wear.

Sources: (1) Some Tennessee Heroes of the Revolution, Pamphlet III, Zella Armstrong, (2) In the Shadow of the Smokies, Smoky Mountain Historical Society, 1993, P. 680, (3) Family Search, the Church of Jesus Christ of Latter-day Saints.

Wear, Colonel Samuel

Samuel Wear's legacy is still very visible in this county, even to this day. He was one of the first white settlers to come to Sevier County and settled on the West Fork of the Little Pigeon River near the mouth of Walden's Creek. The community known as Wear's Valley was named in his honor, and schools and roads bear the name Wear. Many of his descendants are among the county's most influential and prominent citizens.

Samuel was born in 1753 in Rockbridge, Virginia, to Robert (1715-1790) and Rebecca Carrell Wear (1725-1780). He served as a captain in the 7th Virginia Militia and fought in the Battle of Kings Mountain and the Battle of Boyd's Creek under his close friend Colonel John Sevier. Soon after his arrival in Sevier County, he built a fort to protect his family from the Indians because a branch of the Great Indian War Path crossed his land. However, the price of venturing into the Indians' territory proved to be costly to the Wear family for years. (1)

In 1779, Samuel married Mary Thompson, the daughter of James William and Elizabeth Blair

Thompson, in Rockbridge, Virginia. Samuel chose the location for the town of Sevierville, named for his friend John Sevier. He was elected as a delegate to the convention held in Jonesborough, Tennessee, in August 1784 that resulted in the creation of the State of Franklin. Samuel was elected the first clerk of Sevier County and served in that position for twenty-seven years. In January 1796, he was elected as a delegate to help structure the government of the new State of Tennessee and served on the committee to draft the first constitution for the state. (1)

On June 19, 1793, Wear's Fort was the scene of a major Indian attack. During the night, a large party of Indians came into Wear's Cove, killed and stole horses, destroyed growing crops in the fields, and stole bags of cornmeal from Wear's Mill. Two days later, the militia followed the Indians, rescued the horses, and found the bags of cornmeal. Two Indians were killed and a third was wounded. Because civilian volunteers were forbidden by the Territorial governor to fight the Indians, angry Sevier County residents met, probably at Wear's Fort, and chose Colonel Wear to be the commander of a newly formed militia. Very few incidents of Cherokee Indian activity were reported after 1795.

Mary Wear died 3 March 1797 at Fort Wear and was buried at Fort Wear Cemetery. Samuel married Mary Elizabeth Gilliland on 30 September 1799 in Blount County, Tennessee. Mary was born in 1779 in Rockbridge, Virginia, and was the daughter of John and Elizabeth Young Gilliland. John and his father-in-law, Robert Young, fought alongside Samuel at the Battle of Kings Mountain. Robert Young is credited with firing the bullet that killed British Major Patrick Ferguson at the Battle of Kings Mountain. Samuel died 3 April 1817 at Fort Wear, and Mary died 24 September 1840, and both are buried in Fort Wear Cemetery. John Gilliland, Mary's father, is also buried in Fort Wear Cemetery. He was killed by Indians while returning home after visiting his daughter at Fort Wear. (1), (2)

Samuel and Mary's children:
- Elizabeth was born 4 October 1780 in Fort Wear, married General Robert Armstrong III on 19 October 1798 in Knox County, Tennessee, and died on 13 February 1820 in Knox County.
- Robert was born 4 November 1781 in Fort Wear, married Lucretia Thomas on 30 December 1802 in Sevier County, and died 4 August 1846 in Blount County.
- Rebecca was born 28 October 1787 in Fort Wear and married John Witt and died 1836 in Crittenden, Arkansas.
- Samuel, Jr., was born 16 September 1790 in Fort Wear, married Mary Unknown, and died 1837 in Talladega, Alabama.
- John was born 14 March 1793 in Fort Wear, married Susanna Mullendore on 14 March 1793 at Fort Wear, and died 6 July 1868 at Fort Wear.
- Mary Thompson was born 10 September 1795 in Fort Wear, married Colonel Simeon Perry on 15 August 1816 in Sevier County, and died 23 May 1821 in Pigeon Forge.
- Malinda was born 12 November 1798 at Fort Wear, married William Bradshaw on 9 August 1818 in Sevier County, and died 14 December 1852 in Anderson, Texas.

Samuel and Mary Elizabeth's children:
- Pleasant Miller was born 12 October 1802 in Fort Wear, married Tryphenia Whitson Tipton on 8 August 1826, and died 4 January 1870 in Lawrence, Missouri.
- Diana Carrolle was born 1806 in Fort Wear, married David Johnson 1831 in Sevier County, and died 1910.
- Minerva was born 24 October 1806 at Fort Wear, married John Guthrie in 1824, and died 14 June 1844 in Columbia, Tennessee.
- Margaret M. was born 4 April 1813 at Fort Wear, married Reverend David Barclay Cumming on 12 November 1835, and died 14 June 1844 in Missouri. (3)

Sources: (1) Sevier County, Tennessee and Its Heritage, Don Mills, 1994, pp. 6, 8, 22, 23, 24, 380, 381. (2) In the Shadow of the Smokies, Smoky Mountain Historical Society, 1993, p. 680. (3) Family Search, Church of Jesus Christ of Latter-day Saints.

Webb, John

On 1 August 1844, Jesse Webb appeared in Sevier County Court before John Bird, Justice of the Peace, to assist his sister-in-law, Elizabeth McMurtry Webb, with her application for a Revolutionary War Widow's Pension #R11249. Jesse testified that his brother, John, enlisted in the Georgia Militia for a period of eighteen months under Captain John Stuart. Jesse stated that John was called into service a second time and was a spy for at least twelve months under Captain Joseph Null. Jesse further stated that he served in the Revolutionary War with John for at least ten months.

Jesse testified that he was in South Carolina with John and Elizabeth McMurtry when they were married. He added that John and Elizabeth had two children and had lived together as man and wife and the legality of their marriage has never been disputed or called into question. Anna McMurtry Webb, Jesse's wife, also appeared in court on the same date to testify that she witnessed the marriage between her sister, Elizabeth, and John Webb. The application was rejected. On 8 January 1845, Jesse filed an appeal with additional information on John's war record and North Carolina Secretary of State, William Hill, verified that North Carolina Continental Line muster rolls listed John as a private in the 10th Regiment of Captain Stephenson's Company. John was also verified as being a member of the 2nd Company of the Georgia Continental Artillery and drew a warrant for 640 acres of land.

John was born in 1762 in Nanesmond County, North Carolina, to John and Judith Webb. He married Elizabeth McMurtry on 1 February 1781 in North

Carolina. John died 7 October 1842 in Edgecombe, North Carolina. Elizabeth died 10 February 1848 in Sevier County and is buried in Martin Baker Cemetery in Sevier County.

John and Elizabeth's children:
- Thomas was born 8 January 1782 in Greene County, North Carolina, married Sarah Weeks in 1805 in Greene County, and died 2 August 1852 in Sevier County.
- Susannah was born 14 August 1783 in Greene County, married James Williams in 1804 in Jefferson County, Tennessee, and died December 1852 in Moniteau, Missouri.
- Joseph was born 1 October 1786 in Greene County, married Sarah Dillard in 1806 in Sevier County, and died 1841 in Sevier County.
- Jesse was born 27 April 1793 in Greene County and died 1853 in Sevier County.
- Elizabeth was born 27 April 1798 in Greene County, married Martin Caswell Baker 1815 in Sevier County, and died after 1860 in Sevier County.

Sources: (1) Southern Campaign American Revolution Pension Statements & Rosters, transcribed by Will Graves. (2) Family Search, The Church of Jesus Christ of Latter-day Saints. (3) In the Shadow of the Smokies, Smoky Mountain Historical Society, 1993, p. 108.

Weese, Peter Isaac

Peter resided in Sevier County for about two years before moving on to Cocke and Roane Counties. Peter was born 1762 in Hardy County, Virginia (now West Virginia), to Peter Isaac Weese and an unknown mother. Peter was living in Hardy County when he entered the Militia in October 1782 as a substitute for a term of six months under Captain Berry in the Regiment commanded by Colonel Hones. The Regiment marched from Hardy County to Winchester, Virginia, to guard the British soldiers who had been taken prisoner. He was discharged in May 1783 by Colonel Hones. (1)

Peter continued to live in Hardy County several years after the war. On 12 August 1788, Peter married Mary Ann Anteline Smith in Botetourt County, Virginia. She was born 1753 to William and Elizabeth Maier Smith. Peter and Mary Anne moved to Bath County Virginia and lived there several years before moving to Montgomery County, Virginia. About 1821, they moved to Sevier County and lived there for two years (1821-1823) and then they moved to Cocke County, Tennessee. Finally, in about 1825, they moved to Roane County, Tennessee. It is not known where Peter resided in Sevier County. (1)

On 24 July 1833, Peter appeared in Roane County Court to apply for a Revolutionary War Pension #S1734. Family Search lists both Peter and Mary Ann dying on 9 July 1836 in Roane County. (1)

Peter and Mary's children:
- George David was born 4 April 1790 in Virginia, married Luticia Bird on 14 November 1844 in Clinton, Missouri, and died 1860 in Missouri.
- William was born 1790 in

Virginia, married Nancy Susannah 28 January 1830 on Roane County, and died 1860 in Missouri.
- Sarah was born 1792 in Bath, Virginia, married Christopher Marion in 1817 in Bath, and died 5 August 1858 in Fayette County, West Virginia.
- John was born 3 May 1793 in Virginia, married Charity Dennis on 8 March 1827 in Cocke County, and died 15 May 1850 in Gentry, Missouri.
- Landon was born 1795 in Virginia, married Barbara Unkown on 11 January 1821 in Cocke County, and died 15 May 1850 in Gentry, Missouri.
- David was born 1802 in Virginia, married Elizabeth Nida, and died 21 August 1888 in Giles Virginia. [2]

Sources: (1) Southern Campaign American revolution Pension Statements & Rosters, transcribed by Will Graves, (2) Family Search, The Church of Jesus Christ of Latter-day Saints.

Wells, Andrew

Andrew experienced extreme hardships during the Revolutionary War and devastating sadness shortly after arriving home from the war. His grave had been lost over the passage of time. However, his descendants were determined to find his final resting place and bestow well-deserved honor and praise on their heroic ancestor and our patriot.

Andrew was born 16 May 1755 near the Potomac River in Frederick, Maryland, to Robert II (1729-1792) and Esther Brown Wells (1728-?). Robert and Ester were married about 1744 in Maryland. When the French and Indian War ended, Robert and Esther left Maryland and moved to Orange County, North Carolina. They moved again to Edgefield, South Carolina, before the start of the Revolutionary War. (1)

In the fall of 1778 or 1779, Andrew volunteered into service under Captain Drury Pace and Colonel Leroy Hammond, with Andrew filling the position of ensign. He marched to Ferguson Fields near Charleston, South Carolina, where the troops lay in wait, and then at daybreak commenced a battle with the British. General Andrew Williamson commanded the patriots' left wing and General Nathaneal Greene, the right wing, but the Army was defeated by the British, and both Colonel Roberts and Lieutenant Prine of the Continental Army were mortally wounded. Andrew was honorably discharged and returned home. (2)

In the fall of 1779/80, Andrew volunteered under Captain Henry Graybill and Major Middleton, and he filled the position of Lieutenant. The troops scrimmaged with the British near Augusta, Georgia. Andrew was discharged after two months' service and returned home. On the 9th of June of that year, Andrew was at home when two Tory captains came to his house and took him prisoner. He was handcuffed, jailed, and placed aboard the warship Camellia and sailed to Ireland and held as a Prisoner of War for two years, until General Cornwallis surrendered at Yorktown and Andrew was released in an exchange of prisoners. (2)

Shortly after returning home after the war, Andrew's wife died. They had one child, William. Andrew married Elizabeth Williams about 1789. Apparently, Elizabeth died sometime between 1804 and 1805. Andrew continued to live in Edgefield District, South Carolina, until 1805, when he moved to Sevier County and married Eve Houk in 1806. Eve was born in 1781, but the names of her parents and birth place are unknown. (1) In June 1809, William received Land Grant #959 for 233 acres on the waters of Flat Creek, and in 1824, he added another 13.5 acres on the north side of the 233 acres. (1)

On 26 July 1831, Andrew appeared in the Second Judicial Circuit in the Circuit Court of Sevier to apply for a Revolutionary War Pension, #S1600, at the age of seventy-seven years. Because Andrew was able to read and write, he served in various government capacities and was a Justice of the Peace in Sevier County and very active in the Methodist Church. (1), (2)

Andrew died on 1 February 1835 and was survived by his wife Eva Houk Wells. Evidently, she moved West, as records found in Pettis County, Missouri, list Eve Wells with her sons, Michael, Thomas, and John Wells. Originally, Andrew's grave was thought to be lost, but as a result of a diligent search by his descendants, Perry and Elaine Wells of Grandview, Texas, the grave was found on Andrew's land grant property. On Sunday, September 19, 1976, the Spencer Clack Chapter of the Daughters of the American Revolution placed a marker in the old Lafollette (Wells Chapel) Cemetery in memory of

Andrew's Revolutionary War service. (1), (3)

Andrew and first wife's children:
- William was born September 1785.

Andrew and Elizabeth's children:
- Jeremiah was born 22 May 1790 in Georgia, married Mary Manning, and died 19 July 1840 in Jackson, Alabama.
- Andrew J. was born 29 September 1792 in Georgia, married Elizabeth Houk, and died 18 July 1778 in Cooper County, Missouri.
- Coleman was born 10 May 1794 in Wilkes County, Georgia, married Catherine Unknown and died 1840 in Coles, Illinois.
- Katie was born on 7 March 1796 in Wilkes County, Georgia.
- Sallie was born 25 August 1801 in Wilkes County, Georgia.

Andrew and Eve's children:
- Michael was born 14 November 1807 in Sevier County, married Susannah Cowan, and died 1841 in Pettis County, Missouri.
- Nancy Jane was born in 1808 (twin) in Sevier County and married George W. Glass.
- Hannah was born in 1808 (twin) in Sevier County, married Joseph McKinley, and died 2 August 1881 in Missouri.
- George was born 2 October 1810 in Sevier County.
- Rebecca was born 21 January 1812 in Sevier County, married Clarence

Dalyrimple, and died 1850 in Missouri.
- Malinda was born 5 December 1813 in Sevier County, married William McGill, and died in 1862.
- Levi was born 30 October 1815 in Jefferson County, married Anna Strader, and died 1900 in Sevier County.
- Permelia was born 8 September 1817 in Sevier County, married Bentley Potter, and died 15 November 1894 in Missouri.
- Thomas was born 9 September 1819 in Sevier County, married Jerusha Moon, and died 20 August 1845 in Pettis County, Missouri.
- John P. was born 12 January 1822 in Sevier County, married Martha Hughes, and died 25 July 1875 in Bates, Missouri. (3)

Sources: (1) Lost Grave Site of Andrew Wells Believed Found, Beulah D. Linn, Smoky Mountain Historical Society Newsletter, winter 1996, p. 12, 13. (2) Southern Campaign American Revolution Pensions Statements & Rosters, transcribed by Will Graves. (3) In the Shadow of the Smokies, Smoky Mountain Historical Society, 1993, p. 193, (4) Ancestry.com, search Andrew Wells.

Wells, George

George and his father fought side-by-side for years, serving their country in the fight for independence. George was born 15 February 1764 in Rowan County, North Carolina, the son of Barnabus (1748-1822) and Margaret Pool Wells (1750-1792). George entered the North Carolina Militia as a volunteer for three months along with his father on the first of April 1781. They were in the company of Captain William Lopp, and they marched to a house in the county known to be a gathering place for the Tories to prevent them from assembling. At the end of three months, they were discharged by Captain Lopp to return home.

Once at home, George learned that because of Tory activity in the area, it would be safer to be in the Army. George enlisted in the company of Colonel Thomas Wade andproceeded to Anson County, North Carolina, where he joined his regiment at Mount Pleasant and then marched to Cheraw, South Carolina. From there, he marched to the Hills of Santee, met General Nathaneal Greene's troops and continued marching until they reached Eutaw Springs. After the Battle of Eutaw Springs, he joined General Greene's brigade and went in pursuit of the British towards Moncks Corner. They remained in the area between York, South Carolina, and Mecklenburg, North Carolina, watching the Tories and preventing the Tories in the "up country" from communicating with the British in South Carolina. George was encamped near Charlotte, North Carolina, when he learned the British Commander in Charleston had proposed a cease-fire; therefore, George and his father were discharged by Captain Wade.

After the war ended, George moved to Chesterfield, then to Kershaw, South Carolina. He left South Carolina and moved to Blount County, Tennessee, and then to Sevier County. On 9 July 1835, George appeared in Sevier County Court of Pleas and Quarter Sessions to make application for a Revolutionary War Pension, but the application was rejected for failure to prove the required six-month service. On 7 May 1855, at the age of ninety, George filed for bounty land in Sevier County and received 160 acres. (1), (2)

George married his first wife in 1790 in Anson County, North Carolina. Her name is not known. He married Catherine Yearout on 17 September 1828 in Blount County. Catherine was born in 1800 in Sevier County and died 1845 in Sevier County. George married Delilah Walker about 1844 in Sevier County. Delilah was born in 1795 and died after 1860. (3)

The 1850 Sevier County Census lists George Wells, age 85, living in the county along with Deliah, age 55, and five young school age children. (4) George died in 1863, at the age of 99 years, in Sevier County. (3)

George and first wife's children:
- James Bedwell was born 25 September 1804 in North Carolina, married Clarissa Catlett, and died 15 May 1882 in Dandridge, Tennessee.
- George, Jr., was born 1821 in Kershaw, South Carolina.

George and Catherine's children:
- John Walker was born May 1827 in Blount County, married Celia Cagle in 1849 in Sevier County, and died 1916 in Campbell County, Tennessee.
- Lewis was born about 1830 in Sevier

County and married Dorothy "Dolly" Garner on 7 October 1856 in Sevier County.
- Synthia was born 1831 in Sevier County.
- Stephen Ellison was born 1834 in Seymour, Tennessee, married Melinda Cagle, and died in 1864 in the Civil War.
- William was born about 1839 in Sevier County and first married Edna Heartsill and, secondly, married Margaret Bird.
- Clarissa was born 1844 in Sevier County and married Lewis Nichols. (3)

Sources: (1) Revolutionary War Gravesite's of Knox and Surrounding Counties, Stephen Holston Chapter SAR, (2) Southern Campaign American Revolution Pension Statements & Rosters, transcribed by Will Graves, (3) ancestry.com-search George Wells, (4) 1850 Sevier County Census, #840.

White, James

James was born in Shenandoah County, Virginia. The date of his birth and the names of his parents are not known. In March 1776, James entered the service as a private under Lieutenant Jacob Rinker, Captain Jonathan Clark, and Colonel Peter Muhlenberg of the 8th Regiment of the Virginia Regulars. He enlisted for twelve months, left the service the first of April 1777, and was discharged by Colonel Muhlenberg. Also, James marched through Virginia and North Carolina in the Virginia Continental line under General Charles Lee. (1)

James stated in his application for a Revolutionary War pension #S32584, dated 30 August 1832, that he was born in Shenandoah County, Virginia, and was living there when called into the war. After the war, he moved to the French Broad River area in Sevier County and lived there until about 1813 when he moved to Bedford County, Tennessee, and then moved to Jackson County, Alabama. (1) He applied for the pension in Jackson County, and he is listed on the pension rolls of Alabama. A note on the pension certificate states that James died in August 1840 in Jackson County. (2) No additional information is known about James White.

Sources: (1) Southern Campaign American Revolution Pension Statements & Rosters, transcribed by C. Leon Harris. (2) The Pension Roll of 1835, Vol.III, 04 Alabama, U. S. Pension Roll of 1835 for James White.

White, Meady

Some researchers believe Meady and James White, the founders of Knoxville, Tennessee, were brothers. In a book written in 1917 by John Arthur Shields, he states that James Shields married Penelope White, a niece of James White, the founder of Knoxville. This is yet to be proven beyond reasonable doubt, but we do know that Penelope White, the daughter of Patriot Meady White married James Shields, the son of Patriot Robert Shields. Meady was born in 1745 in Bertie County, North Carolina, to Mordecai and Mary Hardy White. Meady served as a private in Captain Alexander Whitehall's Company of the 1st North Carolina Regiment of the Militia commanded by Colonel Samuel Jarris. (1)

In 1770, Meady married Sarah "Mary" Raynor, who was born 1754 in North Carolina. Meady moved to Sevier County in the early 1800s. He signed the 1813 Petition from Rivers South of French Broad and Holston to the General Assembly of the State of Tennessee. This petition asked for leniency on the collection of taxes and land payments from the land owners due to poor economic conditions of the area. (2) Meady, Mary, and Sabra White appear on the 1807 list of church members of the Forks of the River Baptist Church in Sevierville. The date of Meady and Mary's death is not known.

Meady and Mary's children:
- Nancy married John Page Shields in 1790 and was buried in Harrison, Indiana.
- Sabra Ellen was born 1774 in Bertie, North Carolina, married Robert Perry Shields in 1792, and died 16 September

1850 in Pigeon Forge, Tennessee, and is buried in Middle Creek Methodist Cemetery.
- Penelope was born in 1776 in Bertie, North Carolina, married James Shields in 1795, and died in 1841 in Jackson, Indiana.
- William was born in 1789 in Bertie, North Carolina, married Appy Everett in 1813, and died 12 April 1844 in Sevier County.
- Asa was born 23 December 1782 in Bertie, North Carolina, married John Sevier Trotter on 6 October 1803, and died 24 December 1852 in Pigeon Forge and is buried in Middle Creek Methodist Cemetery.
- Aaron was born 1784 in Bertie, North Carolina.
- Winifred was born in 1786 and married Unknown Pearson.
- James White was born October 1800 in Bertie, North Carolina. (3)

Historical Fact: John, Robert, and James Shields are the sons of Patriot Robert Shields.

Sources: (1) Ancestry.com. Revolutionary War Rolls 1775-1783. Publication M246, 138 rolls, record group 93. (2) Smoky Mountain Society Newsletter, fall 1983, pp .73-76. (3) Smoky Mountain Ancestral Quest, smokykin, maintained by Robert L. Beckwith.

Wood, Richard, Rev.

Richard served as pastor of the Forks of the Little Pigeon Church for forty years. In his later years, he had become overweight and afflicted with traumatic troubles, but in spite of the pain and the infirmities of age, he would still preach to his congregations. (1)

Richard was born 1756 in Mecklenburg, Virginia, to William (1730-1787) and Catharine Freer Wood (1731-?). (2) Richard's memorial tombstone at Providence Baptist Church Cemetery shows that he was a soldier in the Revolutionary War. (3)

In 1784, Richard moved to South Carolina, where he was ordained by the Fork of Broad and Paculet Baptist Church in the Union District Association. At the close of the Cherokee War, he moved to Sevier County and in 1789 founded the Forks of Little Pigeon Church (now First Baptist Church of Sevierville). Richard was pastor of the church until his death in 1831 at the age of 75. He attended his last service in August 1830 and died six months later. (1) At the age of 21 years, Richard married Mary Jane Price. (1) Mary Jane, daughter of Joseph and Lucy Burton

Price, was born in 1756 and died 1793 in Sevier County. Richard married Frances "Fanny" L. Libarger on 14 January 1795. (2)

Richard died on 4 February 1831 and was buried in Providence Cemetery in Sevier County. On 19 May 1942, his body was reinterred into the Old McMahan Cemetery in Sevierville by the Tennessee Valley Authority to make way for the building of Douglas Dam. (4), (5)

Richard and Mary's Children:
- Lavina was born about 1780 in Jefferson County, Tennessee.
- Joel was born about 1774 in Granville, North Carolina.
- Richard, Jr., was born in Tennessee.
- Catherine was born 20 February 1776 in Granville, married David Fain, and died 2 May 1859 in Marshall, Tennessee.
- James was born 1778 in Sevier County, married Mary Polly Reneau on 14 October 1807 in Jefferson County, Tennessee, and died July 1832 in Jefferson County.
- Hannah was born in Tennessee.
- Joseph P. was born in 1780 in Sevier County and died in 1826. (2)

Historical Fact: David Fain is the son of Patriot Charles Fain.

Sources: (1) Forks of Little Pigeon Church, Harold Ownby, 1989, Buckhorn Press, Gatlinburg, Tennessee, (2) Family Search, Church of Jesus Christ of Latter-day Saints, (3) findagrave.com, (4) ancestry.com, Tennessee Valley Cemetery Relocation Files, 1933-1990, (5) In the Shadow of the Smokies, Smoky Mountain Historical Society, 1993, p. 172.

Zollinger, Alexander

Alexander moved to the Fairgarden area of Sevier County in the early 1800s and owned over 300 acres of land. Alexander was born 25 March 1761 in Lancaster County, Pennsylvania, to Johann Peter and Maria Barbara Haerbaugh Zollinger. Alexander was drafted into the York County, Pennsylvania Militia at the age of seventeen and served as a private in the 7th Battalion, 8th Company. In 1778, he served under Captain Peter Zollinger and was still in the Militia in 1786. (1) Alexander received a Revolutionary War Pension, #11993 for his service during the war.

Alexander remained in Pennsylvania after the war, and in 1786, married Margaret Baker in Franklin, Pennsylvania. He was living in Augusta County, Virginia, in 1787, and in 1811, he was living in Sevier County. The 1840 Sevier County Census shows his daughter, Margaret, and her family living with Alexander. He is still on the 1850 Census but not his wife, Margaret. It is believed she died in 1849. Alexander died on 4 December 1852 and is buried in Fairgarden Cemetery in Sevier County.

Alexander and Margaret's children:
- Thomas was born 1787 in Franklin, Pennsylvania.
- Margaret "Polly" is born in 1790 in Pennsylvania.
- Elizabeth was born 1794 and married Unknown Gibson in 1814.
- Mary was born 3 December 1804 in Augusta, Virginia, married Willis B. Sharp in 1828 in Sevier County, and died 15 August 1894 in Sevier County.

(2)

Ruth C. Davis

Sources: (1) Smoky Mountain Historical Society Newsletter, summer 1987, p. 62, (2) Family Search, Church of Jesus Christ of the Latter-Day Saints.

A Portrait of Patriots and Pioneers in Sevier County

Index of Patriots and Their Families

Family Member		Patriot
Adams		
	Susan Elizabeth	Josiah Maples
Ah-Lee-sss-kway-tee		Isaac Thomas
Alexander		
	Abigail, Adam, Benjamin, Ebenezer, John	Oliver Alexander
	Margaret, Susan, Jeremiah	William McGaughey
Allen		
	Agnes	Obediah Matthews
	Clement, Jeremiah, Jane, Lucinda	John McKissick
	Deborah	Isaac B. Runyan
Anderson		
	Christiana	Joseph Campbell
	Elizabeth	James Hubbert/ Hubbard
Andes		
	Hannah	Isaac Thomas
Anthony		
	Agnes Ann	Robert Shields
Armstrong		
	Robert	Samuel Wear
Arnett		
	Matilda Maud	Robert Shields
Ashcraft		
	Jacob, Lydia	David Norton
Atchley		
	Abraham, James B., John, Joshua, Jesse, Thomas, William	Abraham Atchley

A Portrait of Patriots and Pioneers in Sevier County

	Abraham	
	Amos Russell, Seth	William Trotter
	Benjamin, Elizabeth, George, Hanna, Isaac, Jane, Joshua Jesse, Lydia, Mary Esther, Noah, Rhoda, Sarah, Thomas	Thomas Atchley
	Jeminah, Lydia Pauline, Martha Jane	Josiah Maples
	Mary	Henry Haggard
Babb		
	Polly	Thomas Buckingham
Baird		
	John Nelson	Ezekial Stone
Baker		
	Henry, Henry, Jr.	Henry Baker
	Malvina, Susannah	Joseph Layman
	Margaret	Alexander Zollinger
	Martin Caswell	John Webb
Ballard		
	Elizabeth	Mordecai Lewis
Barclay		
	David	Samuel Wear
Barefoot		
	Anna	Isaac B. Runyan
Barker		
	Mary	James Pierce
Barnes		
	Jane	William Crowson
Bartlett		
	Mary	James Pierce
Bates		

Bean	James	Edward Murphy
Beatie	Sarah	John Wear
Beavers	Margaret	Samuel Newell
	Major, Mary	Spencer Clack
Benefield	Spencer	John Clack
Bennett	Elizabeth, Mary "Polly"	David Norton
	Lucinda	William Headrick
Benson	Mary Edwards	John Mahan
	Barclay, Benjamin, Isaac, John, Mary May, Robert, Spencer, Jr., William	Spencer Benson
Berry	Charles	James Riggin
	Francis	John Mahan
Bird	Mary "Molly"	George Hudson
	Luticia	Peter Weese
Black	Margaret	George Wells
Blackburn	Esther	Flayl Nichols
	Jane, John, Martha	John Cusick
Blair	Mary	Thomas Millsaps
	Elizabeth	Samuel Wear

A Portrait of Patriots and Pioneers in Sevier County

	Hugh, Mahala, Nancy Jane, Samuel	Samuel Blair
Bleister	Thomas	Ezekial Stone
Blevins	Elizabeth	Jacob Layman
Boaz	Elizabeth, Jonathan	Jacob Troxel
	Abednego, Abednego, Jr., Agnes, Claramon, Drucilla, Meshack, Mignon, Obediah, Peter, Thomas, Zedkijaj	Abednego Boaz
	Claramon	William Lovelady
Bodine	Edmond	John Thurman
	Mary Ann	William Longley
Bohannan	Winey	William Maples
	Elizabeth, Evans, Henry, Henry Jr., James Margaret, Nancy, Sarah, Susannah	Henry Bohannan (Bohanan)
Boggess	Nancy, Susannah	William Ogle Peter Bryan
Bogle	Phoebe	
Bosley	Andrew	John McCroskey
Boyd	Sophia	William Ogle John Sharp
	Ann	

Ruth C. Davis

	Margaret	Samuel and William McGaughey
Booth		
	Phoebe	Joseph Campbell
Bradley		
	Rebecca R.	Andrew Creswell
Bradshaw		
	William	Samuel Wear
Breeding		
	George	John McKissack
Brickey		
	Lydia	Thomas Millsaps
Brimer		
	Barbara, Benjamin, James, John, Sabath, Sarah, Tabitha, Vineyard, William	William Brimer
	Martha Carmichael	Hugh Henry
Brittain		
	William	James Stanfield
Brooks		
	Patsy	Joshua Gist
Brown		
	Esther	Andrew Wells
	John	Joshua Gist
	Rhoda	Robert and Thomas Shields
Browning		
	Mary	John McKissack
Bryan		
	Allen, Margaret, Mary, Peter, Thomas, William	Peter Bryan
	Allen S, Sr.	James Hubbert/ Hubbard
Bryant		
	Gabriel	John McGee

A Portrait of Patriots and Pioneers in Sevier County

Bryson		
	Naomi	Spencer Benson
Buckingham		
	Benjamin, Frances, Nathaniel, Peter, Rebecca, William	Peter Buckingham
Buford		
	Sarah	Charles Fain
Burn		
	Adam	Samuel Blair
Burton		
	Lucy	Richard Wood
Bush		
	Susannah Hardy	James McMahan
Butler		
	Mary	William Maples
Cagle		
	Celia, Melinda	George Wells
Caldwell		
	Sarah A.	Charles Fain
Calhoun		
	Martha, Thomas	John Childress
Calloway		
	Elizabeth Day	Zachariah Isbell
Calvert		
	Rachel	James Hubbert/ Hubbard
	Rachel	James McMahan
Campbell		
	David, John, Joseph, Joseph, Sr., William	Joseph Campbell
	Margaret Jane	John Rains
Cannon		
	James	Henry Rogers
	Martha, Rebecca	Flayl Nichols
Canway		
	Jenny	Charles Fain

Capps		
	Virginia Ellen	Andrew Evans, VA
Carter		
	Amos, John, Samuel, William	Samuel Carter
	Davis	Timothy Reagan
Carmon		
	William H.	Joseph Large
Carrell		
	Rebecca	John and Samuel Wear
Casey		
	Mary "Molly"	David Lindsay
Cate		
	Lucy, Nancy	Peter Bryan
Catlett		
	Clarissa	George Wells
Caylor		
	George, Sr.	William Headrick
Chandler		
	Joell, John, Mary Polly, Nancy, Rebecca, Timothy	Timothy Chandler
Chapman		
	Robert	Robert Chapman
Childress		
	John, Stephen	John Childress
Clack		
	Fanny, Hannah, John Sterling, John, Martha, Naomi, Sterling	John Clack
	Catherine, Frances, John, Malvina, Martha, Raleigh, Rhoda, Spencer	Spencer Clack
	Frances	Joshua Gist
	Catherine, Martha	Henry Rogers

A Portrait of Patriots and Pioneers in Sevier County

Claubough	Micajah, Raleigh Robert	Robert Kerr
Clifton	John III	Henry Haggard
Claunch	Prudence	Spencer Benson
	Ann	Hugh Henry
Clendenon	Margaret	John Gilliland
Coates	Esther	John McGee
Cobb	Rebecca	Joel Davis
Cocke	Richard Caswell	Thomas Buckingham
Cody	Jane	Thomas Buckingham
Collier	Elinor Archdeacon	Abednego Boaz
Collins	Mary	Henry Rogers
Colville	Henry Pleasant	James Pierce
	Nancy Ann	Andrew Evans, VA
	Elizabeth	John Cusick and Samuel Newell
Compton	Ruth	Spencer Benson
Cornstock	Cyrus, Jeremiah, Joseph, William, Zacharia	Jeremiah Compton
Conway	Prudence	Josiah Maples

Cook	Hannah	Ezekial Stone
	John	Joseph Large
Costner	Mary	Richard Varnell
Couchman	Abiline	Burlingham Rudd
Cowan	John	Andrew Evans, NC
	Andrew, Anna, Champion, David, Hugh, James, John, Maria, William	Andrew Cowan
	Jean Glasgow	Joseph Campbell
Cox	Susannah	Andrew Wells
Creswell	Amy	James Mahan
	Andrew, Dorothy, Mary Elizabeth, Margaret V.	Andrew Creswell
	Nancy, Rebecca, Samuel, William E., William H. Sarah Jane	Andrew Evans, VA
Crouch	Martha Susan	David Lindsay
Crowson	Aaron, Abraham, Jacob, Jane, John, Isaac, Mary, Moses, Richard, Thomas William	William Crowson
	Richard Thomas	David Lindsay
	Rebecca	John Mahan
Cuningham	Maximilia	Andrew Evans, NC

Cusick	David, John B., Joseph, Maratha, Rebecca, Samuel	John Cusick
Dalyrimple	Clarence	Andrew Wells
Daniels	Jane	Spencer Benson
Davies (Davis)	Jacob, Jesse, Zachariah	Zachariah Davies (Davis)
Davis	Barbara, Joel, Joel, Jr., Joseph, Jr., Thomas	Joel Davis
Deer	Sarah	Robert Shields
Denbo	John	Joshua Tipton
Dennis	Charity	Peter Weese
Derrick	George, Henry, Jacob, Johann, Jonas, Simon Tobias	Jacob Derrick
DeWitt	Dorcas	John Lovelady
Dickey	Anna, Rebecca	Adam Fox
Dickson	Alexander	Henry Bohannon
Dillard	Sarah	John Webb
Dinsmore	Rachel King	James Pierce
Dixon	Margaret	Richard Varnell
Doty	Elizabeth	Abraham Atchley
Douglass		

Douthit	Mary	John Gilliland
Duggan	Samuel	Isaac Thomas
Dungan	Campbell, Elizabeth, George, Hugh, James, Margaret, Mary Jane, Robert, Robert Jr. Wilson	Robert Duggan
Dunn	Jeremiah, Margaret	James Pierce
Duncan	Cassandra, Margaret	Robert Duggan
	William	William Headrick
	David	William Lovelady
Dunkelberger	John	Oliver Alexander
Durham	Anna Maria	Adam Fox
Dyer	Hulda	John Cusick
Eagleton	Mary Ann	Josiah Maples
Edmondson	John	John McCroskey
Edwards	James	William McGaughey
Eilor	William	Joshua Tipton
Elgin	Anna Catherine	Adam Fox
Elkin	Elizabeth	William Brimer
	Amelia	Henry Haggard

A Portrait of Patriots and Pioneers in Sevier County

Ellard		
	Amos Isaac	John Lovelady
Ellis		
	Jeremiah	Isaac Thomas
	Lucy Ann	John McKissack
Emert (Emmert)		
	Barbara, Catherine, Daniel Elizabeth, Frederick, Frederick Jr., John George, Louisa, Margaret, Mary Phillip	Frederick Emert
	Daniel, Frederick, Louisa Phillip	Timothy Reagan
Emmitt		
	Mary Jane "Mollie"	Joseph Large
England		
	Martha	John McGee
Eppler		
	Jonathan	Isaac Thomas
Evans		
	Andrew, Andrew Jr., David, Elizabeth, James Jesse, John, Mary "Polly", Nancy, Nathaniel, Rachel, Samuel, William	Andrew Evans NC
	Andrew, Ann Henry, Mary Mary Elizabeth, Samuel William	Andrew Evans VA
	Dorothy "Dolly"	Andrew Creswell
	Andrew, James, Jesse	Samuel Newell

Ruth C. Davis

	Martha	Andrew Cowan
	Mary	Robert Duggan
	Nancy	John Cusick
	Mary "Polly"	John Underwood
Everett	Richard	Frederick Emert
Ewing	Appy	Meady White
	Jane	John Wear
Fagala	John Mose	Samuel McGaughey
Fain	Margaret "Polly"	Andrew Creswell
	Charles, Jesse, John, Richard	Charles Fain
	David	Richard Wood
	Elizabeth	Andrew Evans NC
	John, Mary	James Pierce
Faine	Sophia	David Norton
Fancher	Paulina	Samuel Newell
	James S., John West	Henry Haggard
	Mary	James Oldham
Farley	Mary Polly	Thomas Atchley
	Susannah	Flayl Nichols

A Portrait of Patriots and Pioneers in Sevier County

Fouracres		
	Mary Ann	Timothy Reagan
Fox		
	Adam, Catherine, Elizabeth, George, Johan, John, Mark Martha, Matthew, Susanna William	Adam Fox
	Catherine	Robert Shields
	Margaret	Jacob Derrick
Frazer		
	Elizabeth	David Lindsay
Fretwell		
	Susanna	Henry Bohannon
Freer		
	Catherine	Richard Wood
Frye		
	Margaret Ann, George	Burlingham Rudd
Fulton		
	David	David Lindsay
Gallaher		
	Faday	Samuel Carter
Gamble		
	William	William McGaughey
Garner		
	Dorothy "Dolly"	George Wells
Genoa		
	Mary	Abraham Atchley
George		
	Amy	Robert Kerr
Gibson		
	Atlas, Thomas	James Pierce
Gillespie		
	William Cowan	John Sharp
Gilliland		
	Elijah, Harvey, James, John,	John Gilliland

Ruth C. Davis

	Josiah, Mary Elizabeth, Priscilla, Robert	
Gipson	John, Mary Elizabeth	Samuel Wear
Gist	George Washington	Abraham Atchley
	Jane Joshua, Mordecai, Nathaniel, Rachel, Sarah	Joshua Gist
Glass	Mordecai	Spencer Clack
Goodwin	George W.	Andrew Wells
Gosnell	Benjamin, Nancy Ann	James Mahan
Gower	Avarilla	Thomas Buckingham
Graff	Letitia	John Rains
Grant	Eva Marie	Frederick Emert
Graves	Lucinda	John McCroskey
Gray	Elizabeth	John Thurman
Greer	Nancy	John McKissack
Griffin	Jane	William Crowson
Guinn	Eliza	Richard Varnell
Grisham	Susan	John Underwood
Guthrie	Louisa	Richard Varnell
	James	Thomas Atchley
	John	Samuel Wear

A Portrait of Patriots and Pioneers in Sevier County

Guy		
	Elizabeth	Jacob Derrick
Gwinn		
	Fanny	James Stanfield
	John Bryon	Richard Varnell
Haerbaugh		
	Maria Barbara	William Ogle
Haggard		
	Elizabeth	William Ogle
	David, Elizabeth, Henry Henry Jr., James, Joel, Lucy, Mary, Nancy, Noah, Susan, William	Henry Haggard
	James	Thomas Atchley
Haideberg		
	Elizabeth	William Headrick
Hale		
	Joseph	David Lindsay
Hammer		
	Catherine	James McMahan
Hammonds		
	Minerva Ann	John McGee
Haney		
	Elizabeth	Spencer Benson
Hankins		
	Phoebe	Joseph Large
Hardin		
	Elizabeth	Thomas Atchley
Handy		
	Mary	Meady White
Harper		
	James	Joseph Large
	Margaret	Birlingham Rudd

Harris		
	Hannah	James Riggin
Harrison		
	Mary "Polly"	David Lindsay
Hart		
	Lucretia	Isaac Thomas
Hatcher		
	Edward, Nancy Ann	Flayl Nichols
	Hulda	James McMahan
	William	William Crowson
Hawkins		
	Mary Adaline	Zachariah Isbell
Hayes		
	Martha	Robert Kerr
Haynie		
	Keziah, Mary	John Gilliland
Headrick		
	Nancy	Zachariah Davies
	Daniel, Georg, Jacob, John, Henry, Katherine, Rebecca, William	William Headrick
Heartsill		
	Edna	George Wells
Henderson		
	Jerusha	Isaac Thomas
	Mary J., Nancy	James McMahan
	Samuel	Samuel Blair
Hendry		
	Rebecca	James Pierce
Hennessee		
	James	John A. McGee
Henry		
	Albert, Ezekial, Hugh, Isaac, J. Pleasant, Luke, Patrick,	Hugh Henry

	Rachel, Samuel, Sarah C., Thomas, William	
	Hugh, John, Mary "Polly", Samuel, Robert, William, William Jr.	William Henry
Hickey	Rachel	James Hubbard
Hickman	Sarah	James McMahan
	Rachel Elizabeth	Hugh Henry
Hicks	Rachel Elizabeth	William Henry
Hightower	Charles B., George	John Adam Houk
Hill	Gilly	William Crowson
Hillard	Catherine Caty	James Oldham
Hix	Mary	William Crowson
	Hannah	John Lovelady
	Hannah	William Lovelady
Hodges		
	Mary	Andrew Evans, NC
Holland	Nancy	George Hudson
Hooft		
	Cathrine Elizabeth	Zachariah Davies
Hooke	Robert	Oliver Alexander
Houk	Elizabeth, Eve	Andrew Wells

Ruth C. Davis

	John Adam	Timothy Chandler
Houston	Archimedes, Eliza, John, John Adam, John Joseph, Martin, Margaret Elizabeth, Mary, Rebecca, Sally	John Adam Houk
	Esther	Alexander Montgomery
Howard	Esther	Samuel Newell
	Ignatius	James Riggin
Huffaker	Mary	Joshua Gist
	George Fletcher	John Underwood
	George Michael	Andrew Creswell
	Isaac	James Riggin
	Peter Millard	Andrew Evans, VA
Hubbard	Samuel	George Hudson
	Betty	Peter Bryan
	Benjamin, Elizabeth, James, James Jr., Margaret, Phoebe, Polly, Matthew, Robert	James Hubbard
Hudson	Anne Nancy	Robert Kerr
	Amy Anna, Armistead, Benjamin B. Eli, Elijah, Gail, George, George Sr., John, Martha, Mary, Sarah, Thomas,	George Hudson

A Portrait of Patriots and Pioneers in Sevier County

	Lucinda Jane, William	John McKissack
Hughes		
	Clarissa	John Lovelady
	Martha	Andrew Wells
Huskey		
	James, Jane, Mary	Timothy Reagan
	Martha Jane	William Ogle
Hutchinson		
Isbell	Hannah	William Robertson
	Jason, John Miller, Levi, William, Zachariah, Zachariah Sr.	Zachariah Isbell
Jackman		
	Mary Margeret	John Underwood
Jackson		
	Elizabeth	John Rains
James		
	Margaret	James Mahan
	Margaret	John Mahan
	Randolph	John Thurman
Jenkins		
	Hannah, James, Nancy, William	James Jenkins
Johnson		
	David	Samuel Wear
	Ephriam	Hugh Henry
	Elizabeth "Betty"	John Underwood
	Jeffrey	Timothy

		Chandler
	Solomon	Solomon Johnson
	William	William McGaughery
Johnston	Ann Jean Ann, Zachariah	John Sharp
Jones	Elizabeth, John	William Henry
	Frederick	Spencer Benson
	Jane S.	William Maples
	Lucy Williams, Wilson	John Clack
	Nancy	David Norton
Keeler	Elizabeth	John Cusick
	Elizabeth	Robert Duggan
Kellam	Elizabeth	Joshua Gist
Kennedy	Tabitha	Spencer Benson
Keener	Lydia	Zachariah Davies
Keeney	Nancy	James Oldham
Kelly	Anne	Ezekial Stone
Kendle	Elizabeth, William	William Kendle
Kennon	Mary	John Clack
	Mary	Sterling Clack
Kerr	Martha	Spencer Clack

	Jesse, Margaret, Martha, Robert, Robert, Sr. William	Robert Kerr
Kimes	Elizabeth	John Underwood
King	Ellender	Thomas Millsaps
Kindead	Jane	Samuel Newell
Kirby(Kerby)	Christopher, Henry	Christopher Kirby
	Mary "Polly"	John Underwood
Knight(Neidig)	Barbara	Frederick Emert
Lackey	Elizabeth	Samuel McGaughey
	Elizabeth	William McGaughey
Landman	Vina	David Lindsay
Langford	Elizabeth, Thomas	Henry Rogers
Large	Adam, James E., John, Joseph Lucinda, Phoebe, Robert, Sarah, Thomas, Wilson	Joseph Large
Laughlin	John Luke, Mary Jane	Samuel McGaughey
	John Luke, Mary Jane	William McGaughey
Lawson	Andrew	Alexander Montgomery
	Robert	Flayl Nichols
Lay	Abigail	Thomas Atchley

Layman	Elizabeth, Jacob, Susannah	Jeremiah Compton
	Absalom, Ambrose, George, Jacob, Jacob Jr., John, Mary, Michael, Nancy, Preston	Jacob Layman
Lea	Caswell	John Sharp
Lee	Ann	Henry Rogers
Lewis	Magdalena	Jacob Derrick
	Amos, Archibald, Elizabeth George, John, Levi, Margaret, Mary "Polly", Mordecai	Mordecai Lewis
Libarger	Frances "Fanny"	Richard Wood
Lindsay	David, David, Sr., Elijah, Elizabeth, Huldah, James, John, Joseph, Lydia, Mary Ann,. Rachel, Rebecca, Thomas	David Lindsay
	Rachel	John Lovelady
	Hulda	William Crowson
Lindsey	John	Thomas Atchley
Linglan	Elizabeth	William Henry
Long	Mary "Polly"	Hugh Henry
	Moses	Thomas Atchley
	Nancy Ann	William Longley

A Portrait of Patriots and Pioneers in Sevier County

	George Washington	Josiah Maples
	Edward, Nancy	Josial Maples
Longbothtam	Edward, Nancy	William Maples
Longley	Robert	Henry Haggard
	Abigail, Andrew, James, Joel, John, Joseph, Mercy, Sarah, William	William Longley
	Andrew	James Oldham
Love		
Loveday	Isaac	Mordecai Lewis
	Thomas	John Wear
Lovelady		
	Amos	Abednego Boaz
	Amos, Eleanor, Elizabeth, Jesse, Obadiah, Rhoda, Sarah, Thomas, William	William Lovelady
	James, John Sr., John Jr., Sarah, Thomas Sr., William M.	John Lovelady
	Obadiah	John Mahan
	William Morgan	David Lindsay
	Amos, Eleanor, Elizabeth, Jesse, Obadiah, Sarah, Rhoda,	William Lovelady

Lowery	Thomas, William	
McBryant	Mary	Isaac Runyan
McCain	Elizabeth	William Ogle
McCallie	Eli, Margaret	William McGaughey
McCamy	Alexander	John McCroskey
McCarter	William H.	Timothy Chandler
McChesney	James	William Ogle
McClung	Isabella, James	John Sharp
McConnell	Hugh	James Hubbert
McCown	Mary	John McKissack
McCroskey	George	Mitchell Porter
	Dorcas, Elizabeth, Esther, John, John Blair, Lavina, Mary, Robert, Samuel	John McCroskey
McCullah	Robert Scott	John Sharp
McCulley	Elizabeth Kennedy	Andrew Evans, VA
McCullough	Mahala	Abraham Atchley
McDaniel	Elizabeth	Andrew Evans, NC
McDonald	Elizabeth	James Oldham
	Elizabeth	James Hubbert

McGaughey		
	James, Jane, John, Mary Anne, Sarah, William	Samuel McGaughey
	Agnes, Ann, Elizabeth, George, James, Margaret, Mary, Samuel, William	William McGaughey
McGee		
	Clendenon, Elizabeth, James L., Jane, John Alexander, John Jr. Mary, Sarah, Samuel, Richard	John McGee
McGill		
	William	Andrew Wells
McGinley		
	James	Oliver Alexander
McGregor		
	Ezekial M.	John McGee
McKhen		
	Elizabeth	James Pierce
McKinley		
	Joseph	Andrew Wells
McKissack		
	Archibald, Elizabseth, Duncan, James, John, Jonathan, Lucinda, Mary, Nancy, William	John McKissack
	Rachel	Henry Bohannon
McMahan		
	Abraham, James, James Isaac, John Calvin, Mary, Robert, Samuel, Wellington, William	James McMahan
McMurry		
	Elizabeth, Joseph Robert	Andrew Creswell

McMurtry		
	Anna, Elizabeth, Joseph	John Webb
McNabb		
	John Lee	Robert Duggan
Maier		
	Elizabeth, Joseph Robert	John Mahan
Mahan		
	Archimedes, Christian, Edward, James, John, John Jr., Mary Thomas	John Mahan
	Catherine, Elizabeth, Hezekiah, James, Permelia, Thomas Jr.	James Mahan
	Christian	William Lovelady
	Edward	Timothy Reagan
Manifold		
	Elizabeth	John Underwood
Manning		
	Catherine	William Maples
Maples		
	Mary	Andrew Wells
	Ephriam, Nancy	Thomas Atchley
	Elijah, Elizabeth, Ephriam, James, Jesse, John W., Josiah Jr., Josiah Sr., Nancy Ruthea, Thomas, William	Josiah Maples
	Edward, George, James, John Josial, McCampbell, Moses, Peter, William	William Maples
	Sarah	James Oldham

A Portrait of Patriots and Pioneers in Sevier County

Marion		
	Christopher	Peter Weese
Martin		
	David Sr., Letty, Mary	Abraham Atchley
Mason		
	Elizabeth	Samuel McGaughey
Massengill		
	Elizabeth Isabella	Isaac Thomas
Matson		
	John	Flayl Nichols
Matthews		
	Frances	Abednego Boaz
	Obediah, Robert	Obediah Matthews
	Obediah	William Richardson
Maxwell		
	Rebecca J.	Burlingham Rudd
Miller		
	Adam	James Pierce
	David, James	James Mahan
	Hannah Crawford	Zachariah Isbell
	Sarah	Robert Kerr
	William	Spencer Clack
Mills		
	Curtis	John Lovelady
	Frances	William Crowson
Millsaps		
	David, Edward, Isaac, Robert, Thomas, Thomas James	Thomas Millsaps
Mimms		
	Priscilla	Timothy Chandler

Minter		
	Hannah	Joseph Laarge
Mitchell		
	James, Nancy	Mordecai Lewis
Modrell		
	Marjorie	Andrew Evans, NC
Montgomery		
	Alexander, John, John Alexander, Margaret, William H.	Alexander Montgomery
	Elizabeth Ann Houston, Esther Houston, John	John McCroskey
	Jane, John	Samuel Newell
Moon		
	Jane, Mary	William Maples
	Jerusha	Andrew Wells
	Sarah	John Thurman
Moore		
	Dorothy	Andrew Evans, NC
	Martha Torrance	David Lindsay
	Martha	Timothy Reagan
	Mary	James Pierce
	Moses, Mancy	John Wear
	Polly	John Rains
	Sarah	William Crowson
Morgan		
	Lewis	Andrew Evans, NC

A Portrait of Patriots and Pioneers in Sevier County

Morris	Sarah	John Lovelady
	Prudence	Henry Haggard
Morrison	Sarah	Solomon Johnson
	Rachel	William McKissack
Muckley		
	George	Jacob Troxel
Mullendore		
	Abraham, Hettie	Jeremiah Compton
	Nancy	Isaac Runyan
	Susanna	Samuel Wear
Murphy		
	Edward, Elizabeth, Mary	Edward Murphy
Muse		
	Charlotte "Lottie"	Jacob Troxel
Myers(Meyer)		
	Anna Margaretha, Elizabeth, Ludwig, Marie Margaret,	William Headrick
Napier		
	Margaret Eaune	Alexander Montgomery
Neidig(Knight)		
	Barbara	Frederick Emert
Newell		
	Dorcas, Elizabeth Esther, Jame, John M., Joseph, Margaret, Samuel, Susannah, William	Samuel Newell
	Hester, Jane, Susannah	Andrew Evans, NC
Newman		
	Martha	John Underwood

Ruth C. Davis

Nichols	Samuel	William Trotter
	Edward, Flayl, Jesse, John, Martha, Rhoda, Sarah, Simon, Robert, William	Flayl Nichols
Nowlin	Lewis	George Wells
Norton	Mary Polly	James McMahan
	David, Henry, Hiram, James, John, Mary, Rachel, Samuel, Sally, Sophia	David Norton
Nucum(Newcomb)	Martha Patsy	Samuel McGaughey
Nyse	Solomon, Susannah	Solomon Newcomb
Ogle	Katherine Ruth	David Lindsay
	Easter, Isaac, William	Henry Bohannan
Oldham	Hercules, Isaac, John, Rebecca, Mary Ann, Thomas, William	William Ogle
	George, James, John, Moses, Mary, Nancy, Sarah, Stephen, William	James Oldham
Owens	Sarah	William Longley
Palmer	Nancy, William	Samuel Newell
Parker	Elizabeth	William Brimer
	Salley	James Pierce

Parsons	David, Evalina, George, Robert, Susannah	George Parsons
Patterson	Edith Caroline	William Maples
	Priscilla, William Tryon	William Longley
	Sarah Mary	John Sharp
Patton	Susannah	John Webb
Paul	Margaret	Oliver Alexander
Payne	Martha	Flayl Nichols
Penington	Samuel	John McKissack
Perry	Margaret	Robert Shields
	Simeon	Samuel Wear
Pettaway	Rebecca	John Underwood
Pfeffer	Sarah	Jacob Troxel
Pierce(Pearce)	Charlotte, Elizabeth, George, James, Jeremiah, John, Margaret, Mary, Orpah, Sarah, Rebecca, Solomon, Thomas	James Pierce
Pitner	John A.	Andrew Creswell
Pitt	Mary Ann, William	Richard Varnell
Pharis	Elizabeth	Thomas Atchley

Pool		
	Margaret	George Wells
Porter		
	Alexander, Elizabeth, Ester, James, John, Joshua, McKindra, Mary Caroline, Mitchell, Nancy, Sarah, William	Mitchell Porter
	Esther	Isaac Runyan
	James	Joshua Gist
	Sarah R.	Isaac Thomas
Potter		
	Bentley	Andrew Wells
Potts		
	Rebecca	James Oldham
Powell		
	Catherine	Henry Bohannan
	Charlotte "Lottie"	James McMahan
	Eliza	Timothy Reagan
Poythress		
	Tabitha	Henry Haggard
Prentice		
	John	William Lovelady
Price		
	David	James Stanfield
	Joseph, Mary Jane	Richard Wood
	Mary "Polly"	Samuel McGaughey
Pride		
	Samuel	John Shaarp

A Portrait of Patriots and Pioneers in Sevier County

Pryor		
	Anne	Isaac Thomas
Rains		
	Charles, Elixa	John Rains
	Charles, Elizabeth James, John, Josiah, Letitia, Robert, Samuel	
Rambo		
	Jacob, Margaret	Isaac Runyan
Randall		
	Elizabeth	Henry Rogers
Randles		
	John	Andrew Creswell
Randolph		
	Mary	Spencer Clack
	Dorotha, Lucy, Sarah	Henry Haggard
Raney		
	Elizabeth	John Gilliland
Ray		
	Hannah	William Longley
Raynor		
	Sarah "Mary"	Meady White
Reagan		
	Catherine, Celia, Elizabeth, Jeremiah, Joshua, Mary Jane, Rachel, Reason, Rhoda, Richard, Robert, Sarah, Timothy	Timothy Reagan
	Celia, Elizabeth, Robert Nelson, Sarah	Frederick Emert
	Leah	Oliver Alexander
	Rachel	John Mahan

Reams		
	Nancy	Joel Davis
Reece		
	Margaret	Mordecai Lewis
Reid		
	Elizabeth	James Riggin
Reneau		
	Mary Polly	Richard Wood
Renfrow		
	John	James Pierce
Reynolds		
	Jane L.	William Maples
Rice		
	George, Quinton Nix	John Clack
	Mary "Polly"	William Hendricks
Richards		
	Lydia, William	Thomas Atchley
Richardson		
	James, Lydda, Robert	Obediah Matthews
	Joel	Andrew Evans, NC
	Leah, William	William Richardson
	Sarah	Zachariah Isbell
	William	John Thurman
Riggin		
	Elizabeth, Harry, James, Tigue(Teague), Ignatius, John C., Mary "Polly", Sarah	James Riggin
Rittle		
	Angeline	Spencer Benson
Roberts		
	Benjamin	Joel Davis
	Delilah Richie	William

A Portrait of Patriots and Pioneers in Sevier County

		Robertson
Robertson	John	Frederick Emert
	Agnes Nancy	James Pierce
Robeson	Delilah, William	William Robertson
Robinson	Elizabeth	William Ogle
Robison	David	William McGaughey
Rogers	Hannah	Samuel McGaughey
	Bashaba, Elijah, George, Henry, Josiah, Mary,	Henry Rogers
	Elijah, Josiah	Spencer Clack
	Elizabeth	Oliver Alexander
	Elizabeth, Mariam Lee, Matilda Langford	James Riggin
Roome	Hester	John Gilliland
Ross	Martha	John McGee
Roulman	Elizabeth	Oliver Alexander
Routh	Jane	Joseph Large
Rudd	Nancy	Hugh Henry
	Absoly, Andrew, Burlingham, David, George, St. Clair, Stephen, William	Burlingham Rudd

328

Ruth C. Davis

Runyan		
	Aaron, Alexander	Mitchell Porter
	Aaron, Isaac, John, Loami, Tavenor, Ware	Isaac Runyan
Rush		
	Elizabeth	Samuel Carter
Sampson		
	Mary	James Oldham
Sandbridge		
	Nancy Ann Graves, William	John Thurman
Schull		
	Mary	Obediah Matthews
Scott		
	Mary	John Mahan
Scruggs		
	Rebecca Lindsay Conway	George Hudson
Seager		
	Anna Elizabeth	Jacob Troxel
Selvidge		
	Charlotte Temple, George W., Nancy	Jacob Layman
Semore		
	Jinny	Mitchell Porter
Sewell		
	James	James Oldham
Shahan		
	Rebecca	Joseph Campbell
Sharp		
	Ann, Amy, James, John, Martha, Mary, Narcissa, Sally	John Sharp
	Elizabeth	William Maples
	Mary McChesney	John McCroskey
	Willis B.	Alexander Zollinger
Shell		
	Catherine	Spencer Benson

A Portrait of Patriots and Pioneers in Sevier County

Shields		
	Arnett, Robert	Frederick Emert
	Benjamin, David, James, Jennet, Jesse, John, Joseph, Richard Robert, Thomas, William	Robert Shields
	James, John Page, Robert Perry	Meady White
	Jennet, Robert	Joshua Tipton
	John, Joshua, Thomas, Robert	Thomas Shields
	Joshua	Joshua Tipton
	R. S.	John Thurman
	Robert	Mordecai Lewis
Shook	Sarah	William Crowson
Short	Comfort	Spencer Benson
Shotwell	Amelia	Henry Bohannan
Shults	Johann Jr.	Frederick Emert
	Barbara, Julia Ann	Timothy Reagan
Simmons	Rebecca	John McKissack
Simms	Sarah	James Riggin
Simpson	Asbury	Samuel McGaughey
Skillman	Isaac	David Lindsay

Smallwood		
	William	William Smallwood
Smith		
	Elizabeth Emily	Thomas Atchley
	Mary Anne, William	Peter Weese
	Patrick	David Lindsay
Snider		
	Elizabeth	John Thurman
Snoddy		
	William Glasco	Andrew Creswell
Speer		
	Elizabeth Ann	James Riggin
Spurlock		
	John, Judath Catherine	Charles Fain
Stallions		
	Elizabeth, Sarah	Burlingham Rudd
Standifer		
	James, Sarah	John Clack
Stanfield		
	Cornelius, Delphia, James, Mary Ann	James Stanfield
Stapleton		
	Catharine Margaretha	Jacob Derrick
Steel		
	Augustine	William Longley
Stephens		
	Leah, William	James Oldham
Stewart		
	John Lumpkin	John McKissack
Stinson		
	John L.	Samuel McGaughey
Stockton		
	Nancy, Richard	Robert Shields
	Nancy	Thomas Shields

Stone	Nancy	Joshua Tipton
	Ezekial, Hannah, Rebecca, William	Ezekial Stone
Stover	Barsheba	William Trotter
Strader	Anna	Andrew Wells
Sullins	Lydia	Richard Varnell
Sutton	Joseph	Adam Fox
Swafford	Mary	Thomas Millsaps
Sweeney	Mary Elizabeth	John Rains
Taylor	Ruthea	William Maples
Teffeteller	Charlotte	John McCroskey
Temple	Ellen	Burlingham Rudd
	Mary Jane	Abraham Atchley
Terry	Hetty Jane	Timothy Chandler
	Christina	John Thurman
Tinder	Frances	Thomas Burlingham
Tipton	Elizabeth	Samuel Blair
	Agnes, Elizabeth, John Joshua, Mordecai, Rhoda, Sarah	Joshua Tipton

Ruth C. Davis

	Benjamin, John B.	John Cusick
	Joshua	Robert Shields
	Lydia	Jacob Derrick
	Rachel	Samuel Blair
	Rhoda	Thomas Shields
	Tryphenia Whitson	Samuel Wear
Thomas		
	Dennis, Elizabeth, Ellis, Elsie, Henry, Isaac, Jesse, John, John Henry, Lucretia, Mary Ann	Isaac Thomas
	Elijah	John Mahan
	Henry Massengill	Mitchell Porter
	Jonathan, Mary Patience	William Crowson
	Lucretia	Samuel Wear
	Martha	John Thurman
	Rachel	Timothy Reagan
Thompson		
	James William	Samuel Blair
Thurman		
	Ailsey, Barnabas, Graves, Jabez, John, Lucy, Martha, Richard, Sarah, Samuel, Susannah, William	John Thurman
Threewit		
	Mary	William Crowson
Tinker		
	Sarah	Jacob Troxel

A Portrait of Patriots and Pioneers in Sevier County

Todd		
	Sara Jane	Zachariah Isbell
Toomey		
	James	William Trotter
Trigg		
	Clement, Elizabeth	Timothy Reagan
Trosper		
	Rebecca	James Mahan
Trotter		
	Angelia, Arminta, Clabourn, Diane, James, Mariah, William	William Trotter
	John Sevier	Henry Haggard
	John Sevier	Meady White
	Samuel	Jacob Troxel
Troxel		
	Barbara, David, Eliza, Jacob, Magdalena, Martin, Samuel, Sarah, Thomas, William	Jacob Troxel
Tucker		
	Sarah	John McCroskey
Tunes		
	Unknown	John Thurman
Underwood		
	Catherine	Hugh Henry
	Elizabeth, Enoch, George, Harvey, Hugh, James, Joel, John, Martha Mary, Nancy, Thomas	John Underwood
Urquhart		
	Hannah	James Mahan
Vance		
	Cynthia	John Cusick
Varnell		
	Jesse, Joseph, Richard,	Richard Varnell

Vaughn	Sarah, William	
	Elizabeth	Hugh Henry
Veach	Mary, William	Burlingham Rudd
Veatch	Martha	Robert Shields
Vinson	Mary Elizabeth	Robert Shields
Wade	Eliah, Jane	William Crowson
Walker	Mary Margaret	Mitchell Porter
	Delilah	George Wells
	Martha	John McGee
Wall	Rebecca	Mordecai Lewis
Wallace	Randolph	Randolph Wall
Walsh	Ruth	Oliver Alexander
Waters	Anthony	John Gilliland
Watkins	Dicey Elizabeth	James McMahan
Watts	Martha	John Clack
Wayland	Loucinday	Burlingham Rudd
Wear	Ann Usher	Timothy Chandler
	Diana, Elizabeth, John, Malinda, Mary, Margaret, Minerva,	Samuel Wear

	Pleasant, Rebecca, Robert, Samuel	
	Hannah M.	William Lovelady
	Jane Elizabeth, John, Rebecca, Robert, Samuel	John Wear
	Jane Elizabeth	John Lovelady
	John	John McCroskey
	Robert	Isaac Thomas
	Samuel	John Gilliland
Weese	Barbara, David, George, John, Landon, Peter, Sarah, William	Peter Weese
Webb	Elizabeth	Joseph Large
	Elizabeth, Jesse, John, Joseph, Susannah, Thomas	John Webb
Weeks	Sarah	John Webb
Wells	Andrew, Coleman, George, Hannah. Jeremiah, John, Katie, Levi, Malinda, Michael, Nancy Jane, Permelia, Rebecca, Robert, Thomas, Sallie, William	Andrew Wells
	Barnabus, Clarissa, George, James, John, Lewis, Stephen, Synthia, William	George Wells

West		
	Elizabeth	David Lindsay
	Penelope	Mitchell Porter
Wilder		
	Elizabeth	William Maples
Wilhelm		
	Alsey	Abraham Atchley
Williams		
	Bathsheba	Thomas Millsaps
	Elizabeth	Andrew Wells
	John	William Henry
	Mary	Joseph Large
Wilson		
	Margaret	Robert Duggan
	Matthew	Andrew Evans, NC
	William	John McCroskey
Winton		
	Elizabeth, Mary	Alexander Montgomery
Witt		
	John	Samuel Wear
Whaley		
	Lydia Jenkins	William Henry
	Sarah	Burlingham Rudd
	William M.	William Ogle
Whitaker		
	Polly	Oliver Alexander
White		
	Aaron, Asa, James, Meady, Mordecai, Nancy, Penelope,	Meady White

A Portrait of Patriots and Pioneers in Sevier County

Surname	Given Name(s)	Spouse
	Sabra Ellen, William, Winfred	
	Anne/Anna	James Oldham
	Elizabeth "Betsy"	John Thurman
	James	James White
	Nancy	Isaac Runyan
	Nancy, Penelope, Sabra Ellen	Robert Shields
Wildman	Rhoda	Joseph Large
Wilkinson	Nathan	John Wear
Wilson	Margaret	Robert Shields
Wood	Catherine, Hannah, James, Joel, Joseph, Lavina, Richard, William	Richard Wood
	Jane	Ezekial Stone
	Katherine	Charles Fain
	Martha	William Crowson
Wright	Betsy Ann	David Norton
Wynn	Ashley	Mitchell Porter
Yadon	Mary "Polly", Sarah Sally	Andrew Evans, VA
Yearout	Catherine	George Wells
Yell	Pearcy	Joshua Gist
Young		

Ruth C. Davis

	Elizabeth, Robert	John Gilliland
Ziegler	Elizabeth, Robert	Samuel Wear
	Mary	Mordecai
Zollinger	Alexander, Elizabeth, Johann Peter, Margaret "Polly", Mary, Thomas	Alexander Zollinger

A Portrait of Patriots and Pioneers in Sevier County

Ruth C. Davis

Sources

"Alabama, Revolutionary War Residents, 1776-1783." *Search*, search.ancestry.com/search/db.aspx?dbid=60921.

Alderman, Pat. *The Overmountain Men, 1760-1795*. Overmountain Press, 1970.

Allen, Penelope Johnson. *Tennessee Soldiers in the Revolution*. Reprinted for Clearfield Co. by Genealogical Pub. Col, 2008.

AncestrySupport, support.ancestry.com/s/family-trees.

"Annals of Southwest Virginia, 1769-1800." *Search*, search.ancestry.com/search/db.aspx?dbid=49061.

"Application." *National Society Sons of the American Revolution*, www.sar.org/faq/application/.

Beasley, Jim. *Ancestors in Middle Tennessee and Smoky Mountains*.

Bryan, Jerry. *Jerry's Personal Genealogy Page*, jerrybryan.com/genealogy/genealogy1.html.

Bulletin of Fauquier Historical Society, 1921-1924.

"Census and Voter Lists." *Ancestry*, www.ancestry.com/search/categories/35/.

"Census Records of The Church of Jesus Christ of Latter-Day Saints." *FamilySearch Wiki*, wwwp.familysearch.org/wiki/en/Census_Records_of_The_Church_of_Jesus_Christ_of_Latter-day_Saints.

Chilton, Joe. "Family Search." *GEDCOM - FamilySearch Developer Center - FamilySearch.org*, 1994, www.familysearch.org/developers/docs/guides/

gedcom.
Clerc-Fakhar, Kay. *Longley Family*.
Descendants of Henry Haggard, alagenealogy.com/Patriarchs/Haggard, Henry.htm.
East Tennessee Land Grants. Tennessee State Library and Archives.
Eli and Betsy McCarter Family, ebmfamily.tripod.com/index.html.
"Family Article Index." *Dennis Nicklaus Genealogy Article Index*, freepages.rootsweb.com/~nicklaus/genealogy/articles.html.
"Family Search." *Find A Grave Index - FamilySearch.org*, www.familysearch.org/search/collection/2221801.
"Family Search." *GEDCOM - FamilySearch Developer Center - FamilySearch.org*, www.familysearch.org/developers/docs/gedcom/.
"Family Tree Maker - Free Downloads and Reviews - CNET Download.com." *Download.com*, download.cnet.com/s/family-tree-maker/.
"Genealogy Resources on Geni." *Genealogy Resources*, William Headrick, www.geni.com/genealogy-resources.
Southern Campaigns American Revolution Pension Statements ... Translated by Will Graves, revwarapps.org/r1182.pdf.
Grubb, Cheryl. *Richard Varnell Family*, www.next1000.com/family/GRUBB/varnell.R.html.
Gwathmey, John H. "Historical Register of Virginians in the Revolution, Soldiers, Sailors, Marines, 1775-1783." *The William and Mary Quarterly*,

vol. 19, no. 1, 1939, p. 110., doi:10.2307/1923066.

Gwathmey, John H. *Historical Register of Virginians in the Revolution: Soldiers, Sailors, Marines, 1775-1783*. Genealogical Pub. Co., 2010.

Hammett, C. "Welcome to the TNGenWeb Project." *Welcome to the TNGenWeb Project*, 2001, tngenweb.org/.

Haun, Weynette Parks. *North Carolina Revolutionary Army Accounts: Secretary of States Papers*. W.P. Haun, 1995.

Henderson, Cherel B. *Smoky Mountain Historical Society Newsletter*, 1987.

Henderson, Cherel. *James Hubbert, Sevier County's Paradoxical Pioneer*, Smoky Mountain Historical Society Newsletter, Sevierville, Tennessee1987, 1987.

Hennessee, David. "David Lindsey." *Minipickles.com*.

Hennessee, David. "Our Family Genealogy Pages." *Our Family Genealogy Pages*, thehennesseefamily.com/.

"Historical Military Records." *Fold3*, www.fold3.com/.

"Historical Register of Virginians in the Revolution : Soldiers, Sailors, Marines, 1775-1783." *Find in a Library with WorldCat*, www.worldcat.org/title/historical-register-of-virginians-in-the-revolution-soldiers-sailors-marines-1775-1783/oclc/2808722.

In the Shadow of the Smokies: Sevier County, Tennessee Cemeteries. The Society, 1993.

Index of Revolutionary War Pension Applications; Compiled from Pension and Bounty Land Records of the Veterans Administration Archives in the National Archives. 1964. William Headrick

Isaac Barefoot Runyan. Wikitree.
JEFFERSON COUNTY, TENNESSEE - GRANT BOOK No. 1 - 1792-1794, www.mountainpress.com/books/tn/details/tn-0002w.html.
Jowers, A. *Sevier County, Tennessee Genealogy and History*, www.genealogytrails.com/tenn/sevier/.
Linn, Beulah D. *Jacob Layman, Revolutionary Soldier*. Sevierville, TN.
Linn, Beulah D. "Mordecai Lewis,Militiaman in the Continental Army." *Sevier County News-Record & Gatlinburg Press*.
Linn, Beulah D. "Trotter-Revolutionary Soldier." *Sevier County News-Record & Gatlinburg Press*, 19 Aug. 1975, Accessed 8AD.
Linn, Beulah D. "Robert Duggan, Revolutionary Soldier." *Sevier County News-Record & Gatlinburg Press* , 10 June 1976.
Linn, Beulah. "Joshua Tipton-Forgotten Revolutionary Soldier." 22 July 1976.
Linn, Beulah D. "Lost Grave Site of Andrew Wells Believed Found." *Smoky Mountain Historical Society Newsletter*, 1996, p. 12.
McMahan, Carroll. "Revolutionary War Hero John Gilliland Is Buried in Pigeon Forge ." *Mountain Press*, May 2016.
McMahan, Carroll. "William Ogle." *The Mountain Press*, 8 May 2016.
"MONTGOMERY Family Tree and MONTGOMERY Genealogy Records." *Family Tree Circles*, www.familytreecircles.com/surname_MONTGOMERY.html.
Murray, Joyce Martin., and Martin Richard. Murray. "Greene County, Tennessee Deed Abstracts." *Amazon*, J.M. Murray, 1996,

www.amazon.com/Greene-County-Tennessee-Deed-Abstracts/dp/B0028U0YMO.

National Society of the Daughters of the American Revolution. *DAR Patriot Index Vol. II*. National Society of the Daughters of the American Revolution.

"Navy Report Book # 8." *Reddit*, www.reddit.com/r/navy/comments/g8ix36/navy_report/.

"North Carolina and Tennessee, Early Land Records, 1753-1931." *Search*, search.ancestry.com/search/db.aspx?dbid=2882.

"Norton Family Resources, History, DNA and Research." *Norton Family Resources, History, DNA and Research.*, www.nortonfamily.net/.

"Oliver Alexander." *WikiTree*, 23 Dec. 2019, www.wikitree.com/wiki/Alexander-4476.

"Our Family Genealogy Pages." *Our Family Genealogy Pages*, boazhistory.com/.

"Our Family History." *Our Family History*, oldham.one-name.net/.

OWEN, THOMAS MCADORY. *HISTORY OF ALABAMA AND DICTIONARY OF ALABAMA BIOGRAPHY*. FORGOTTEN BOOKS, 2015.

Ownby, Harold. *Forks of Little Pigeon Church*. Gatlinburg, Tennessee, 1989.

Reagan, Donald B. *The Book of Ragan/Reagan*. D.R. Reagan, 1993.

REVOLUTIONARY WAR PATRIOT'S - Stephen Holston. www.stephenholston.org/Revolutionary War Patriot Pensions & Gravesites.pdf.

"Roster of South Carolina Patriots in the American Revolution: Bobby Gilmer Moss." *Genealogical.com*, library.genealogical.com/preview/roster-of-south-carolina-patriots-in-the-american-revolution.

"Southern Campaigns Revolutionary War Pension Applications & Rosters." Translated by C. Leon Harris Revwarapps@att.net, *Southern Campaigns Revolutionary War Pension Applications & Rosters*, www.revwarapps.org/.

Riggin, Sharol. *Teage Riggen and His Riggen-Riggin Riggins Descendants*. Gateway Press, 1987.

Robinson, Phoebe. "David Lindsey." *Alabaster Reporter*, 17 Sept. 2018.

"RootsWeb.com Home Page." *RootsWeb.com Home Page*, www.rootsweb.com/.

Sevier Revolutionary War Soldiers of Tennessee, TNGenWeb Project (TNGenNet), www.tngenweb.org/revwar/records/s/sevier.html.

Sharp, Joseph. *Revolutionary Soldiers, Sevier County*.

Smith, Nadine. "Barbourville Mountain Advocate." *Paperboy Online Newspaper Directory*, 8 May 2003, www.thepaperboy.com/newspaper.cfm?PaperID=2146109678.

"Smoky Mountain Historical Society Journal and Newsletter." *Smoky Mountain Historical Society Journal and Newsletter | Database of the Smokies*, 1983, dots.lib.utk.edu/?q=biblio/smoky-mountain-historical-society-journal-and-newsletter.

"Smoky Mountain Historical Society Journal and Newsletter." *Smoky Mountain Historical Society Journal and Newsletter | Database of the Smokies*, 1984, dots.lib.utk.edu/?q=biblio/smoky-mountain-

historical-society-journal-and-newsletter.
"Smoky Mountain Historical Society Journal and Newsletter." *Smoky Mountain Historical Society Journal and Newsletter | Database of the Smokies*, 1987, dots.lib.utk.edu/?q=biblio/smoky-mountain-historical-society-journal-and-newsletter.
"Smoky Mountain Historical Society Journal and Newsletter." *Smoky Mountain Historical Society Journal and Newsletter | Database of the Smokies*, 1990, dots.lib.utk.edu/?q=biblio/smoky-mountain-historical-society-journal-and-newsletter.
"Smoky Mountain Historical Society Journal and Newsletter." *Smoky Mountain Historical Society Journal and Newsletter | Database of the Smokies*, 1998, dots.lib.utk.edu/?q=biblio/smoky-mountain-historical-society-journal-and-newsletter.
"Smoky Mountain Historical Society Journal and Newsletter." *Smoky Mountain Historical Society Journal and Newsletter | Database of the Smokies*, 1999, dots.lib.utk.edu/?q=biblio/smoky-mountain-historical-society-journal-and-newsletter.
"Smoky Mountain Historical Society Journal and Newsletter." *Smoky Mountain Historical Society Journal and Newsletter | Database of the Smokies*, 2002, dots.lib.utk.edu/?q=biblio/smoky-mountain-historical-society-journal-and-newsletter.
"Smoky Mountain Historical Society Newsletter." *Smoky Mountain Historical Society Newsletter: Smoky Mountain Ancestral Quest*, 1983, www.smokykin.com/tng/showsource.php?sourceID=S9.

"Some Tennessee Heroes of the Revolution : Armstrong, Zella : Free Download, Borrow, and Streaming." *Internet Archive*, Baltimore : Genealogical Pub. Co., 1 Jan. 1975, archive.org/details/sometennesseeher00arms. Vol. No 2

"Sons of the American Revolution." *SAR*, members.sar.org/user/edit.

Sues Stories: The McGaughey Family. suessimplestories.blogspot.com/2016/05/the-mcgaughey-family.html.

"The Church of Jesus Christ of Latter-Day Saints." *FamilySearch Wiki*, wwwp.familysearch.org/wiki/en/The_Church_of_Jesus_Christ_of_Latter-day_Saints.

"The Family Chronicle and Kinship Book, Octavia Zollicoffer Bond, Hardcover." *Worthpoint*, www.worthpoint.com/worthopedia/family-chronicle-kinship-book-octavia-1788950712.

The Virginia Land Office - Library of Virginia. www.lva.virginia.gov/public/guides/Research_Notes_20.pdf.

U.S. Revolutionary War Bounty Land Warrants Used in the U.S. Military District of Ohio and Related Papers (Acts of 1788, 1803, 1806). National Archives, National Archives and Records Service, General Services Administration, 1971.

"U.S., Revolutionary War Rolls, 1775-1783." *Search*, search.ancestry.com/search/db.aspx?dbid=4282.

Underwood, Stella, et al. "Ferries on the French Broad River in Sevier County." *Smoky Mountain Historical Society Newsletter*.

United States, Applications for Headstones for U.S. Military Veterans. 2014.

"Washington County, Tennessee Deeds 1775-1800. (Vol. #1)." *Southern Historical Press, Inc.*, southernhistoricalpress.com/products/washington-county-tennessee-deeds-1775-1800-vol-1.

Williams, Theresa. "Forks of the Little Pigeon River Cemetery and Park History." *Anonymous*, 21 July 2014, sevierville.bar-z.com/location/forks-little-pigeon-river-cemetery.

"Www.Smokykin.com." *Www.Smokykin.com - Home Page: Smoky Mountain Ancestral Quest*, urlm.co/www.smokykin.com.

Zachariah William Isbell, Jr. (1745 - 1799) - Genealogy. www.geni.com/people/Zachariah-Isbell-Jr/6000000000435218584.

Modern Language Association 8th edition formatting by CitationMachine.net.

Made in the USA
Middletown, DE
16 May 2021